The View from Everywhere

PHILOSOPHY OF MIND SERIES

SERIES EDITOR: David J. Chalmers, *New York University*

The Conscious Brain
Jesse Prinz

Simulating Minds
The Philosophy, Psychology, and
Neuroscience of Mindreading Alvin
I. Goldman

Supersizing The Mind
Embodiment, Action, and Cognitive
Extension
Andy Clark

Perception, Hallucination, and Illusion
William Fish

*Phenomenal Concepts and Phenomenal
Knowledge*
New Essays on Consciousness and
Physicalism
Torin Alter and Sven Walter

The Character of Consciousness
David J. Chalmers

The Senses
Classic and Contemporary Philosophical
Perspectives
Fiona Macpherson

Attention Is Cognitive Unison
An Essay in Philosophical Psychology
Christopher Mole

The Contents of Visual Experience
Susanna Siegel

*Consciousness and the Prospects of
Physicalism*
Derk Pereboom

Consciousness and Fundamental Reality
Philip Goff

The Phenomenal Basis of Intentionality
Angela Mendelovici

Seeing and Saying
The Language of Perception and the
Representational View of Experience Berit
Brogaard

Perceptual Learning
The Flexibility of the Senses Kevin
Connolly

Combining Minds
How to Think about Composite
Subjectivity
Luke Roelofs

The Epistemic Role of Consciousness
Declan Smithies

*The Epistemology of Non-Visual
Perception* Berit Brogaard and Dimitria
Electra Gatzia

What Are Mental Representations?
Edited by Joulia Smortchkova, Krzysztof
Dołęga, and Tobias Schlicht

Phenomenal Intentionality
George Graham, John Tienson, and
Terry Horgan

Feminist Philosophy of Mind, Keya Maitra
and Jennifer McWeeny

The Border Between Seeing and Thinking
Ned Block

The View from Everywhere Realist
Idealism without God Helen
Yetter-Chappell

The View from Everywhere

Realist Idealism without God

HELEN YETTER-CHAPPELL

OXFORD
UNIVERSITY PRESS

Oxford University Press is a department of the University of Oxford.
It furthers the University's objective of excellence in research, scholarship,
and education by publishing worldwide. Oxford is a registered trade mark of
Oxford University Press in the UK and in certain other countries.

Published in the United States of America by Oxford University Press
198 Madison Avenue, New York, NY 10016, United States of America.

© Oxford University Press 2025

All rights reserved. No part of this publication may be reproduced, stored in a retrieval system, transmitted, used for text and data mining, or used for training artificial intelligence, in any form or by any means, without the prior permission in writing of Oxford University Press, or as expressly permitted by law, by license or under terms agreed with the appropriate reprographics rights organization. Inquiries concerning reproduction outside the scope of the above should be sent to the Rights Department, Oxford University Press, at the address above.

You must not circulate this work in any other form
and you must impose this same condition on any acquirer

Library of Congress Cataloging-in-Publication Data
Names: Yetter-Chappell, Helen, author.
Title: The view from everywhere : realist idealism without God / Helen Yetter-Chappell.
Description: New York, NY : Oxford University Press, [2025]. |
Series: Philosophy of mind series | Includes bibliographical references.
Identifiers: LCCN 2024056630 (print) | LCCN 2024056631 (ebook) |
ISBN 9780197795026 (hardback) | ISBN 9780197795057 |
ISBN 9780197795040 (epub)
Subjects: LCSH: Idealism. | Realism. | Mind and body—Religious aspects.
Classification: LCC B823 .A39 2025 (print) | LCC B823 (ebook) |
DDC 141—dc23/eng/20250128
LC record available at https://lccn.loc.gov/2024056630
LC ebook record available at https://lccn.loc.gov/2024056631

DOI: 10.1093/9780197795057.001.0001

Printed by Marquis Book Printing, Canada

For Richard
(even though his credence in idealism is irrationally low)

Contents

Preface	ix
1. Berkeley without God	1
1.1 Berkeley's Theistic Idealism	6
1.2 Idealism without God	11
1.3 God-minus	12
1.4 The Plan	18
2. The Phenomenal Tapestry	24
2.1 Overview	25
2.1.1 Unifying Distinct Perspectives	30
2.2 Theories of Phenomenal Unity	36
2.2.1 Co-Consciousness and Subsumptive Unity	37
2.2.2 Experiential Parts	39
2.2.3 Kantian Unity	42
Unity and Objectivity	45
2.2.4 Property Binding and Phenomenal Spatial and Temporal Relations	48
2.3 Threads of Reality	51
2.3.1 How "Thick" Is the Tapestry?	57
2.3.2 Cognitive Phenomenology and Reality	62
2.4 Conclusion	63
3. Idealism and the Mind-Body Problem	65
3.1 The Options	66
3.1.1 Reductionism	66
3.1.2 Immanent Non-Reductionism	67
3.1.3 Transcendent Non-Reductionism	68
3.2 Local vs. Extended	70
3.2.1 Transcendent Non-Reductionism: Local vs. Extended	70
3.2.2 Immanent Non-Reductionism: Local vs. Extended	73
3.2.3 Reductionism: Local vs. Extended	74
3.2.4 Is Idealist Reductionism Tenable?	77
3.3 Which Way to Turn?	80
4. Perception	84
4.1 Naïve Idealism	85
4.1.1 Transitivity	88
4.1.2 Bridging Laws and Indices	96

viii CONTENTS

4.2 How Much Do We Overlap with the Tapestry? — 98
  4.2.1 Two Extremes — 100
    No Hidden Assumptions — 100
    Any Hidden Assumptions — 101
  4.2.2 A Middle Ground — 102
  4.2.3 Hidden Assumptions in Practice — 107
    Three-Dimensionality — 107
    Back-Sides — 109
    Occlusion — 109
4.3 Illusion — 110
    Cognitive Phenomenology and Illusion — 111
    Veridicality and Illusion — 112
    Illusions of Generation — 113
  4.3.1 Afterimages — 113
4.4 Conclusion — 116

5. Science, Structure, and Spacetime — 118
5.1 The Neutrality of Laws — 119
5.2 The Microphysical Structure of Physical Reality — 124
5.3 Profligacy — 132
  5.3.1 Simplicity and the Laws of Nature — 136
5.4 Spacetime — 139
  5.4.1 Relationalism — 140
  5.4.2 Substantivalism — 141
  5.4.3 Temporal Phenomenology — 142
  5.4.4 Temporal Flow — 144
5.5 Conclusion — 146

6. The Virtues of Idealism — 148
6.1 Living in Eden — 149
6.2 Why Not Naïve Realism? — 154
  6.2.1 Perceptual Naïve Realism — 155
  6.2.2 Color Naïve Realism — 165
  6.2.3 Johnston's Manifest World — 171
6.3 Theoretical Virtues or Wishful Thinking? — 174
6.4 Assessing the Competition — 181
  6.4.1 Panpsychism — 182
    (a) Consciousness: Exhaustive or Not — 182
    (b) What's Fundamental: Small, Medium, Large — 183
    (c) Macro-Minds — 183
  6.4.2 Phenomenalism — 186
  6.4.3 Theistic Idealism — 191

Bibliography — 195
Index — 203

Preface

Everything is just pictures offset by a frame or two.

When my (then) two-and-a-half-year-old told me this, I was flabbergasted. Could he possibly have said what I think he did? Could he possibly understand what he had just said?[1] He was insistent. "Everything—[his] bed, the ceiling, the table—it's all pictures offset by a frame or two." The following day, my question was answered. He put a water bottle down on the kitchen floor, and walked around it using a pretend camera to take pictures of it from all angles. He smooshed the imaginary photographs together with a *bzzzzt* and handed me the result: "Here Mama, here's a bottle-like-thing for you."

One of two things seems to follow: either idealism is genetic or Berkeley is right that idealism is the pretheoretic view of common sense.

While the view my son came to as a two-year-old is not quite the view developed in this book, it has striking similarities.

I first began thinking about the ideas developed in this book in 2012, while sitting in on a graduate seminar on perception taught by Mark Johnston and Frank Jackson. Mark supplied my first exposure to a "naïve" view of perception. I was mystified. It was a way of thinking about our relation to the world that was completely at odds with my background conception of how the world works. And I couldn't wrap my mind around it.

But I think an important part of philosophy is being able to step outside of one's own worldview and appreciate the perspective of the other side. I think of it like having a collection of "worldview hats" that one can put on to see the world through different eyes. The hats don't become *mine* by virtue of doing this, but—if I'm successful—wearing them can enable me to understand what motivates the other sides and how my perspective looks from their perspective.

---

[1] We later worked out that he'd acquired the concept of pictures being offset by frames from a Smarter Every Day video he'd seen that mentioned fast-frame differencing—in which you "take one layer of video and put another layer of video on top of it and then offset it by a frame or two." You can then look only at the pixels that are different in the second frame, allowing you to detect motion that would otherwise be imperceptible to us. The conception of objects *as* pictures offset by a frame or two seems to have been entirely his own.

X PREFACE

I wanted very much to understand Mark's perspective and to develop a "naïve view of perception" hat. Eventually, I found that I could do so ... but only given the background assumption that the world was intrinsically experiential. I could make sense of the naïve view of the world ... but only as *naïve idealism*.[2]

So my initial thoughts about idealism were a form of play: seeing how far I could develop this curious not-my view. But as I've crafted my idealist hat, I've come to the conclusion that the virtues of idealism shouldn't be ignored.

A challenge you face when you construct worldview hats is this: What do you do when you have a collection of them? Do you keep your initial hat as *your* hat, and only wear the others to silly hat parties? Do you abandon your first hat and find a better one? How can you know which is better? Does it feel better when you have it on? Does it look better from the perspective of your first hat? What *should* you do?

I've tried to say something about this in Chapter 6, proposing that it's sometimes possible and desirable to evaluate matters with a bare head.

One might think that, having written this book, I must be a card-carrying idealist. I am not to that point yet. But I put a significant degree of confidence (perhaps 30%) in something like the view described in the book being true.

This book has benefited enormously from feedback I've received over the years from others. Here is a non-exhaustive list of some whose engagement I've benefited from:[3] David Yetter, Plato Tse, Galen Strawson, Hwan Ruy, Howard Robinson, Michael Pelczar, Kenneth Pearce, Ivan Ivanov, Tyron Goldschmidt, Philip Goff, Keith Frankish, Nevin Climenhaga, Lok-Chi Chan, and David Chalmers. I've also benefited enormously from comments on work presented at the UNC Idealism Summit, the Rice Philosophy of Mind Conference, Uriah Kriegel's Autumn of Consciousness Workshop, the Idealism and the Mind-Body Problem at NYU Shanghai, and colloquia at National Taiwan University, Sun Yat-sen University, Mount Holyoke College, Florida International University, the University of Birmingham, and the University of Reading.

Work on this book was supported by a University of Miami Humanities Fellowship (2020–2021). And the book was made stronger thanks to the feedback of my 2022 graduate seminar at the University of Miami, which read an

---

[2] Though, in the end, I've concluded that this view may be much closer to Mark's view than I initially appreciated (§6.2.3).

[3] Alas, I suspect I've forgotten many who've given invaluable feedback. Apologies for not giving you the credit that's due.

early draft of this book. In one of my seminars, Wali Hussaini described my view as "the view from everywhere," inspiring the title of the book.

Thanks also goes to three fantastic anonymous reviewers for Oxford University Press who raised some really fun and tricky challenges, and whose feedback prompted me to get clearer on the structure of the phenomenal tapestry and its relation to the structure of the laws of nature. The front cover is a partially completed tapestry, *Nest (Golden-Winged Warblers are Happy in their Minnesota Habitat)*, designed and created by weaver Robbie LaFleur, who provided assistance in selecting cover art.

Finally, my greatest gratitude is to my husband, Richard Yetter Chappell: my most frequent and best philosophical interlocutor, my emotional support, and my greatest advocate. I have been bouncing the ideas in this book off of Richard for the past decade. He has read and given feedback on countless versions of draft chapters and the book as a whole. I'm sure there are uncredited objections and examples that I owe to Richard. Thanks also to my son, Elian, for his more-than-maximal love, his faith in his mama, and many interesting philosophical discussions. I can't wait to read your book explaining why I'm wrong![4]

Some of the ideas in this book appear in other papers. I first wrote about core idea developed in this book in: "Idealism without God" (2018a) in *Idealism: New Essays in Metaphysics*, ed. Goldschmidt & Pearce (Oxford University Press). My "naïve idealist" theory of perception is developed in "Get Acquainted with Naïve Idealism" (2024a), in *The Roles of Representations in Visual Perception*, ed. French & Brogaard (Synthese Books). And I make the positive case for embracing idealism in "Idealism and the Best of All (Subjectively Indistinguishable) Possible Worlds" (2024b), in *Oxford Studies in Philosophy of Mind*, ed. Uriah Kriegel, Vol. 4.

Like its namesake, this book contains a great deal of speculation about the world and how we fit into it. Some of it will seem wild, but the world is a strange place, and nothing but radical speculation gives us hope of coming up with any candidates for truth. (Nagel 1986, 10)

Of course, as Nagel tells us, this "is not the same as coming up with the truth." Perhaps our world does not number among the idealist worlds. I will be content if you agree that idealism should be taken seriously as a viable *candidate* for truth. Few are antecedently inclined to grant any non-negligible credence to idealism; I hope this book will change that.

---

[4] The age of naïveté is fleeting!

1

Berkeley without God

I look outside my window. I see dull green of palm leaves, the richer green of a mango tree, a glimpse of blue sky. The rhythmic flow of Vivaldi helps to focus my mind as I write. A black kitten sits curled up in my lap, warm and soft. There is nothing out of the ordinary about this scene. This is the world we live in: a world of soft, warm kittens, greens and blues, pitch and timbre.

At least, this is the world we think that we live in. But philosophers are very good at denying the obvious: at turning the world we live in upside down and giving reasons to justifying doing so. Consciousness is an illusion. You shouldn't lie to the murderer who's come to the door to kill your father. Whether you survive may be merely a matter of convention. We don't have free will (in the sense of being the ultimate source of our actions).[1]

When it comes to the nature and character of the world we live in, there are compelling empirical reasons to think that we must give up on the world that seems so clear to us. As David Chalmers (2006) puts it:

> Science suggests that when we see a red object, our perception of the object is mediated by the reflection or radiation of light from the surface of the object to our eyes and then to our brains. The properties of the object that are responsible for the reflection or radiation of the light appear to be complex physical properties, such as surface spectral reflectances, ultimately grounded in microphysical configurations. Science does not reveal any primitive properties in the object, and furthermore, the hypothesis that objects have the relevant primitive properties seems quite unnecessary in order to explain color perception.

---

[1] Counterintuitive claims due to illusionists (e.g., Frankish 2016; Kammerer 2019), Immanuel Kant, and compatibilists.

The View from Everywhere. Helen Yetter-Chappell, Oxford University Press. © Oxford University Press 2025. DOI: 10.1093/9780197795057.003.0001

2   THE VIEW FROM EVERYWHERE

We do not need leaves to *be green* in order to explain why they appear green to us. Furthermore, there is no gaping hole left in the scientific picture of the world by leaving them out. We've got complex microphysical configurations and light, and surely that's enough. We can happily do away with warmth, in favor of molecular kinetic energy, pitch in favor of frequency, color in favor of surface reflectance profile.

We can. We can embrace a world without color, a world without warmth, a world without pitch or solidity or sweetness. We can embrace a world beyond our grasp, a world entirely alien to us save for its dispositions and structure. We *can*. And yet. . . .

What if we didn't have to? What if it turned out that a world of color, sweetness, and sound—the very world we took ourselves to know so well—is perfectly compatible with science? What if it turned out that the complex causal chain from light to surface reflectance properties to our retinas and brains . . . was compatible with our *directly, unmediatedly grasping* shape and color? What if we could embrace the world as-it-seems . . . and have our science, too? That is the promise of idealism. That is what this book aims to deliver. Idealism offers a way of understanding the world, on which the nature of reality is intelligible: we don't merely grasp empty structure, but the nature of that which instantiates this structure. Idealism reveals that we don't have to dismiss the way the world seems as "mere appearances." We don't have to take ourselves to be cut off from reality. Idealism renders it intelligible how we can literally and directly grasp the world around us. And—as I'll argue—idealism is *uniquely* able to capture these common-sense intuitions. Embracing the naïve picture of the world requires embracing idealism.

There are times when we must abandon what "common-sense tells us." We find that there is no "further fact" to personal identity beyond constantly evolving physical and psychological states. There is nothing that can ground our common-sense intuitions about personal identity, and so we must abandon them. We find that we are not the ultimate sources or origins of our actions, but are like conscious computers, acting in accordance with their programming. (Both these examples are obviously controversial. Feel free to fill in with something else counterintuitive, which you think we have no choice by to accept.) There are other times when we simply *cannot* reasonably deny common sense. The existence of consciousness is like this. We can coherently debate the nature of conscious experiences. But we cannot intelligibly deny their existence. To do so would be, to borrow a favorite term of Galen Strawson's (2006), *silly*.

The reality of the sensible world is not in this latter group. It is not unintelligible or silly to think that the world we live in is nothing like it seems. The space of possible worlds is vast. It includes worlds of a spectral nature, and it includes materialist worlds: worlds of insensible matter.[2]

Some of these materialist worlds are worlds that appear to their inhabitants just as our worlds appear to us. We are not logically required to be idealists.[3] But neither are we logically required to be materialists. The space of possible worlds also includes idealist worlds: worlds constructed out of phenomenology. This book offers a blueprint for constructing such a phenomenal world—a world that is not only fundamentally phenomenal but is subjectively akin to the world we ourselves inhabit.

If I'm right that there are both idealist and materialist worlds that subjectively appear to their inhabitants the way that our world appears to us, the question is not *must* we embrace idealism (or materialism). Rather, the question to ask is: how confident should we be that *the actual world* is among the idealist worlds, versus among the materialist worlds?

There are times when we must abandon our common-sense views. There are times when they conflict with empirical reality or are logically inconsistent. But we should not abandon common-sense willy-nilly. We should not abandon it without a damn good reason for doing so.

This book will develop a complete idealist worldview: showing that idealists can offer compelling accounts of the nature of reality, the mind-body problem, and the nature of perception. And this book will argue that neither science nor scientific theory offers reason to reject idealism, as they are neutral concerning the metaphysical nature of reality. We do not find a damn good reason for rejecting common-sense.

This is the same promise that Berkeley found in idealism. As Berkeley summarizes his view in the Third Dialogue (1996, 172):

> I am of a vulgar cast, simple enough to believe my senses, and leave things as I find them. To be plain, it is my opinion that the real things are those very things I see, and feel, and perceive by my senses. These I know; and, finding they answer all the necessities and purposes of life, have no reason to be

---

[2] "Materialism" has (at least) two meanings. It can be used as a theory of the nature of the world, or as a theory about the nature of consciousness. Traditional mind-body dualism is a version of materialism in the first sense, but not in the latter. Here and throughout this book, I'll use "materialism" to contrast with idealism—denoting the theory about the nature of reality. I'll use "physicalism" to specify the view that consciousness is grounded in matter.

[3] See Chapter 6 for brief discussion of my expansive conception of modal space.

4 THE VIEW FROM EVERYWHERE

solicitous about any other unknown beings.... It is likewise my opinion that colours and other sensible qualities are on the objects. I cannot for my life help thinking that snow is white, and fire hot. You indeed, who by SNOW and fire mean certain external, unperceived, unperceiving substances, are in the right to deny whiteness or heat to be affections inherent in THEM. But I, who understand by those words the things I see and feel, am obliged to think like other folks.[4]

So idealism offers the promise of a reality that captures common-sense: a world that is intelligible; a world that is as it appears; a world that we grasp and know directly.

But while the idealism developed in this book is similar in spirit to Berkeleyan idealism, I will not be defending Berkeleyan idealism. Berkeley's idealism is constrained by his theological commitments, and (perhaps because of this) he does not offer an adequately fleshed out account of reality and our place within it. Berkeley is not alone in this. Previous work on idealism has often focused on offering "refutations of realism" and "vindications of idealism," at the expense of offering a well-developed positive alternative. This book is different. I won't argue that all worlds subjectively like our own are idealist worlds. Instead, I'll flesh out the details of how there could be an idealist world akin to ours. I'll consider not only the nature of the world, but its *structure*, and *how beings like us could relate to such a reality*.

The idealism I'll develop is a *realist idealism*, which—unlike Berkeley's idealism and that of neo-Berkeleyans like Foster (1982, 2008) and Robinson (1985, 1994, 2022)—is not essentially theistic.[5]

Realist idealism is a form of *realism*. It no more denies the reality of the physical world than realist materialism does—it simply gives a different account of the *nature* of the physical world. An analogy may clarify: most physicalists about consciousness do not take themselves to be *doing away with experience*, but to be giving an account of the *nature of experience*. The concept of experience is substrate neutral. Similarly, the realist idealist is not (by definition) doing away with the physical world. Rather, they are giving an account of the nature of this world. It's an account that one may disagree

---

[4] Berkeley goes on to claim that idealism provides an answer to skepticism, and that the denial of idealism is as ridiculous as the denial of our own being. I don't think we should put stock in either claim.

[5] Though, despite the title of the book, the view is not essentially atheistic. It is simply neutral as to the existence of God. We'll return to this point in §6.4.3.

with. But it is no more a contradiction in terms than materialist phenomenal realism is.

Of course, one might reject the substrate neutral conception of experience. One might insist that *by definition*, phenomenal realism requires that experiences are non-material. Likewise, one might *define* realism (about the external world) as requiring that the world is non-experiential. In this case, realist idealism would be a contradiction in terms. Perhaps *real* realism requires matter that has OOMPH—and being phenomenal just isn't sufficiently oomphy.[6] I don't understand what this oomphiness is supposed to be.[7]

Beyond this, the parallel to phenomenal realism suggests that substrate-biased accounts of realism are a mistake. While I think that physicalism is incompatible with phenomenal realism, I take this to be a *substantive* claim—not something that we can know to be true simply by definition. What's important about phenomenal realism is its commitment to capturing the what-it's-like of experience—not its commitment to what experiences are made of.

Likewise, insofar as external world realism is a view that's worth caring about, it's not because it claims there's some substrate that we should all be committed to. If not a particular substrate, what is the core idea of realism? What's worth committing ourselves to is simply the idea that reality is independent of *our* minds.[8]

For the realist, my mind (human minds, animal minds, finite minds) do not constrain, construct, or shape reality. Our minds are but incidental.[9] This—more than the alleged oomphiness of insensible matter—strikes me as the important insight of realism.

---

[6] A similar intuitive commitment to "oomphiness" might lead one to define realism in such a way that digital realism and ontic structural realism become contradictions in term.

[7] Though I do understand wanting more than mere structure. We want the *qualities* that inhere in the structure!

[8] This accords with Nagel's (1986) account of realism. In arguing against idealism and in support of realism, Nagel writes, "I leave aside views, also called idealist, that hold reality to be correlative with minds in a much wider sense—including infinite minds, if there are such things.... The realism I am defending says the world may be inconceivable to *our* minds, and the idealism I am opposing says it could not be" (90–91).

[9] Not all forms of idealism are realist in this sense. Thomas Hofweber (2022) has recently defended an anti-realist form of idealism, on which totality of facts is constrained by human minds. Donald Hoffman (2019) defends a "consciousness realism," according to which physical objects are *our* conscious experiences, and do not exist when unperceived. And Foster (2008), insofar as he grants a privileged role to *human* sensory experience, also is not a realist (though I think one can also read Foster as emphasizing the importance of human sensory experience, without *privileging* it).

6 THE VIEW FROM EVERYWHERE

So the realist idealist is a realist. But they are also an *idealist*. What is the nature of this real physical world? For the idealist, it is fundamentally experiential.[10] On the view developed in this book, physical reality is a vast, non-agential unity of consciousness—independent of all ordinary minds—weaving together sensory experiences of colors, shapes, sounds, smells, and so on into the trees, stars, teacups, and bodies that fill the world around us. The world we inhabit is not a construction out of our own experiences, nor is it constructed out of merely possible experiences. Much as the materialist's world, it exists regardless of our beliefs, experiences, and existence. It existed before life evolved in our universe, and will (presumably) continue to exist long after we are gone. Unlike the materialist's world, it is a world of phenomenology—a world that is constructed out of the very thing we're directly acquainted with, the very appearances that form our conception of the world.

Berkeley is—as I read him—also a realist idealist, with similar ambitions to capture our common-sense view of the character of our world and our acquaintance with it. But the two views diverge from there. (i) This book develops an idealism that is nontheistic (in contrast to Berkeley's essentially theistic idealism). I offer (ii) a radically different and more minimal conception of subjects; (iii) a fleshed-out solution to the mind-body problem; (iv) a novel account of perception (though similar in motivation to Berkeley's); and (v) a wholly different way of understanding natural laws, which is more akin to standard materialist theories than Berkeley's theistic account. The motivations and broad shape are familiar, but the details are both novel and developed in far greater depth. Since Berkeley is also a realist idealist, I will use *nontheistic idealism* as shorthand for the view developed in this book.

It will be helpful to begin with Berkeley's positive view, to situate nontheistic idealism in relation to its more familiar predecessor.

1.1 Berkeley's Theistic Idealism

The details of Berkeley's positive position are the subject of significant debate. There is disagreement as to the nature of sensible objects, how Berkeley's

---

[10] The traditional framing casts idealism as the view that reality is fundamentally *mental*. I opt for the weaker assertion that reality is fundamentally experiential, as I'll remain neutral as to the precise relationship between experiences and minds. While I think it's plausible that experiences require experiencers (and hence minds, in some sense), I also want the view to be compatible with the possibility of free-floating experiences. This is an issue we'll return to in §1.3.

God ensures the persistence of reality, and whether objects persist when not perceived by ordinary minds. Given that my aim is neither to interpret nor to defend Berkeleyan idealism, I will not dwell on the nuances of Berkeley's idealism. Rather, I'll offer a brief overview of a few possible interpretations of Berkeley, in order to clarify the relation between his view and nontheistic idealism.

Sensible objects, for Berkeley, are collections of—or constructions out of—ideas (roughly, sensory phenomenology). As Berkeley puts it:

> what are [sensible objects] but the things we perceive by sense? and what do we PERCEIVE BESIDES OUR OWN IDEAS OR SENSATIONS? and is it not plainly repugnant that any one of these, or any combination of them, should exist unperceived? (Principles 4)
>
> Take away the sensations of softness, moisture, redness, tartness, and you take away the cherry, since it is not a being distinct from sensations. A cherry, I say, is nothing but a congeries of sensible impressions, or ideas perceived by various senses: which ideas are united into one thing (or have one name given them) by the mind, because they are observed to attend each other. (D3, 193)

One might object: we perceive non-mental external objects! Surely our ideas are but reflections of these external objects, that resemble the objects themselves. But, Berkeley argues, "an idea can be like nothing but an idea." As Philonous puts it:

> [H]ow can that which is sensible be like that which is insensible? Can a real thing, in itself INVISIBLE, be like a COLOUR; or a real thing, which is not AUDIBLE, be like a SOUND? In a word, can anything be like a sensation or idea, but another sensation or idea? (D1, 146)

So if we are to have a world of color and sound, a world of the sort ours seems to be, we are left with a world of sensations. But this picture is not complete for Berkeley, for "[a] little attention will discover to us that the very being of an idea implies passiveness and inertness in it, insomuch that it is impossible for an idea to do anything, or, strictly speaking, to be the cause of anything" (Principles 25). Since extension, figure, and motion are but ideas themselves, they cannot cause our (other) sensations.

8   THE VIEW FROM EVERYWHERE

But "[w]e perceive a continual succession of ideas, some are anew excited, others are changed or totally disappear. There is therefore some cause of these ideas, whereon they depend, and which produces and changes them." Since ideas are causally inert, and Berkeley takes himself to have shown the incoherence of material substance, he concludes that "the cause of ideas is an incorporeal active substance or Spirit" (Principles 26).

Mind (spirit) is not merely posited to account for causation. It is something that we are taken to be directly acquainted with. I am aware not just of ideas flitting through my mind, but of my own *willing*, and the effects that it has on these ideas. I can imagine a child running, imagine him tripping over a stone and falling on the grass. As Berkeley sees it, these ideas aren't just things that happen to me; I can produce and *change* them.

> [B]esides all that endless variety of ideas or objects of knowledge, there is likewise something which knows or perceives them, and exercises divers operations, as willing, imagining, remembering, about them. This perceiving, active being is what I call MIND, SPIRIT, SOUL, or MYSELF. By which words I do not denote any one of my ideas, but a thing entirely distinct from them, WHEREIN THEY EXIST, or, which is the same thing, whereby they are perceived—for the existence of an idea consists in being perceived. (Principles 2)

While in imagination, I can create, change, and get rid of ideas at will,

> I find the ideas actually perceived by Sense have not a like dependence on my will. When in broad daylight I open my eyes, it is not in my power to choose whether I shall see or no, or to determine what particular objects shall present themselves to my view; and so likewise as to the hearing and other senses; the ideas imprinted on them are not creatures of my will. (Principles 29)

Berkeley concludes that "[t]here is therefore some other spirit or will that produces them." This other spirit is God. God plays three central roles in Berkeley's metaphysics: He accounts for (i) the persistence of reality, and (ii) phenomenological difference we find between ideas of imagination and those of sense.

> The ideas imprinted on the Senses by the Author of nature [God] are called
> real things; and those excited in the imagination being less regular, vivid,
> and constant, are more properly termed *ideas*, or *images of things*, which
> they copy and represent. (Principles 33)

Further, (iii) God underwrites Berkeley's understanding of laws of nature.

> The ideas of Sense are more strong, lively, and distinct than those of the
> imagination; they have likewise a steadiness, order, and coherence, and are
> not excited at random, as those which are the effects of human wills often
> are, but in a regular train or series. (Principles 30)

Berkeley takes the liveliness and coherence of our ideas of sense to reveal the wisdom and benevolence of the mind from which they originate. Laws of Nature, then, are the "set rules or established methods" whereby God produces ideas of sense in us.

I take it to be fairly uncontroversial that Berkeley endorses the picture described thus far. But the precise manner in which Berkeley takes God to perform roles (i) and (iii) is contentious. First, there's the question of how God ensures the persistence of reality. At least four interpretations have been offered as to God's role in (i).

The *Perception Interpretation* holds that God's *experiences* sustain reality: God is always perceiving (or, more neutrally, experiencing[11]) the totality of reality. And, Ronald Knox's famous limerick would have it, "that's why the tree continues to be // since observed by, Yours faithfully, God."[12] John Foster (1982, 30) embraces this reading, writing that "God has an all-embracing perception of a vast spatiotemporal arrangement of sensible qualities—a perception, of course, of which he is the causal agent, rather than the passive recipient."

The *Conception Interpretation*, proposed by George Pitcher (1977), takes God to sustain reality, not through his perceptions, but through his thoughts—"i.e. by having ideas of them in His understanding" (175).

The *Phenomenalist Interpretation* of Berkeley holds that it's God's *dispositions* that sustain reality: to say that the tree continues to exist alone in

---

[11] As Pitcher (1977, 167) notes, perceptions must be caused (in part) by something outside of the perceiver, and no external being can affect God.

[12] As quoted in Downing (2011).

10 THE VIEW FROM EVERYWHERE

the quad is to say that, although God is not continually perceiving the tree, his will is responsible for ensuring that were we to attend in the right way, we *would* perceive the tree.

The *Phenomenalist Interpretation* is radically different from the previous two interpretations and seems at first incompatible with them. But Kenneth Winkler (1989) argues that the *Phenomenalist Interpretation* and the *Conception Interpretation* are compatible and mutually supportive. Given that Berkeley plausibly agreed with his contemporaries in the denial of "blind agency," for God to will that we have appropriate perceptions, God must have an idea of what it is that he's willing us to perceive. Thus, on Winkler's interpretation, the tree's continued existence depends on both dispositions and on his ideas. God both has an idea of the tree *and* wills that, under the right circumstances, we should perceive it.

A related interpretive question concerns the relation between our ideas and the corresponding divine ideas (assuming there are such ideas). When I have ideas of sense, do I literally share the same (numerical) idea as God? Possible readings of Berkeley include (i) that God does not have the same (numerical) ideas as me—but simply excites distinct ideas of sense within me; (ii) that God does have the same (numerical) ideas as me; and (iii) that the question of whether two ideas are numerically identical is unintelligible. Each interpretation has strikingly different implications for the nature of reality and its persistence. But since my interest here is not in Berkeley interpretation, I will set this question aside.[13]

So this is Berkeley's view in a nutshell: the trees, stars, bodies, and so on that populate our world are bundles of sensations (ideas). In addition to sensations, there also exist minds. Through introspection, we find that sensations (and the real things they constitute) are causally inert, whereas minds are *active*—affecting the world through acts of volition. Real things are those sensations which are "imprinted on our senses" by God. Perhaps God shares these experiences, or perhaps he just ensures that we have them in the appropriate circumstances. Regardless, the rules that God follows in imprinting these ideas on our senses are Laws of Nature, and account for the regularity of the world we live in.

---

[13] (i) fits naturally with the *Conception Interpretation* and the *Phenomenalist Interpretation*. (ii) fits naturally with the *Perception Interpretation*. (iii) seems compatible with any of these interpretations. Personally, I'm inclined toward (iii) as a reading of Berkeley, but I am philosophically most attracted to option (ii). Given that I'll take the *Perception Interpretation* as a jumping-off point for developing my nontheistic idealism, I'll start from an assumption of (ii).

1.2 Idealism without God

However it is that God accounts for the persistence and stability of reality, it is clear that God plays an enormously central role in Berkeley's metaphysics. In fact, Berkeley thought that idealism offered a novel argument for the existence of God: since ideas of sense can't be caused by other ideas or our own minds (and insensible matter is incoherent), they must be caused by some other spirit. And given the incredible complexity and regularity of ideas of sense, this other spirit must be incredibly wise, powerful, and good ... and hence, is God. But one philosopher's modus ponens is another's modus tollens. Few philosophers are persuaded by Berkeley's arguments for idealism, and it seems plausible that the theistic implications are a significant barrier to philosophers embracing idealism.[14]

Whatever your views about the existence of God, logically weaker claims are more likely to be true. An idealism that remains neutral as to the existence of God is theoretically superior to one that is inseparable from theism. So does idealism really require God? Is God—an omnipotent, omniscient, omnibenevolent creator—really, as Berkeley argues, the only remaining candidate to account for our ideas of sense? Or is there a more theologically and ontologically neutral way of accounting for these regularities?

I think that Berkeley has overstated his case. I think that we can have a coherent realist idealism without God, which captures the common-sense picture of the world and our relation to it that Berkeley sets out to deliver.

A theologically neutral account has two main advantages: first, ecumenicalism is a dialectical virtue. Not only will theologically neutral views have broader appeal as a matter of sociological fact, it has the virtue of making assumptions that are no more robust than necessary. Second, there's a methodological advantage. It's difficult to speculate freely about the structure and contents of the mind of God. Doing so seems a matter for theologians or mystics. Once we embrace the idea that there is a traditional God who accounts for the persistence and stability of the physical world, it's tempting to leave things at that. "God is aware of the totality of reality. He excites relevant ideas in me. *How* does he do this? What are his experiences

---

[14] The 2020 philpapers survey of philosophers found that 18.8 percent of faculty in target departments lean toward theism, and a mere 6.6 percent lean toward idealism (Bourget and Chalmers 2023).

12 THE VIEW FROM EVERYWHERE

like? Surely it's hubris to speculate!" The story ends there. The details of the theory are concealed within the "black box" of God's mind.

But this leaves crucial details of the metaphysics as mysteries. My experiences are all had from a single perspective. But God's mind encompasses *all* perspectives (human and otherwise). How could such a multi-perspective experience be structured? How does God account for the coherence and consistency of different individuals' experiences? How is it that I consistently perceive only the greenness of leaves, as opposed to their redness (which my color-inverted twin perceives)? These are details that a complete theory ought to flesh out.

Moving away from God gives us license to speculate about how such a fundamentally phenomenal world could hang together and what it could be like. It gives us license to speculate and to flesh out the details. And, as I'll argue in §6.4.3, the value of this is preserved, even if one ultimately adds God back into the picture. Even if we subsequently return to a more traditional theistic conception of reality, contemplation of idealism without God can help us to flesh out the details of a possible idealist world with far greater depth and precision.

So let's consider what an idealism without God might look like. I'll take Berkeleyan idealism as my starting point. This will yield a number of possible ways of thinking about nontheistic idealism, depending on which interpretation of Berkeley we begin with. The view I'll develop in this book corresponds to a nontheistic fleshing out of the *Perception Interpretation*.

1.3 God-minus

If real things are identified with divine dispositions—as opposed to with the *experiences* that God is disposed to create in us—then subtracting God yields a nontheistic phenomenalism. Reality is identified with a collection of dispositions. Without God to ground these dispositions, they are simply *ungrounded, brute* (cf. Pelczar 2019).

Alternatively, suppose that real things are collections of sensory experiences had by us, where God's volition accounts for the regularity of our experiences. Then, in the absence of God, we are left—as Tom Stoneham (2002) suggests of nontheistic Berkeleyanism—with real objects popping in and out of existence, with no explanation for this.

BERKELEY WITHOUT GOD   13

This is more radical and, I think, less plausible than a standard Millian phenomenalism. For Mill (1865), reality is comprised of Permanent Possibilities of Sensation (roughly, dispositions for there to be certain experiences under the right circumstances). My chocolate cake continues to exist when closed in the refrigerator, because these possibilities of sensation exist regardless of whether anyone is actually having a chocolate cakey experience. But on this second reading of Berkeley without God, the chocolate cake is identified with actual experiences had by finite beings. The chocolate cake may be experienced whenever I open the refrigerator door; but it does not literally persist when the door is closed.

We can also consider what happens when we subtract God from the view that reality is a collection of ideas *had and sustained by God*. The answer to this might seem obvious and unilluminating. Suppose we start with the *Perception Interpretation* and (per impossibile) vaporize God. In doing so, we obviously vaporize the physical world. But there's another way we can make sense of the *Perception Interpretation* without God.

Many attributes of God are not essential to the metaphysical role he plays in sustaining reality.[15] It's not essential that God be omnibenevolent. (God could, on occasion, have wicked thoughts, and still sustain our world.) It's not essential that God be all-powerful. (God could be unable to change the laws of physics or perform miracles, and yet sustain our world.) It's not essential that God be all-knowing, as it's not essential that God have doxastic attitudes at all. It is God's *experiences*, not his beliefs, desires, intentions, or anything about him as an agent, that are relevant to physical reality's continued existence. Rather than "vaporizing" God, a more promising way to construct a nontheistic idealism is to peel away the attributes of God that aren't essential for sustaining a reality, and see what sort of world we're left with (Yetter-Chappell 2018a).

If God sustains the external world through continual experiencing of it, what's essential to reality is his sensory phenomenology[16]: the experience of the pine needle's greenness, its shape, the smell of pine, the roughness of the bark, and so on. Of course, reality is not a disjoint collection of colors, shapes,

---

[15] Cf. Mary Calkins (1927), 141–143, who argues that "it is far from evident that a spirit adequate to produce nature should be 'eternal, infinitely wise, good and perfect.'"

[16] Note: I use "sensory phenomenology" here to distinguish the relevant sort of phenomenology from cognitive phenomenology. I use this to delineate experiences that are qualitatively akin to those that we gain through our senses. I don't mean to suggest that God has sensory organs or perceives anything independent of himself. I do not propose that God perceives *by* sense, merely that he has experiences qualitatively akin to those that *we* so perceive. It's still controversial to think of Berkeley's

14   THE VIEW FROM EVERYWHERE

textures, sounds, and smells. The greenness of the needles seems to inhere in their shape; the roughness of the bark seems bound up with the brownness. Reality has *structure*. God's experiences are no more disjoint than reality is. God's experiences, too, must have structure. (Without structure, God would not experience reality as a *whole*. Without structure, God would not experience *trees*, but merely green, brown, rough, soft, thin, fat, jumbled among all other features of existence.) And for the *Perception Interpretation*, the structure of God's experiences is presumably what gives reality its structure.

When we strip away features of God that are inessential to his role in grounding the world, we retain the structure of the remaining phenomenology. And this provides the structure of our world. What we're left with is a structured collection of sensory experiences: a unity of consciousness, weaving together sensory experiences of colors, shapes, sounds, smells, sizes, and so on, into the trees, chairs, black holes, and central nervous systems that fill the world around us. We might call the resulting structure *God-minus*.

Whereas I only experience reality from a single perspective—restricted by my spatial location and sensory apparatus—God is not so limited. God would not merely perceive the side of the tree visible from my window, but the tree in its entirety: top, bottom, sides, roots, and all. God would not merely perceive the human-visible spectrum, but ultraviolet, infrared, radio waves, and gamma rays: the entire electromagnetic spectrum. God would not merely perceive the greenness of the tree (which I perceive), but the indistinctness (perceived by the red-green colorblind), and the redness (perceived by my inverted twin). God contains multitudes. And the phenomenal unity that is God-minus would retain all this phenomenal complexity.

We saw that God performs a number of roles in Berkeley's metaphysics: he accounts for (i) the persistence of reality; (ii) phenomenological difference we find between ideas of imagination and those of sense; and (iii) laws of nature. God-minus seems equally well suited to playing the first two roles.

First, the persistence of reality. The tree persists in all its richness, even when no one's about in the quad. Why? Because there is unified sensory

---

God as having such experiences. Berkeley holds both that God can "suffer nothing," and also that our experiences of great heat are one sensation inseparable from pain. We might take God to have experiences that are qualitatively akin to our own only in a weak sense (i.e., not qualitatively *identical* to ours). Or we might disagree with Berkeley, either about God's "suffering nothing" or about the unity of great heat and pain. At the end of the day, my interest is not in defending Berkeleyan idealism or even to defend a neo-Berkeleyanism (de dicto). It's of little importance whether the starting point is one that Berkeley strictly would have adopted, so long as we wind up with an attractive form of realist idealism.

BERKELEY WITHOUT GOD   15

phenomenology as-of a tree in all its glory, whether this is perceived by any ordinary minds or no, and *that's* what the tree is. What about the phenomenological difference between ideas of imagination and those of sense? To flesh this out, we'd need an account of perception (to be developed in Chapter 4). But the rough idea is that—just as on the traditional Berkeleyan view—ideas of sense are not generated by my will, but come from God-minus. Given that God-minus is not an agent, and has no volition, these ideas are not "imprinted" on my mind by another will. Rather, I shall propose that we literally overlap with reality, sharing (partaking in) the ideas of God-minus.

But while God-minus can account for the stability of reality in roughly the same manner as God (on this interpretation of Berkeley) it cannot facilitate an analogous account of laws of nature. Having stripped away will and benevolence from the phenomenal unity, we cannot hold that laws of nature are *rules ordained by God.* (God-minus has no thought or will.) Laws of nature cannot be taken to display "the goodness and wisdom of that Governing Spirit whose Will constitutes the laws of nature" (Principles 32). So nontheistic idealism will need to offer a radically different account of laws of nature. I'll argue in Chapter 5 that the nontheistic idealist is in precisely the same position as the nontheistic materialist. And any account of laws that is available to such materialists is equally available to the nontheistic idealist.

This is, in a nutshell, the view that will be developed in this book: Reality is a vast unity of sensory phenomenology,[17] the phenomenal content and structure of which corresponds to the sensory experiences that would be had by the God of the *Perception Interpretation.* Just as God is not limited to a single perspective, but perceives reality from all perspectives, so too, this phenomenal unity includes phenomenology as-from all perspectives. And just as God's experiences are (presumably) not an incoherent jumble of sensations, but have structure, so too, this phenomenal unity has structure. This phenomenal unity is governed by laws analogous to those posited by materialists.

Unlike Berkeley, I've said nothing about Spirits. The entire picture, thus far, has been constructed out of phenomenology and relations between phenomenology. This naturally raises the question of *who* has the experiences of God-minus. We began with God, and imagined stripping away all doxastic

---

[17] Again, I use "sensory phenomenology" simply to distinguish from cognitive phenomenology.

16 THE VIEW FROM EVERYWHERE

attitudes and agency, as well as traditional divine attributes. Is the result still a mind? This is a question that I'll remain neutral on throughout the book. I see three candidate positions, which I'll label *Robust Mind*, *Thin Mind*, and *No Mind*.

One might think that experiences require experiencers, reasoning that experiences are essentially experienc*ed*—and for something to be experienc*ed* there must be an experienc*er*. As Frege (1956) puts it, "[t]he inner world presupposes the person whose inner world it is" (299). "Can there be a pain without someone who has it? Being experienced is necessarily connected with pain, and someone experiencing is necessarily connected with being experienced" (305).

But embracing an essential connection between experiences and subjects doesn't in itself tell us what subjects *are*. One option would be to follow Berkeley and take subjects to be something over and above— ontologically distinct from—the experiences that they experience. This would give us an ontology of experiences and minds. On this picture, the experiences that constitute our world would be collectively had by a cosmic mind—God-minus—where God-minus is a *Robust Mind* that experiences reality.

By contrast, Galen Strawson (2003) argues that subjects might be nothing over and above the experiences themselves—provided that we properly understand experiences as things that are by their very natures experienced. Strawson holds that experience is necessarily experience-for: he takes the idea of an experience without an experiencer to be an incoherent failure to grasp what experience is. Nevertheless, it does not follow from this that experiences are somehow distinct from subjects.

> It is not . . . clear that we can know that this . . . involves some sort of genuine ontological . . . distinction, as opposed to a merely conceptual distinction. . . . For there is a real distinction between two phenomena (so that genuine ontological plurality is in question) if and only if they can possibly "exist apart," and a merely conceptual distinction between them if and only if they are conceptually distinct but cannot possibly exist apart, like trilaterality and triangularity. And when we confine our attention to thin subjects . . . it seems quite unclear that the actual subject S of any given actual experience E can exist apart from E, even in thought. (Strawson 2003, 294–295)

This way of understanding the relation between subjects and experiences yields a different and more minimal picture of reality. Reality is constituted by a vast phenomenal unity. The experiences that make up our world are experience*d*, and hence there is an experienc*er* of these experiences. But this does not entail any addition to our ontology. There is a unity of sensory phenomenology. And, given an appropriate understanding of phenomenology, this entails that the unity is experienced. But there need not be some ontologically independent entity that does the experiencing. There is simply the sensory unity. The experiences that constitute reality are (essentially) experiences of a *Thin Mind*, which brings to our ontology nothing over and above the bundle of experiences themselves.

A third way to understand nontheistic idealism would be to deny any essential connection between experiences and minds: to embrace the idea that there could be free-floating phenomenology. If this were right, reality would simply be constituted by an experiencer-less phenomenal unity. This is the *No Mind* reading. One might question whether this is really a form of idealism, given that minds and mentality are in no way central to the picture. This doesn't worry me, per se. I don't care whether minds or mentality are essential to the picture, but with whether *phenomenology* is—as I'll argue that this is essential to capturing the common-sense picture of the world that motivates idealism. The difficulty with the *No Mind* view is that it's not clear that experiencer-less experiences are coherent. As Strawson argues, being experienced seems to be the essence of an experience. And it's not clear how something could be experienced without there being an experiencer. Still, the *No Mind* view is structurally identical to the earlier interpretations, and so it will be interesting to keep it in the back of our minds going forward. (I'll suggest in §6.2.3 that the *No Mind* view may be akin to Mark Johnston's [2007] picture of reality.)

I myself am partial to the *Thin Mind* view. I see no reason to add robust minds to our ontology. In fact, I'm not sure I understand what it is that robust minds are supposed to be. Like Hume, "when I enter most intimately into what I call myself, I always stumble on some particular perception or other, of heat or cold, light or shade, love or hatred, pain or pleasure. I can never catch myself at any time without a perception, and can never observe anything but the perception" (2000, 165).

But if you are attracted to the *Robust Mind* view, everything written in this book is also compatible with this. You should feel free to interpret the rest

18 THE VIEW FROM EVERYWHERE

of the book accordingly. (The resulting view will be closer to the traditional Berkeleyan view than on the thin reading.)

Thus far, I have focused on the nature of the physical world that we inhabit. But I have said nothing about creatures like us and how we fit into this picture of reality. Developing such a view is the second main aim of this book and will be central to showing how idealism can make good on its promise to give us a world that not only is as it appears, but which we can *grasp directly*.

The central idea is that in perception, the perceived aspects of reality are bound by the unity of consciousness relation into two distinct phenomenal unities: God-minus (physical reality) and the mind of the perceiver. In perception, the perceived features of reality become a part of your mind in just the same way that your aches and pains are. Your acquaintance with them is equally direct. Central to this is giving accounts of (a) our minds and (b) their relation to the physical world, that renders this intelligible. This is the task of Chapters 3 and 4.

1.4 The Plan

Thus far, I've characterized reality in a top-down way, beginning with God and then eliminating the features that weren't essential to ensuring the persistence of reality. Doing so enabled us to quickly get to the heart of nontheistic idealism. But starting with a black box and subtracting from it doesn't help to illuminate the contents of the box. And this is essentially what we have done in characterizing reality in terms of God-minus. Chapter 2 develops an alternative way to understand nontheistic idealism. Rather than beginning with God-minus (the phenomenal unity) and trying to deconstruct the contents and structure of the physical world, we'll begin with the aspects of the phenomenal unity—phenomenal greenness, warmth, roughness, sweetness, middle C—and see how they can be woven together into a world like ours. I'll describe reality as a phenomenal tapestry, weaving simple bits of phenomenology into a complex structure akin to God-minus. By considering how such a tapestry of reality might be constructed, we'll come to a better grasp of the structure of idealist reality, and the way in which the different phenomenal threads hang together. This will be essential in future chapters for developing detailed accounts of perception and the compatibility of idealism and science.

My aim is to show how there could be an idealist world that is precisely the way we take our world to be. As such, I'll take our world[18] as a guide. There could be all sorts of different idealist worlds: worlds with alien properties, worlds with floating pink elephants that only certain people can see, worlds with conceptualizations built into the very fabric of reality. But I don't take such worlds to be *our world*. My aim is not to make claims about what idealist worlds *must* look like, rather I'll endeavor to give most plausible snapshot of *our* world as an idealist world.

In Chapter 3 I begin the work of situating *us* in idealist reality, considering what the mind-body problem looks like within an idealist framework. For idealists, our bodies are bits of phenomenology within the phenomenal tapestry (God-minus). But how do experiences, thoughts, and conscious subjects-of-experience like us fit into the picture? Are my pains, desires, and perceptions parts of the phenomenal tapestry? Are they primitive or do they reduce to other bits of phenomenology, such as those that constitute my brain?

Idealism, per se, is not a position on the mind-body problem. It is simply a view about the nature of physical reality. In fact, idealism does not directly constrain the options available in addressing the mind-body problem. There are, I will argue, idealist analogues of reductive physicalism, dualism, and panpsychism. But embracing idealism does render reductive accounts of the mind-body transparently implausible (a result that, I'll argue, points toward a novel argument against physicalism).

I'll argue that idealists ought to embrace a nonreductive solution to the mind-body problem, in conjunction with a novel externalist account of psychophysical bridging laws. This externalist account of bridging laws holds special appeal within an idealistic context, as it will facilitate the direct contact with reality defended in Chapter 4.

Chapter 4 shows how an epistemically powerful theory of perception is made available through the conjunction of the nontheistic idealism (Chapter 2) and the externalist account of bridging laws (Chapter 3). Externalist bridging laws function to "expand" our minds, ensuring that the perceived facets of reality are *literal constituents* of our mind. As a result, our perceptual contact with reality is just as direct as the contact we have with our own minds. We are not merely acquainted with a representation of the world or a sense datum corresponding to it: we are directly acquainted

---

[18] Our empirical observations and intuitions about what our world is like.

20   THE VIEW FROM EVERYWHERE

with *the world* itself. The greenness of the leaves and the roughness of the bark are aspects of reality . . . and, in perception, they are also aspects of me. I dub this theory "Naïve Idealism." This account of perception bears obvious similarities to naïve realism. I return to this issue in Chapter 6, where I argue that such direct contact with reality is only intelligible if the world is fundamentally phenomenal.

In addition to fleshing out an idealist account of veridical perception, I offer accounts of hallucination and illusion. The latter diverges markedly from Berkeley's purely cognitive account, and shows that idealists have the resources to give a more common-sense explanation of illusions, on which (at least) some involve defective phenomenology, as opposed to merely defective judgments.

Chapter 5 turns to compatibility of idealism and the scientific worldview, including the physical structure of reality, the nature of space and time, and laws of nature. Idealism gives us a world of color, warmth, and sound. But, I argue, the idealist does not need to deny that there are also microstructural facts about the surfaces of objects that cause (only) certain wavelengths of light to be reflected. The idealist does not need to deny that there are molecules and molecular kinetic energy. The idealist does not need to deny that vibrations cause compression waves to propagate through the air, to my ear, causing me to hear sounds. This chapter looks at how the idealist makes sense of these microphysical truths (hint: they're collections of structured phenomenology), and at the relation between microphysics and the macroscopic entities we're directly acquainted with.

Next, we turn to the regularities we find in nature. As we've seen, when we move away from theistic idealism, we lose Berkeley's explanation of these regularities. The phenomenal tapestry (God-minus) is not an *agent* with a *will*. Laws of nature cannot be taken to display "the goodness and wisdom of that Governing Spirit whose Will constitutes the laws of nature" (Principles 32), as God-minus has no such will. Nontheistic idealism needs to offer a different account of laws of nature. But the task facing the nontheistic idealist is no different from that facing the nontheistic materialist. And any account of laws that is available to such materialists is equally available to the nontheistic idealist, for physical laws are—rightly—neutral as to the metaphysical nature of that which they govern. The idealist need simply understand the elements being related in accordance with idealism: as phenomenal. And there's nothing in any of the standard accounts of laws that prevents us from doing so.

I'll argue that idealism is compatible with both substantivalism and relationalism. The idealist relationalist denies that spacetime exists as an independent aspect of physical reality. The threads of the tapestry stand in spatial relations to each other, and that's what it is for there to be space. These relations are *phenomenal* relations insofar as they are relations among phenomenal elements. For the substantivalist idealist, there is an absolute spacetime that exists independently of the (phenomenal) objects within it. This might seem incoherent. (Surely qualia don't exist within space!) But it's only incoherent given a materialist understanding of space. It doesn't make sense to think of qualia as existing within a *physical* space. But the substantivalist idealist understands spacetime differently: as the sort of four-dimensional array that houses phenomenal properties. I propose two ways to make sense of this, one of which holds the promise of reconciling eternalism with common-sense intuitions about temporal passage.

We'll also consider the biggest challenge to idealism: that of ontological profligacy. Nontheistic idealism entails that physical objects have a huge number of phenomenal aspects. The leaf includes not only phenomenal greenness, but phenomenal indistinct-coloredness (as perceived by the red-green colorblind), phenomenal redness (as perceived by my inverted twin), phenomenal infrared (as perceived by the snake), and so on. I'll argue that this sort of ontological profligacy is not such a terrible cost after all.

Chapter 6 concludes with an exploration of the theoretical virtues that come from embracing the conjunction of a nontheistic idealist metaphysics and a naïve idealist theory of perception. In contrast with materialism, idealism offers a picture of reality and our place within it according to which (i) the nature of reality is intelligible to us. Not only is reality intelligible, (ii) it is as it appears, and (iii) its nature and character is something that we can grasp directly. The intuitive picture of the world that we began the book with is vindicated. The upshot of this is that we can have our science (Chapter 5) and common-sense too.

One might have thought that we didn't need to uproot our metaphysics in order to achieve this. This is the claim of naïve realism. Naïve realists about perception take us to directly grasp the character of the world, and yet take reality to be material (i.e., not fundamentally experiential). Property naïve realists take appearance properties to be mind-independent primitive properties possessed by physical objects. If these naïve realist views are tenable, one needn't embrace idealism in order to capture common-sense.

22 THE VIEW FROM EVERYWHERE

But naïve realism isn't tenable. Chapter 6 argues that that perceptual naïve realism can only be rendered intelligible if the external world has the correct nature: if it's fundamentally phenomenal. This is because the acquaintance relation on which the naïve view depends can only intelligibly relate us to phenomenal items. If we want to account for the epistemic access we naïvely take ourselves to have on the world, we must embrace a phenomenal conception of reality. We must embrace idealism.

Nor does property naïve realism offer a viable way of capturing the world of common-sense. We will see that property naïve realists must either arbitrarily privilege certain appearances over others, or abandon the idea that colors are manifest in their appearances. Further, they face serious challenges in explaining how we can be *aware of* color—undercutting the rationale for embracing the view. The world of common-sense is available to us if *and only if* reality is fundamentally experiential.

The upshot of this chapter, and of the book, is *not* that you *have to* be an idealist. I have already noted: you don't. My aims are, rather, (a) to present a fully fleshed out idealist picture of reality and our place within it, and then (b) to assess this picture holistically against alternative conceptions of reality and our place therein. Chapters 2–5 develop the idealist's positive picture of the world. Chapter 6 turns to the second aim. If I'm right that there are both idealist and materialist worlds that subjectively appear to their inhabitants the way that our world appears to us, the question is not *must we* embrace idealism, but rather: how much confidence should we have that *the actual world* is among the idealist worlds, versus among the materialist worlds? I argue that the best way to do this is compare the complete worldview on offer from idealism against the complete worldview on offer from materialism. When we do this, idealism looks far more compelling than most philosophers suppose.

The book concludes by assessing nontheistic idealism against other "mind-first"[19] alternatives, including panpsychism, phenomenalism, and theistic idealism.

While I'll often write about "nontheistic idealism" as though it were a single unitary view, it is actually a family of related views, members of which will be noted in passing throughout the book. One way of looking at the book

---

[19] This is a term coined by Michael Pelczar to capture what's in common between theories like idealism, phenomenalism, and panpsychism, in which consciousness plays a central role. While not all of these theories make consciousness fundamental, none of the theories can be stated without making reference to consciousness.

is as a mix-and-match recipe for constructing a plausible idealism. There are a number of choice points throughout the book. We've already seen one: whether the physical world is a mind or not, and (if so) whether it's a robust addition to our ontology. Each way of answering this question will lead you to a different ultimate account of the world—perhaps with different costs and virtues. Other choice points concern whether cognitive phenomenology is part of the physical world (Chapter 2), the relationship between our minds and the physical world (Chapter 3), the nature of spacetime (Chapter 5), and whether to reintroduce traditional divine attributes (Chapter 6). At each point, I'll make the case for the position that strikes me as the most plausible, and will stipulate my answer for the rest of the book. But readers may disagree. I encourage readers to make their own judgments at these choice points: to see what sort of idealism you wind up with, and to assess how it fares in relation to the virtues discussed in Chapter 6.

The space of possible worlds is vast. The space of idealist possible worlds is vast. Just as when considering the choice between materialism and idealism, when considering different forms of idealism, it seems to me that the question is not *must* we embrace this version of idealism or that one, but rather, which sort of idealist world is the actual world most likely to be? It seems to me that the physical world we live in doesn't include cognitive phenomenology (Chapter 2). It seems to me that our non-perceptual experiences are not a part of the physical world (Chapter 3). But your mileage may vary. Drive it your way.

2
The Phenomenal Tapestry

In the previous chapter, we explored a top-down way of construing idealist reality: as God-minus. Our intuitive grasp of what God's mind encompasses gave us the ability to quickly capture the heart of the view. But although this captures the essence of the view, it also obscures many details that a thorough metaphysics should flesh out. God's mind—and so the phenomenal unity that is God-minus—encompasses all perspectives (human and otherwise). But how could such a multi-perspective experience be structured? What would such a multi-perspective unity of consciousness be *like*?

In this chapter, I aim to address these questions, by developing an alternative way of conceptualizing this idealist reality. Rather than beginning with the phenomenal unity (God-minus), and trying to deconstruct its contents and structure, we will begin with the phenomenal components (or aspects) that intuitively constitute reality, and see how they can be woven into a world like ours.

I find the metaphor of a tapestry illustrative. The green of the leaf I see out my window, the white of the clouds beyond it, the sound of Sarasate playing on the radio are like threads of a vast phenomenal tapestry. In an ordinary cloth tapestry, fiber threads are woven into a complex structure that ensures both that the cloth hangs together and that the appropriate threads to form the picture are always at the fore. Similarly, for the idealist, phenomenal threads are woven into the structure of reality: the phenomenal tapestry of our world. This gives us another way of understanding the very same structure described in Chapter 1. In the one case, we begin with a completed tapestry (God-minus); in the other, we begin with pieces of thread, and weave them together. But the end result in each case is the same.

By considering how the different phenomenal threads hang together, we will come to a better grasp on the structure of idealist reality. It is important to note that although I will write of the "tapestry of reality" being *constructed* or *woven* from phenomenal threads, I do not thereby mean to take a stand

The View from Everywhere. Helen Yetter-Chappell, Oxford University Press. © Oxford University Press 2025. DOI: 10.1093/9780197795057.003.0002

on which of these is more fundamental. I intend this locution, and the view developed here, to be compatible with both smallism (to borrow a term from Sam Coleman 2006) and priority monism (Schaffer 2010, Goff 2017). On a smallist reading, the phenomenal threads are fundamental. The existence of, and qualitative nature of, the tapestry is explained by the existence of these threads and the relations they stand in to one another. On a priority monist reading, the tapestry is fundamental, and the threads exist derivatively.

This book takes no stand on whether the tapestry or the threads are fundamental—or, indeed, on whether there is a real metaphysical difference between (otherwise identical) smallist and priority monist worlds. The worldly structure that I'm interested in is structure about which all sides on the fundamentality debate can agree. As a toy example, consider a block tower. We can all agree that block A is on the top, blocks B and C support A, and so on . . . regardless of whether the blocks or the tower is fundamental. This is the sort of structure that I'm interested in. Which blocks are on top of which blocks? Which threads are bound to which threads? What are the threads like and what is it that binds them? There's a sense in which a priority monist can agree that a tapestry is woven out of threads. It is precisely this sense in which I use the term "woven," and it is this sort of structure that is the focus of this book.

In comparing reality to a tapestry, two immediate questions arise: What are the threads? And how are these threads structured? In the next section I'll offer a schematic overview of the answers to both questions. In §2.2 I will consider the structuring relations in more detail, and in §2.3 will return to the question of what the threads are.

2.1 Overview

To the nontheistic idealist, the physical world is a vast phenomenal unity. As such, it is something of a sort that we're intimately acquainted with. We might hope that reflection on our own minds and how they are unified could prove illustrative in making sense of the structure of the tapestry of reality. I think this is right when it comes to understanding the *structure* of reality, but it is of limited use when it comes to understanding the *contents* of our world.

The tapestry of reality is vastly richer than the phenomenal unities we're directly acquainted with. Consider my cup. What's included in the phenomenal unity (physical reality) isn't merely the sensations *I* have when

26   THE VIEW FROM EVERYWHERE

perceiving the cup from a particular vantage point. There is, after all, no reason to think that I (or humans more generally) have a uniquely epistemically privileged grasp of reality. The bat, the bee, and the color-invert all have an equally good claim on grasping the nature of reality. Thus, our phenomenal tapestry must include experiences as of the cup from every possible perspective it could be viewed from—binding together experiences as of the cup from every possible angle and as of from every possible sort of perceiver.

This is another way of fleshing out the multitude of experiences that would comprise God-minus. God doesn't merely experience the world from my perspective, or from all human perspectives, but from *all* perspectives. Thus, these two ways of fleshing out the phenomenal components of reality should be coextensive. These bits of phenomenology, very roughly, comprise the threads of the tapestry of reality.

While I have tried to give a sense of the scope of the phenomenology that makes up the tapestry by appeal to the phenomenology that could be had by possible perceivers, the threads should not be understood as merely possible experiences, but as *actual* experiences qualitatively akin to those that would be had were there to be such perceivers. So the tapestry includes *experiences* as though from every possible perspective, *not* possible-experiences from different perspectives.

But reality isn't merely a collection of colors, shapes, textures, odors, and sounds, any more than a sweater is merely a pile of yarn. Reality has *structure*. Blueness inheres in the vast expanse of sky, greenness in the teardrop-shaped leaf; the smell of bread baking pervades the air, as warmth does the water of your bath. All this seems to be laid out in space: the green bushiness of the palm trees lies *below* the blue of the sky; the noise of construction comes from the campus, to my left. And all these things seem to be parts of a *single* reality.

What provides the structure of reality? Given a phenomenal conception of reality, the same unifying relations that structure ordinary minds like ours plausibly also structure reality.[1] Return to our Berkeleyan starting point. God's mind is very much a black box to us, but it is presumably not a fragmented heap of disconnected phenomenology, willings, and so forth. Without structure, God would not be an agent, but a jumble of disconnected

---

[1] The precise relations necessary to structure an individual's experiences are disputed. Tye (2003) distinguishes between object unity, spatial unity, subject unity, introspective unity, and phenomenal unity. Bayne and Chalmers (2003) appeal to objectual unity, spatial unity, subsumptive unity, access unity, and phenomenal unity.

attitudes and experiences. Without structure, God would not experience reality as a *whole*. Without structure, God would not experience *trees* but merely green, brown, rough, thin, fat, jumbled among all other features of existence. When we strip away features of God so as to be left with God-minus, we retain the structure of the remaining phenomenology. While my interest is not in Berkeley per se, or in an account that accurately captures traditional Christian theology, it is plausible within such a tradition that the relations that structure God's mind are akin to those structuring our own minds—for it is held that God created us in his image and likeness. So let us grant that (at first pass)[2] the same relations that structure our minds also structure God-minus and our tapestry. What are these relations?

At the broadest level, we have the unity of consciousness relation. Within a finite agent's mind, the unity of consciousness relation binds together all the experiences of the individual into a single overarching experience. When you have an experience of seeing a bird hopping from branch to branch, feeling the breeze against your skin, and hearing the leaves rustling, you have a single overarching experience of which all these experiences are aspects.[3] This is different from a scenario in which one person sees the bird hopping, another feels the breeze, and a third hears the rustling. In the first scenario, but not the second, the experiences are all phenomenally unified: bound into a single experience by the unity of consciousness relation. (At present, I'm simply stipulating that the unity of consciousness relation is whatever relates experiences in this way. Precisely how to make sense of this relation is a topic about which much has been written, and to which we'll return in §2.2.) The suggestion is that for the idealist, the unity of consciousness relation does more than structure *our minds*: it structures *reality*. Within the minds of finite agents, the unity of consciousness binds together experiences into those belonging to a single subject. Within the tapestry of reality, this relation binds experiences from all perspectives into a single *world*.

But the unity of consciousness is not the only relation to structure my experiences, nor can it be the sole relation that structures reality. In addition to my experiences all seeming to be aspects of a single overarching

---

[2] Things will ultimately be more complicated, as reality structures *all* perspectives, whereas our minds only structure a single perspective. Making sense of this will require phenomenal indexing, to which we will return.

[3] I don't mean to commit to the claim that the overarching experience is *made up out of* stand-alone experiences. This is simply the most natural way of describing the scenario. Readers who do not take experiences to have experiential parts should feel free to redescribe appropriately. We will return to the question of whether there are experiential parts in §2.2.2.

28   THE VIEW FROM EVERYWHERE

experience, some facets of my experience seem more intimately related. When I look at a tree, I experience the greenishness of the tree as bound up with the leaf-shape and the brownishness as bound up with the trunk-shape. Color and shape are not free-floating. Nor does the warmth of the bath float free from its wet-feel. We take this to mirror relationships that are present in reality. Reality is not (to borrow a term from Goff 2017) *blobby*. The warmth of the bath is bound up with its wetness, and the roughness with the trunk of the tree in an especially intimate way.

Within psychology, the "binding problem" is a collection of problems relating to our capacity to integrate information. In visual perception, many perceived features of objects are processed in a distributed fashion across the brain, analyzed by separate neural subsystems, raising the question of how the information about these features can be brought back together to form a perception of a unified object (Treisman 2003). While my concern here is not with the underlying neurophysiology, the conscious relation that results from this process is precisely what we need to make sense of the structure both of our minds and of the tapestry of reality. Psychologists distinguish a variety of different sorts of feature binding. The one that is essential to making sense of the structure of reality is property binding, which (as the name suggests) binds together different properties into a structured whole.[4]

While my experience of a leaf might simply bind together shape and color, in the tapestry of reality, the tree will bind together shapes and colors from many different perspectives into a much more complex structure. This poses a distinct challenge: in my experience, the leaf is green all over; in my inverted twin's experience, the leaf is red all over. But both these experiences (arguably) have equal claim to being part of the tapestry of reality. So within the tapestry, the leaf is both green all over and red all over: an absurdity. Note that this challenge could equally well be leveled against God. If God perceives everything from all possible perspectives, God will perceive the leaf as both red all over and green all over; God's mind contains a contradiction!

If you suspect, at this point, that there's something misguided about the objection, you're right to do so. The question is *how* the structure of reality

---

[4] Another sort of feature binding, binding of parts, involves "integration in a structured relationship of the separately codable parts of a single object," for instance, binding together the eyes, nose, and mouth as parts of a face (Treisman 2003, 98). I'm wary to include this among the relations structuring reality, as this seems to blur into including cognitive phenomenology—perceiving things *as objects*—into the tapestry. For reasons that will become clear in §2.3.2, this is something I think we should avoid. The spatial relations I will discuss next will give us a weaker relation of a related sort, namely, the nose, eyes, and mouth being *included within the space of* the face.

can be made sense of such that this isn't a contradiction: how might the mind of a god be structured so as to render this intelligible?

Return to our tapestry analogy. An ordinary tapestry is woven out of threads. A thread is not a single strand of fiber. Rather, multiple individual strands are twisted together (and sometimes bonded with chemical agents) to form the thread. This offers a compelling analogy for the tapestry of reality. Reality is not woven directly out of bits of phenomenology. Rather, bits of phenomenology *indexed to a perspective* are bonded into the "threads" out of which reality is woven. The green phenomenology I have as I look at the leaf of the tree is indexed to a perspective: $green_{[perspective1]}$. The red phenomenology my i-twin has as she looks at the leaf is indexed to another perspective: $red_{[perspective2]}$. These two bits of indexed phenomenology (along with phenomenology indexed to all other possible perspectives) are akin to the individual fibers that make up a thread. This indexed phenomenology is bonded into the thread out of which the leaf is woven: $green_{[perspective1]}$ + $red_{[perspective2]}$ + . . . Thus, it is not true to say that the leaf is red all over and green all over *simpliciter*. Rather, the leaf is green all over from *perspective 1*, and red all over from *perspective 2*. This is clearly not a contradiction, nor is it problematic.

I think of indices as akin to hashtags for bits of experiential content. But the hashtags are thin. Unlike #metoo—which carries some of its content with it—the indices merely structure the existing content. So the indices shouldn't be thought of as further experiential content. There is not the greenish phenomenology *and* the perspective1 phenomenology, which need to be conjoined. Nevertheless, the indices do affect the phenomenology of the tapestry as a whole insofar as it affects the structure of the content.

I propose that we think of phenomenal strands as having two distinct hashtags, which we can think of as corresponding to perceptual system (ps) and spatial location (lo).

The plate I'm currently looking at—which appears circular to me from this spatial vantage point, but elliptical from others—might be a bundle of indexed phenomenology like so:

$$circle_{\#ps1,\#lo1}, \; horizontal\text{-}ellipse_{\#ps1,\#lo2}, \; vertical\text{-}ellipse_{\#ps2,\#lo1}, \; circle_{\#ps2,\#lo2} \cdots$$

(Here, perceptual system 2 corresponds to a creature for whom shapes are smooshed along the x-axis in relation to my experiences.)

30 THE VIEW FROM EVERYWHERE

In addition to the unity of consciousness relation (which binds all of reality into a single world) and property binding (which binds together all the aspects of the tree into a single entity), there are spatial relations. All my experiences appear to belong to a single shared space. And this shared experiential space has spatial structure: the green bushiness of the palm is *below* the blue sky; the noise of construction is coming from the campus to *my left*; your eyes are located *within* the bounds of your face. And we take this perceived spatial structure to mirror a real structure that exists within reality. As before, the suggestion is that the same relations that structure our experiences also structure the tapestry of reality. There are also temporal relations, including diachronic unity and temporal ordering relations. We'll set these aside until Chapter 5, when we develop a realist idealist account of time. As for the other relations that structure reality, the proposal will be that the same relations that structure our experiences of time also account for the temporal structure of reality.

The tapestry of reality is vastly more complex than our minds. Each thread of my experience might be thought of as a single strand of phenomenology.[5] By contrast, the threads of reality are complex structures constructed out of indexed phenomenology. But the very same relations are at work in weaving these threads into our experiences and the world we inhabit. While the contents are richer and the structure more complex, we don't need any new tools to explain how it's held together.

2.1.1 Unifying Distinct Perspectives

As I've described it, physical reality is akin to a tapestry woven out of phenomenology, and structured via the same phenomenal relations that structure our own minds. But this phenomenal tapestry is vastly richer than our own minds. To accommodate this richness, I've suggested that the phenomenology is indexed to different perspectives.

But this might give one pause. Sure, phenomenology from a single perspective can be co-conscious and phenomenally property-bound together. But can *indexed* phenomenology from *divergent perspectives* really be related

---

[5] Though I'll complicate this in the following section by suggesting that even our own experiences might not be so simple—but might be better thought of as small, unified collections of indexed strands.

in this way? Is it really coherent for greenness-from-here and grayness-from-there to be not just co-conscious but *property-bound*?

Idealists might simply respond that it isn't reasonable to expect humans to be able to wrap their minds around the phenomenal tapestry, since we're not creatures who perceive things from multiple perspectives simultaneously—but that this isn't a reason to doubt the possibility of such phenomenal unities. I don't think this is an unreasonable move. We can't know what it's like to be a bat or an octopus. It seems undeniably and wholly expected that there would be epistemic limitations preventing us from knowing what it's like to be Physical Reality. But given how central the possibility of such unity is to the nontheistic idealist's project, I think it's reasonable to want something *more*. Fortunately, I don't think the position is quite as hopeless as it might seem, as there are limited ways in which *we* integrate multiple perspectives.

At a first pass, one might appeal to Berkeley's example of the warm and cold hands placed in an intermediate bucket of water. The water is simultaneously experienced as cold-from-R-hand-perspective and hot-from-L-hand-perspective. And I am simultaneously co-conscious of both experiences. So it clearly is possible for divergent perspectives to be co-conscious. The limitation of this analogy is that—while the divergent experiences are co-conscious—it's not clear that they're property-bound. I certainly take the hot experience and the cold experiences to be experiences of the same water. But plausibly, the *phenomenology* isn't what unifies the hot-experience and the cold-experience. Rather, there's an intellectual *judgment*, based on other visual and tactile data that I'm receiving, that leads me to conclude that both experiences are of the same thing. But the phenomenal tapestry as I've described it is a purely sensory unity. Insofar as judgment is required to make sense of these temperature experiences as constituting a single object, this doesn't help illuminate how divergent perspectives could be property-bound within the phenomenal tapestry.

A better analogy is binocular vision. You have an experience of the world when you close your right eye. You have a subtly different experience of the world when you close your left eye. Your two eyes, functioning independently, offer two subtly different perspectives on the world. When we have both eyes open, our experience seems to encompass both eye-perspectives. Suppose you're looking at a teacup. You don't have two separate (but co-conscious) experiences, as in the case of the water. Rather, the experiences are *integrated*. Nothing is lost from the right-eye experience or the left-eye experience. But the phenomenology of these two more limited perspectives

32   THE VIEW FROM EVERYWHERE

is *fused* into a single property-bound experience.[6] Curiously, when we fuse the right-eye perspective and the left-eye perspective, we also get more: we get *depth*. The two perspectives don't wind up superimposed on one another. Rather, they are integrated in a way that includes both experiences and gives us additional phenomenology: an experience of the relation between the two simple perspectives. It's natural to wonder whether something similar might be true for the phenomenal tapestry: whether the integration of phenomenology from different "mini" perspectives might yield distinct relational phenomenology not present in any smaller perspective.

This might not seem like much. For humans, our eyes are close enough together that it's difficult[7] to notice the differences between them. But no matter how subtle the differences, they raise the same quandary: an angle cannot be 90 degrees and 91 degrees at the same time; an ellipse cannot have an eccentricity of .3 and .35 at the same time. Our experience of binocular vision illustrates that it's possible for multiple *apparently conflicting* perspectives to be unified into a single unity of consciousness, *and for their phenomenology to be property-bound*. While the phenomenal tapestry includes far more content and far more diversity, this is arguably a mere difference in degree from what we ourselves experience.

We can develop this by imagining different variations of humans and other actually existing creatures. It's hard to imagine that our eye spacing is essential for phenomenal integration. (*Only eyes that are 70 mm or fewer apart can yield integrated visual phenomenology!*) Some of us have broader faces and wider-set eyes than others. And presumably there is no problem with the integration of experiences for friends with wider-set eyes. Taking things a step further, many prey animals have eyes on the sides of their heads—which, nevertheless, presumably feed into a single unified visual experience. We can now imagine shifting the eyes to locations that are further askew. Imagine eye positions such that one sees a dinner plate from above and another sees it from an angle. One eye will capture an image of a circle; the other will capture the image of an ellipse. And—if the eyes function analogously to ours—the

---

[6] Try tilting your head to the side, so one eye is above the other. Then look at a teacup so that you can see both the mouth of the cup and the body. If you close the top eye, you will see a narrower ellipse. If you close the bottom eye, you will see a wider ellipse. Alternating between one eye and two eyes open, you'll get a feel for how there can be a single experience that quite literally encompasses two perspectives.

[7] But not impossible!

two images will be woven into one phenomenal experience, without losing information from either.[8]

If two experiences that vary to a small degree along dimension d can be phenomenally integrated, it's hard to see how we could block off the possibility of phenomenal integration among experiences that vary to a larger degree along dimension d.

One might question, on empirical grounds, whether such a spectrum principle is legitimate. Within human binocular vision, too much variation in the inputs to both eyes ceases to yield binocular fusion, but instead yields either binocular rivalry or binocular superimposition. This typically takes the form of binocular rivalry, in which we either alternate between experiencing R-eye image (R) and L-eye image (L), or we experience a piecemeal image made up out of bits of R and bits of L (Palmer 1999, 216).[9] There is a line *for us* between inputs that generate binocular vision and those that generate binocular rivalry. It might be reasoned that this line that holds for us holds of metaphysical necessity; hence radically different phenomenology within the tapestry cannot possibly be integrated.

But the necessity claim is baseless. While some similarity may be required to yield integration, *how much* similarity is sufficient is contingent on how the individual organism processes information. Compare: to me, a 100 g weight appears indistinguishable from a 101 g weight. But while these appear the same to *me*, this is contingent on human processing. The two weights might seem radically dissimilar to a creature with different processing. Likewise, while our eyes have about 140 degrees of binocular overlap, most birds have only 20 degrees of overlap (Maier et al. 2022, 346). Given the plausible assumption that birds have a single, integrated visual experience, there is clearly no *metaphysical* barrier to the integration of experiences that are far more dissimilar than those humans can integrate.

---

[8] I do not mean to commit myself to any claims about the neurobiological mechanisms at work in human binocular vision. It is an open question whether or to what extent the information taken in by our two eyes is processed independently prior to being brought together into a single image (Palmer 1999, 211–212; Maier et al. 2022). The crucial point for our purposes is not the functional mechanisms that generate binocular fusion, but the simple fact of it: the fact that in binocular vision, we have a single phenomenal experience that encompasses phenomenology as-from different perspectives.

[9] Though when the two eyes see different inputs very briefly (less than 200 ms), one experiences a superimposition in which both images are overlayed into a single image (e.g., vertical stripes seen by one eye and horizontal stripes seen by the other will appear as a single image of a checkerboard pattern) (Blake and Tong 2008).

34   THE VIEW FROM EVERYWHERE

It's not surprising that binocular fusion would require some degree of commonality between the images being fused. And it's not surprising that the amount of commonality that's required be a contingent matter that can vary depending on the psychology of the creature. But even if each individual creature necessarily has *some* threshold for the commonality that's required for integration, we can't reason from this to the necessity of any given threshold.

One need only look to other biological organisms to find plausible examples of integration that radically outstrip what we experience, and offer plausible models for the phenomenal tapestry. While we have only two eyes— only two visual perspectives to integrate—there is no metaphysical barrier to the integration of far more perspectives. Many insects and crabs have compound eyes. Compound eyes have thousands of tiny lenses (ommatidia) that function independently, all sending signals to the brain that are integrated into a single image of the world.[10] We could imagine lesioning all but one of these ommatidia. This is a distinct (if highly limited) spatial vantage point on the world.

While I don't want wade into questions of insect consciousness, it's difficult to imagine there's a principled barrier to there being phenomenally conscious creatures who have compound eyes. And—given the integration of sensory information within creatures like bees—it seems highly plausible that such creatures could have visual experiences that appear singular and unified, much as our own do. So having compound eyes doesn't logically entail a multiplicity of visual experiences any more than having two eyes does. If experience from n perspectives can be phenomenally integrated, it's hard to see how we could block off the *possibility* that n+1 perspectives could be.

The possibility of such "compound" perspectives can further help us make sense of the phenomenal integration of radically dissimilar phenomenal experiences.

It seems incoherent to imagine that an image of my bathroom could be integrated with an image of my bedroom. But suppose we are not integrating these two images in isolation but, rather, overlapping images extending from bathroom to hall and hall to bedroom. This looks perfectly intelligible. We could imagine laying out a dozen different images, all overlapping with one another, such that they fit into a panoramic view (cf. Pelczar 2022, 13).

---

[10] Sensory integration within bees has been most extensively studied. See Gatto et al. 2022; Leonard and Masek 2014.

THE PHENOMENAL TAPESTRY   35

Alternatively, we can imagine spacing eyes every 65 mm around your head. The eye at 12 o'clock will take in completely different information from the eye at 6 o'clock. In isolation, it may be impossible for the 12 o'clock eye's perspective to be integrated with that of the 6 o'clock eye. (There is no commonality between these two inputs.) But given the intervening eyes, the way their phenomenology fits together is perfectly intelligible. Likewise, for the bee, with its near spherical visual field (Horridge 2009).[11]

What can we take from this? (1) It is possible for incompatible perspectives to be integrated. This happens with us in binocular vision. (2) While our own binocular vision can only integrate two perspectives, it is possible for many such perspectives to be integrated. This happens with compound eyes. (3) While our own binocular vision can only integrate perspectives that yield very similar phenomenology, it is possible for the integrated perspectives to be *radically* different. This is most readily intelligible in cases where there are many subtly different perspectives such that there are intermediary cases between each radically dissimilar pair.

This is enough to vindicate the possibility of the phenomenal tapestry. Sure, I might not be able to wrap my mind around what it's like to unify all possible perspectives. But that's hardly surprising! What I can do is to extrapolate from my own case (and those of actually existing animals) and see that the sorts of things that need to be possible for such a phenomenal unity are in fact possible. Indexed phenomenology from divergent perspectives really can be integrated as required.

This raises the question of whether the tapestry has one perspective or many. Following the analogy from binocular vision, it seems most natural to take there to be a distinct perspective associated with the phenomenal tapestry. When I look out through my eyes, I seem to have a single perspective on the world. I don't experience my right-eye perspective and my left-eye perspective as distinct experiences. They are integrated in such a way that they yield *one* experience of a cup, rather than two. This phenomenal integration is what it is for me to have a single perspective. Likewise, when the dragonfly looks out at the world through its compound eyes, it's plausible to assume that it has another single perspective on the world: a perspective in which it seems to be presented with *one* pond, rather than thousands. If the phenomenal tapestry is unified in an analogous way, it seems appropriate to

---

[11] It's also plausible that such a creature would get more than a mere panoramic image: getting a panoramic plus depth from the variations among adjacent pairs. Hence, it's possible that the phenomenal tapestry would be more than the sum of its component perspectives.

36 THE VIEW FROM EVERYWHERE

think of the tapestry as having *its own* perspective on the world—not a perspective in the sense of a cognitive outlook or an attitude towards the world, but in the minimal sensory respect of having unified phenomenology.

My perspective might be thought of as a perspective from right-eye-and-left-eye (R-and-L). This perspective from R-and-L does not obliterate the phenomenology that would be had by R (or L) alone. It encompasses and binds together phenomenology as-from both perspectives.[12] The phenomenal tapestry encompasses vastly more perspectives than my limited example of binocular vision. But the idea is the same: it binds together the phenomenology as from every possible perspective. It isn't a view from here or there, from R or L or R-and-L: it's a view *from everywhere*.

2.2 Theories of Phenomenal Unity

With the basic relations that structure reality in hand, we turn to considering the nature of these relations. Much has been written about the unity of consciousness, in particular. Given that I take the same unity of consciousness relation which unifies our minds to also unify reality, it will be important to determine whether this relation is suited to the task. I will not aim to take a stand on the nature of this relation, but will instead aim to show that regardless of what theory of the unity of consciousness is correct, the relation can fulfill this world-unifying role—with one noteworthy exception. While I will not offer a complete survey of all possible accounts of the unity of consciousness, I will look at a few representative accounts, which I believe can be generalized: Dainton's co-consciousness, Bayne's subsumptive unity, Tye's No Experiential Parts account, and several Kantian accounts of the unity of consciousness.

Readers who are unbothered by the nature of the unity of consciousness—and are happy to grant that this relation is capable of playing the world-unification role within the phenomenal tapestry—should feel free to skip ahead to §2.2.4.

---

[12] Again, if you doubt this, experiment with opening and closing one eye at a time.

2.2.1 Co-Consciousness and Subsumptive Unity

Barry Dainton (2000) and Tim Bayne (2010) each offer compelling, well-developed accounts of what phenomenal unity consists in. We'll see that each proposal is well suited to the task of unifying the tapestry of reality.

On Dainton's account, phenomenal items are united by a primitive experiential relationship, which he calls "co-consciousness." While the relationship is primitive and unanalyzable, it is not mysterious, as it is a relationship with which we are intimately acquainted—finding co-conscious experiences every time we attentively inspect our total phenomenology. As Dainton puts it, whenever we introspect, we find that all the experiences we are having at that moment are "fused" into a single unit of experience. While we are directly aware of co-consciousness in our experiences, the co-consciousness relation is not a further experiential ingredient. It is not more experiential content, which somehow needs to be related to the other experiential content. Rather, it is the glue that binds our experiences to one another, which we are aware of insofar as we are aware of the experiences *being bound*. Finally, the co-consciousness relation can relate two or more experiences, with no upper bound on the number of experiences that can be so fused.

Bayne's account of unity as subsumption views the phenomenal unification of simpler experiences as akin to the part-whole relation.[13] On Bayne's account, two token experiences e1 and e2 are subsumptively unified when they are both subsumed by a further token experience, e3. This broader experience e3 is a whole that contains e1 and e2 as parts, "nestled like Russian dolls within each other" (Bayne 2010, 21). Subsumption is reflexive; so e3 subsumes itself, avoiding the need to posit a further state to unify e3 with e1 and e2. As for Dainton's relation of co-consciousness, the subsumption relation is not a further experience but nevertheless makes a difference to our overall phenomenology by unifying experiences. As Bayne (2010, 31) puts it: "Phenomenal unity is a phenomenal relation in the sense that it makes a phenomenal difference, but not in the sense that it has its own phenomenal character that makes an additional contribution to what it is like to be the subject in question. Finally, while our unity of consciousness contains experiences as parts, Bayne is explicit that the view is neutral as to the question of whether the whole or the parts are ontologically fundamental:

---

[13] The basic account was first developed in a coauthored piece with David Chalmers (2003).

38 THE VIEW FROM EVERYWHERE

> To say that the phenomenal field contains experiential parts is to make no
> claim whatsoever about the relationship between those parts and the whole
> of which they are parts. We could take the experiential parts of a phenom-
> enal field as more fundamental than the phenomenal field itself, but we
> could also hold that there is a sense in which the overall phenomenal field is
> more fundamental than its parts. (Bayne 2010, 36)

Both of these approaches seem well suited to the task of unifying the tapestry
of reality. Take Dainton's co-consciousness: much as my experiences of the
hopping bird, wind, and rustling leaves might all be related by a primitive co-
consciousness relationship—fusing them into a single experience of reality-
as-I-currently-experience-it—so too, a far greater number of experiences
could be fused together. There is, after all, no upper bound on the number
of experiences that can be related by co-consciousness. Likewise, for Bayne's
subsumptive unity. Just as my experiences of the bird, the wind, and the
leaves can all be subsumed by a broader total-Helen-experience, so too the
experiences of all possible perspectives on reality might be subsumed by a
massive total-reality-experience.

One might worry that within the tapestry, we are not relating experiences,
but experiences-indexed-to-perspectives. Perhaps this is the wrong sort of
thing for co-consciousness to apply to. But this need not worry us: while
experiences within the tapestry *are* indexed to perspectives (and this is important for making sense of more fine-grained structure to reality), indexing
is not essential to the unity of consciousness. The unity of consciousness relation unifies experiences, and these experiences happen to be indexed. But
there's no reason to think that this must interfere with the unity relation. The
indices are simply incidental as far as the unity of consciousness relation is
concerned.

Dainton and Bayne both argue that the unity of consciousness relation
is transitive—or, at least, that it's transitive within the context of synchronic
unity (Dainton (2000), 88–112; Bayne (2010), 36–45). While this does not
pose any challenges to the phenomenal tapestry model of reality, we will see
that it is incompatible with the account of perception that I think pairs best
with the tapestry. On this account, in perception our minds literally overlap
with reality. So the perceived aspects of the tree are both phenomenally unified with the tapestry, and also with my mind. In order for this to be possible
without all aspects of my mind and all aspects of reality being phenomenally unified, the unity of consciousness cannot be transitive. So while we

THE PHENOMENAL TAPESTRY   39

can embrace the core of Dainton's and Bayne's accounts of the unity of consciousness, we must disagree about transitivity. I will return to this in §4.1.1, arguing that there are, in fact, no grounds for embracing transitivity as essential to the unity of consciousness.

2.2.2 Experiential Parts

Both co-consciousness and subsumptive unity are naturally viewed as accounts on which phenomenal unities have experiential parts.[14] The aspects of my overall experience (trees, sky, construction noises) are themselves experiences: an experience of blueishness, an experience of greenishness, an experience of loud rumbling. But this is not true of all accounts of phenomenal unity.

Michael Tye defends an account of the unity of consciousness, on which phenomenal unities have no experiential parts. As he puts it:

> [T]here really are no such entities as purely visual experiences or purely auditory experiences or purely olfactory experiences in normal, everyday consciousness. Where there is phenomenological unity across sense modalities, sense-specific experiences do not exist. They are the figments of philosophers' and psychologists' imaginations. And there is no problem, thus, of unifying these experiences. There are no experiences to be unified. ... There is a single multimodal experience, describable in more or less rich ways. (Tye 2003, 28)

While I could have had an experience that only included the visual aspects of my total experience, it does not follow from this counterfactual claim that my actual experience contains a merely visual experience as a part. What follows, according to Tye, is simply that I could have had an experience that is constituted in totality by a visual experience qualitatively identical to the visual *aspect* of my actual experience. This view is motivated with an analogy:

> Suppose it is lunchtime and I have a sudden and strong desire for a pint of beer with a ham sandwich. In having this desire, of course, I have a desire

---

[14] Bayne himself rejects experiential parts, in favor of holism, though he grants that both approaches are compatible with subsumptive unity (2010, 225–249).

40 THE VIEW FROM EVERYWHERE

> for a pint of beer. It is also true that I have a desire for a ham sandwich. But patently I don't have three sudden desires here. . . . These remarks apply mutatis mutandis, I want to suggest, to the problem of the unity of conscious experience, as it is usually conceived. There are not five different or separate simultaneous experiences somehow combined together to produce a new unified experience. (Tye 2003, 26–27)

I think Tye's example is illuminating. It's intuitively right that there is only one desire, not three. But consider a further case: You have a sudden strong desire for a pint of beer with a ham sandwich. "No," you then think, "make that a cider." When you change your mind about your beverage of choice, it's intuitively only the drink-desire that has changed. You still have the same token sandwich-desire. Your first desire wasn't intuitively replaced by a new desire with a qualitatively identical aspect. But this isn't possible if the first desire token was a holistic desire for the sandwich and beer together.[15] There's a conflict between what our intuitions say about Tye's initial case, and what they say about this modification.

What should we make of this? First, it seems clear that our intuitions about how to individuate desires aren't very reliable. Introspection might directly reveal to us the content of our desires, but it doesn't thereby give us privileged insight into how to individuate them.[16] Second, there arguably *is* no privileged way to individuate such desires. There is no privileged way to individuate given to us from a first-person perspective, and it's difficult to see how a third-person perspective could be of use in settling the matter.

The same seems to me to be true of individuating experiences. I'll admit that unlike the case of desires, where it seems to me that intuitions conflict, I have no intuitions whatsoever as to whether I have a single experience E*, with phenomenal aspects e1–e5, or five phenomenal experiences E1–E5, with a single unifying experience E* that binds them all together. This is another case where neither first-person nor third-person resources seem to have the capacity to settle the dispute—arguably because there is nothing to settle. Reality doesn't include one distinct glow for experiences, and another for aspects of experiences. And considerations of simplicity don't tell one way or another. For it is no more (or less) simple that there be a single

---

[15] At least, this isn't possible, assuming the objects of desires play a role in their individuation. And intuitively, one couldn't have a single token desire that shifted its object over time.

[16] Cf. S. Hurley (2003), 73–74; Tye (2003), 33–34.

THE PHENOMENAL TAPESTRY 41

experience, with five aspects, than that there be one overarching experience, with five sub-experiences.

For an idealist, the question of whether "big experiences" have experiential parts is closely related to the question of whether the whole or the parts are metaphysically prior. The view that there are No Experiential Parts[17] (NEP) fits naturally with a view on which the whole is prior, while the view that our experiences do decompose into parts that are themselves experiential (EP) pairs naturally with a bottom-up view of metaphysical priority.

It's natural (if not positively required) for an idealist to hold that experientiality is fundamental: experientiality doesn't emerge from non-experiential parts. Furthermore, it's plausible that idealism commits us to holding that experientiality is the fundamental building block of reality. We can now argue from NEP to the conclusion that the whole is metaphysically fundamental.

1. For an idealist, experientiality is fundamental: experientiality doesn't emerge from non-experiential parts.
2. Furthermore, experientiality is the fundamental building block of reality. Reality doesn't have fundamental nonexperiential parts.
3. So if reality has fundamental parts, they are experiential parts.
4. NEP: There are no experiential parts.
5. So reality doesn't have fundamental parts.

The challenge to this argument is that it's not obvious that idealism strictly commits one to (2). Idealism could be taken to require the weaker claim that the fundamental building blocks of reality are things that would be experiences, were they to occur in isolation. What counts as an experience for proponents of NEP is an extrinsic matter: were I to have had my visual experience without any of the other experiences I'm currently having, I would have had a purely visual experience, even though I do not actually have any purely visual experiences. A proponent of NEP could hold that these would-be-experiences are fundamental, and are the building blocks of reality.

Still, while NEP doesn't strictly entail that the whole is metaphysically prior, it is the most parsimonious way of making sense of the view. Given that

---

[17] As Tye (2003) puts it, "[t]here are not five different . . . experiences somehow combined together to produce a new unified experience." Rather, "there is just one experience here." We might be able to think about just the visual aspect of my overall experience. But this is not itself an experience—it is an abstraction from an experience.

42 THE VIEW FROM EVERYWHERE

experientiality is fundamental, it's natural to think that the smallest experiential unity would be the smallest fundamental unit, simpliciter.

Nothing that I say elsewhere in the book hangs on whether there are experiential parts,[18] just as nothing I say elsewhere in the book hangs on whether the tapestry or the threads are metaphysically prior. Experiential parts views and no-experiential parts views are both equally well suited to binding together the phenomenal tapestry. It is not my task here to take a stand on issues of metaphysical priority. Readers who think there are experiential parts can embrace EP about the unity of consciousness and embrace the smallist conception of reality that naturally follows. Readers who reject the idea of experiential parts can embrace an NEP view of the unity of consciousness, which will naturally bring them to a holistic conception of reality. To me, it all seems much of a muchness.[19]

2.2.3 Kantian Unity

While there are a number of accounts of the unity of consciousness that are compatible with the phenomenal tapestry, not all are. In particular, on a standard conceptualist reading of Kant (2003), the unity of consciousness presupposes the possession and application of concepts. This runs against the idea that the unity of consciousness can bind the tapestry together, since the phenomenal tapestry is stipulated to be constructed out of pure sensory experiences—lacking concepts, conceptualization, or anything intellectual. At the very least, the tapestry would need to be far richer than the bare collection of sensory phenomenology I've described.

One response to this would be to accept that Kant's conceptualized account of unity is incompatible with the phenomenal tapestry, and to simply set Kant aside. Indeed, there are good reasons for skepticism about Kant's positive account of synthesis.[20] It is not my aim to show that my project is

---

[18] Although we will see in Chapter 4 that there are some slight differences for the account of perception, depending on one's stance on experiential parts. According to NEP, whether something counts as an experience is an extrinsic matter that depends on the overall state it is embedded in. So the blueness of the sky might not be an experience for the tapestry as a whole, while *that very aspect* constitutes an experience for an observer for whom that is the totality of their present mental state.

[19] I myself am skeptical that there is a substantial disagreement between smallist and holist variants of idealism, much as I am skeptical of there being a substantial dispute between proponents of EP and NEP.

[20] One basis for doing this is that Kantian synthesis faces a regress worry that is not shared by the accounts of unity we've looked at thus far.

compatible with *every possible* account of the unity of consciousness. And we have already seen that there are several accounts of the unity of consciousness that are compatible with my project. Inasmuch as one finds any of the previously discussed views plausible, this is not a great cost. Still, I would like to remain as neutral as possible as to the nature of the unity of consciousness.

Another response to the Kantian would be to modify the phenomenal tapestry to give it the resources that are required for Kantian unity. We could make the tapestry richer in a way that would allow for synthesis and Kantian unity. The resulting view would be closer to Berkeley's God, as it would require concepts and rationality. It would also entail that conceptualization is built into reality, not merely imposed by us. But plausibly much of the details of Chapters 3–6 will be untouched by this.

Finally, one could argue that while concepts may be required for a certain sort of unity, there are other—more minimal—sorts of unity that do not require this. One basis for doing this lies in a nonconceptualist interpretation of Kant.[21] For example, Colin McLear (2015) argues for a Sensibilist reading of Kant on which not all objective representations require synthesis.

According to Kant, the pure intuitions of space and time cannot be grasped discursively via synthesis, as to do so we'd need to first grasp an infinite number of spatial parts to construct the whole out of. McLear (2015, 91) concludes that Kant embraces *two* sorts of unity:

> The unity of aesthetic representation—characterized by the forms of space and time—has a structure in which the representational parts depend on the whole. The unity of discursive representation—representation where

Kant holds that representations can only be unified when they have been synthesized. In synthesis, individual representations are first apprehended sequentially. The mind retains previously apprehended representations, and these past representations are recognized as related to the present ones by way of a priori concepts [the categories]. (And hence application of a priori concepts [the categories] is necessary for the unity of apperception.)

But this positive account of synthesis faces challenges, in particular the threat of an infinite regress. As Van Cleve (1999, 86) writes: "Kant holds that we cannot apprehend the parts of a manifold straight off in one act. Instead, we must apprehend the parts successively, retain memory images of them, and see what they all add up to. But how are we supposed to survey these images? A manifold of images presents the same problem we had to begin with. Either we must perform a threefold synthesis on it, in which case we are off on an infinite regress, or we can take it all in at once, in which case we could have done likewise with the original manifold."

This regress problem is distinctive to the Kantian account of unity. The regress problem does not simply arise from holding that there are experiential parts; rather, it arises from holding that these experiential parts are apprehended separately, and then conjoined. And none of the other accounts of unity we've considered is committed to this.

[21] See, e.g., Hanna (2005), Allais (2009), McLear (2015).

44 THE VIEW FROM EVERYWHERE

the activity of the understanding is involved—has a structure in which the representational whole depends on its parts.

He then extends this reasoning to argue that discursive unity is not required for intuitions[22] more generally. As he reads Kant,

> [We] have two forms of unity: aesthetic and discursive. An intuition has aesthetic unity in that it presents to consciousness a shaped, located, solid, and colored region of space, the consciousness of which, though episodic, may nevertheless persist over some period of time. Here the subject is consciously *en rapport* with features of her environment. But she is not yet in a position to make any propositionally structured claims about this tract of her environment. Being in a position to make such claims requires that the second, discursive, form of unity be present in her experience. (McLear 2015, 105)

Without discursive unity, we can still have representations *of* objects, but we can't represent objects *as* objects. Since *we* both (a) represent objects (directly) and (b) represent objects *as* objects, we need both varieties of unity to make sense of the unity of *our* conscious experiences.

But if concepts are only required to represent objects *as* objects, omitting them from the tapestry is only problematic insofar as the tapestry contains representations-*as*. And—as I'll argue in §2.3.2—the tapestry does not contain such representations. We can perfectly well accept that "intuitions [or the sparse phenomenology from which the tapestry is constructed] without concepts are blind" (Kant A51/B75): the tapestry is blind, inasmuch as it is without perceptions-as or judgments.

Putting Kant's views aside, it seems to me that the raw sensory inputs that we get from the world must include a sort of unity if our empirical judgments are to be justifiable. There must be something about this raw sensory intake *in virtue of which* we're justified in making subject-predicate judgments about the world. If the redness is not presented to me as inhering in the shape of the apple, it is difficult to see how perception could justify my belief that the apple is red. And this sort of unity presupposes a more general

---

[22] Intuitions are objective representations that represent particulars, and do so directly (i.e., without making use of other representations). When I have an intuition of, e.g., a tree, I represent the tree, but I do not represent it *as a tree*. (By contrast, representing *as* is not direct, but is mediated by concepts.)

THE PHENOMENAL TAPESTRY   45

sort of unity, namely that the redness and the apple shape are experienced *together*. So, inasmuch as we grant the existence of nonconceptual conscious sensations,[23] it is difficult to deny that such experiences are presented to us with a minimal kind of phenomenal unity. And it is this kind of unity that I take to be required for the tapestry.

Unity and Objectivity

Let's turn to a neo-Kantian account of the unity of consciousness: that of Susan Hurley (1994). At first glance, Hurley's view, too, might seem to pose trouble for nontheistic idealism. We'll see that it does not. Hurley's account places a plausible restriction on possible accounts of the unity of consciousness but poses no challenge to the unity of consciousness's application to the tapestry. I'll conclude this section with some general remarks about how idealists should approach phenomenal unity.

Susan Hurley (1994) argues that the unity of consciousness requires objectivity. We can't, as Hurley puts it, "get anything rich enough to determine the separateness or unity of consciousness if we restrict ourselves . . . to the subjective viewpoint" (60).

The thought "the sky is blue" and the thought "the tree is green" do not jointly entail that there is a thought "the sky is blue and the tree is green." The latter thought follows only if the same subject is doing the thinking in both cases. Likewise, Hurley notes, the thought "I am thinking that the sky is blue" and the thought "I am thinking that the tree is green" don't entail the thought "I am thinking that the sky is blue and the tree is green." Again, the latter thought follows only if it is the same "I" who is thinking both thoughts. Her point is that merely adding more *content* to the thoughts—as when we add to the content that it is "I" who is doing the thinking—doesn't settle whether the thoughts truly are being had by the same subject. As Hurley (1994, 61–62) puts it, "something outside of content, something objective, is needed. . . . [W]hat is needed will not be got from the contents of consciousness, from subjectively accessible materials, alone."

On the face of it, this might seem in tension with my project, for my project aims to construct reality out of the same materials our minds are woven from. If our minds require objectivity to unify them, then the tapestry will require objectivity also. But objectivity is often thought to require something outside

---

[23] Again, it's the subject of debate among Kant scholars whether Kant grants that there are such raw sensory inputs, or whether (for Kant) consciousness essentially requires conceptualization. See Van Cleve (1999), 74–76.

46 THE VIEW FROM EVERYWHERE

of our minds. How can the tapestry secure such objectivity, if the tapestry *constitutes* reality?

Hurley is surely right that we need more than content to account for phenomenal unity, and that (in a sense) something objective is needed. But talk of objectivity and subjectivity is ambiguous. One might take "objective" to mean "outside of the *contents* of consciousness." In this sense, it clearly follows that something objective is needed to individuate phenomenal unities. But it does not follow that this something must be outside of the bounds of our own introspective awareness (i.e., subjectively accessible materials.) For instance, Dainton's co-consciousness relation does not bind together phenomenal content using more content; it binds them together with a *relation*. We are introspectively aware of this relation insofar as we are aware of the *fusion* of different phenomenal contents. So Dainton's view does not run afoul of the just-more-content objection.[24] If God were to look down at all of the subjective experiences being had across the universe, he would surely say it is *objectively* true that this relation was binding together certain experiences, and not others. In this sense, Dainton does provide something objective (the co-consciousness relation) that accounts for unity.

But there's also a clear sense in which it is not objective: Dainton's account of the unity of consciousness is given in terms of subjectively (introspectively) accessible materials alone. So there is a difference between being outside of *the contents* of consciousness and being outside of *subjectively accessible* materials. Hurley demonstrates the need for the first, but not the second. And only the second would be problematic for my project.[25] Something more than mere content is needed to account for unity. But this does not show that something *extra-mental* is needed.

For all that I've said, it's entirely possible that there are other neo-Kantian views that are both plausible and unsuited to doing the work of binding

---

[24] See (Dainton (2000, 244–247) for Dainton's reply to Hurley.

[25] Hurley also argues that objectivity is required to account for the difference between cases involving phenomenal overlap and cases of phenomenal duplication. Introspectively, my experiences would be the same whether my mind partially overlaps with yours or not: whether we share a single overlapping experience or have duplicate experiences. Likewise for you. This is a case where not only are the contents of my experience the same regardless of whether we overlap, the relations that I'm aware of are also the same. (And likewise for you.) Nevertheless, in this case mental ingredients plausibly *are* sufficient to make sense of the distinction between overlap and duplication, for the *structure* of the relations will be different in the two cases. Again, God looking down upon the world would note that the one scenario involves overlapping relations; the other situation involves duplicate contents. This is perfectly intelligible from a God's-eye perspective without appealing to anything outside of our minds.

together the tapestry. I'll end this discussion with three general notes about the unity of consciousness as it relates to ontological idealism.

First, in assessing other neo-Kantian approaches to the unity of consciousness, it's important to keep in mind that they may—following Kant—presuppose a very different, more intellectualized, understanding of what is to be unified. Such views are only incompatible with nontheistic idealism if they also deny the possibility of bare, unconceptualized phenomenology being phenomenally unified.

Second, any theory of unity of consciousness that will work for my purposes must be compatible with realism about phenomenology. Theories that don't satisfy this requirement aren't suited to the idealist's task for a very fundamental reason: they are incompatible with a world that is fundamentally phenomenal. But I also take phenomenal realism to be an independently motivated desideratum for a successful account of the unity of consciousness.

Third, we should be looking for a general account of the unity of consciousness, not one that is restricted to accounting for the unity of *human* consciousness. The account should be able to account for the phenomenal unity of animals' experiences (something that many take Kant to deny), the unity of God's experiences, and (more generally) the unity of any set of mental states/events that plausibly could be unified. My own intuitions about what mental states/events can be phenomenally unified might diverge wildly from those of (neo-)Kantians, but I'm inclined to think that we can imagine, for instance, a unity of experience whose sole content is a tie-dyed color patch, with no concepts, no comparisons, no cognizing whatsoever. Since these bits of color phenomenology are spatially related to one another, they must be unified as part of the same phenomenal space. But there is nothing cognitive to the experience, even in whatever sense a cat's experiences might be cognized. If you agree that such experiences are possible, our account of unity must be able to explain them.

Finally, while I would like to remain as neutral as possible as to the nature of the unity of consciousness, all that my project strictly requires is a single plausible account of the unity of consciousness that is able to unify bare phenomenology of the sort described above. We have already seen that there are not one, but several accounts of the unity of consciousness that both (i) offer plausible accounts of phenomena and (ii) are compatible with my project. I encourage the reader to pick their preferred one of these to use when evaluating my project and its implications—or to pick a different account

48 THE VIEW FROM EVERYWHERE

and see whether it's compatible with the project, and if not, how nontheistic idealism might be tweaked to render it compatible with this view of unity.[26]

2.2.4 Property Binding and Phenomenal Spatial and Temporal Relations

The unity of consciousness ensures that all our experiences are experienced as aspects of a single overarching phenomenal experience. Suppose you and I go to see *Swan Lake*. I watch the ballet but have earplugs in. You listen to the music but have a blindfold on. There is an experience of the dancing, and there is an experience of the music. But there is no experience of *dancing to music*. You take off your blindfold, and voilà: *dancing to music*. This is what the unity of consciousness gives us. Within the tapestry of reality, the unity of consciousness binds experiences from all perspectives into a single *world*. Without the unity of consciousness binding together all aspects of the tapestry, we would have not one tapestry, but many: not one world, but many.

But, as we've seen, the unity of consciousness is not the only relation that structures our experiences, nor can it be the only relation that structures idealist reality. Some facets of my total experience are more intimately related than others. Color and shape are not free-floating. When you look at the Japanese flag, you don't just have an experience of {white, red, circle, rectangle}. The redness seems to be bound up with the circle, and the whiteness seems to be bound up with the rectangle. Each set of properties seems to be *bound together* in a more intimate way than the way in which the music and the dance are. This phenomenon is not specific to visual perception. As I hold and look at my teacup, I do not merely have an experience {blue, hard, warm, smooth, cylinder}. All these properties seem tightly bound in a way that goes beyond all being experienced together. They present in a way that invites us to think of them as forming (or inhering in) a single object. We've called the relation that these phenomenal elements stand in *the property binding relation*.

---

[26] For instance, a view that takes subjects to be ontological primitives, and takes experiences to be unified insofar as they belong to the same subject, would yield a view in which the tapestry is a robust subject, somewhat closer to Berkeley's idealism. A view on which conceptualization is required for unity would entail that the tapestry possesses concepts. Whether the other parts of the theory will be compatible with these views, and whether the same benefits can be gained by them, is an interesting further question.

THE PHENOMENAL TAPESTRY   49

It is undeniable that there is such a relation. We need to simply look to our own experiences of the world to find it. The suggestion is that this same relation is present in the tapestry, providing structure to reality. *Our* minds do not generate this additional structure. The structure is there within the world. The redness and the circle on the Japanese flag *really do* stand in a tighter relationship than the whiteness and the circle.

This accounts not only for the appearance of objects at a moment, but for the coherent unfolding of these objects over time. Suppose I am watching a tennis match. I see the racket come into contact with a (yellow) ball, and the ball flies over the net. My inverted twin is also watching the match. She sees the racket come into contact with a (blue) ball, and the ball flying over the net. There weren't two balls that needed to fly over the net: one yellow and one blue. There was a single ball, a single hit, a single force acting on the ball. Property binding is what accounts for this.

I think the analogy of the tapestry is an illustrative one. Imagine an ordinary wool tapestry. You pick up a single thread of the tapestry and lift it into the air . . . and all the adjoining threads are lifted up with it. Why? Because the threads have a *structure* that binds them all together. You don't need a separate force to act on each thread because the threads themselves are not separate. By moving one thread, you move them all. Or consider another analogy. Suppose this particular tapestry depicts a Japanese flag. Your five-year-old decides that the tapestry is too plain, and uses a marker to draw a line bisecting the circle. They draw *one single line* through the middle of the circle. In doing so, they don't just bisect the circle, they also bisect the redness. To accomplish this, they don't have to draw two lines: one bisecting the redness and one bisecting the circle. A single line is enough. This isn't magic, it's the result of the tapestry's structure.

This is not unique to physical tapestries. We can *imagine* a red circle and *imagine* drawing a line through it. An imagined line bisecting the circle cannot help also bisecting the redness (and vice versa). Why? Again, because of the structure: because the redness and the circularity are bound together via the property binding relation. These phenomenal aspects are literally fused into a single experiential entity. A single phenomenal alteration to the circle phenomenology affects everything that is property-bound with the circle.

These examples are very simple ones. The phenomenal tapestry is vastly more complicated than either an ordinary wool tapestry or an ordinary mental image, and includes experiences indexed to numerous

50 THE VIEW FROM EVERYWHERE

different perspectives. But the basic idea is the same: property binding literally fuses experiences together—the yellow of the tennis ball, the blue, the echolocation-experience, etc.—such that acting on one phenomenal thread entails acting on the others in a corresponding way. While a single piece of yarn from a pile can be picked up in isolation, once it is woven into a tapestry, you cannot pick up a single thread without picking up all the others that it is bound to. Likewise, if phenomenal redness is property-bound with phenomenal circularity, you cannot act on the redness without acting on the circularity. This is true whether we are talking about two phenomenal aspects in your mental image . . . or a million in the tapestry of reality. (This point will play a prominent role in accounting for the simplicity of the laws of nature in §5.3.1.)

Phenomenal unity explains why there is *a* tapestry, *a* world. Property binding explains why this world is populated with structures that can qualify as objects, rather than unintelligible collections of fragmented phenomenology. But there is more structure to our world than this, just as there is more structure to our experiences of the world. The tree's leaves appear *above* its trunk, the red circle in the Japanese flag seems *surrounded by* white. Again, it is undeniable that our experiences have such spatial structure.[27] And again, this structure is intuitively not something that our minds construct, but a feature of the world itself. (Though Kant would obviously disagree![28])

The tapestry includes far more than the experiences of any ordinary perceiver. The properties bound together by the property binding relation will be far more numerous than those bound together in my experience. The tapestry will include not just the dancers from the angle I'm observing from in the center right balcony, but also the view from the boxes on the left, from the orchestra, from the wings of the stage, from behind, and so on. And the spatial relations from all these perspectives will cohere. How might this work? Michael Pelczar (2022, 13) offers a nice example. He imagines a group of Bedouin travelers, camped around the Great Sphinx:

> The traveler viewing the Sphinx from the East has an experience with a certain phenomenal shape and size, and the one viewing the Sphinx from

---

[27] By saying that experiences have spatial structure, I am not claiming that experiences exist within physical (non-phenomenal) space. The claim is rather that the phenomenology itself has a certain structure.

[28] None of the remainder of the project hinges on this claim. If you're inclined to agree with Kant, you can omit this as well as temporal relations as features of the tapestry. I simply aim to show that the spatial structure we intuitively take the world to have is compatible with idealism.

THE PHENOMENAL TAPESTRY   51

the South has an experience with a different phenomenal shape and size, but there is some overlap in the spatial quality of the Eastern and Southern experiences, corresponding to the part of the Sphinx both viewers can see (the monument's southeastern quadrant). There's a similar overlap between the experience of the person who views the Sphinx from the South and the one who views it from the West; and likewise for the Southern viewer and a viewer standing between him and the Western viewer, etc. In short, the travelers' experiences fit together, like overlapping regions of the surface of the Sphinx itself.

For the idealist, the travelers' experiences don't merely overlap *like* regions of the Sphynx itself. These experiences—or experiences qualitatively identical to them, which are aspects of the tapestry—*are* (aspects of) the Sphinx itself.

Finally, there are temporal relations. When I hear Tchaikovsky's sobbing lament in Act IV and see Odette's arms fluttering to break free of Von Rothbart, I do not have a static experience (or even a collection of static experiences); rather, I have an experience that flows and unfolds temporally. Once again, this temporal structure is intuitively not generated by my mind—Kant notwithstanding—but is a feature of the world. Insofar as this is the case, the idealist should take these same temporal relations that structure our experiences to structure the tapestry of reality. I'll return to temporal relations in Chapter 5, where I'll survey several realist idealist accounts of space and time. But roughly, the relations are diachronic phenomenal unity (binding together experiences as-of different moments into a single temporal structure), and temporal ordering relations: before, after, simultaneous with.

In short, the very same relations that structure our minds also structure the phenomenal tapestry: synchronous and diachronic unity of consciousness, property binding, and phenomenal spatial and temporal relations. There are no controversial resources required to do this structuring, as the structuring simply requires relations that everyone (at least, every realist about phenomenology) must embrace, regardless of their account of the nature of reality.

2.3 Threads of Reality

We began this chapter with a characterization of reality as a tapestry, in which phenomenal threads are woven together into the structure of reality. This picture of reality raised two immediate questions: first, what are the

52   THE VIEW FROM EVERYWHERE

threads? And second, how are these threads bound together? We have just addressed the second question, of how the threads are structured (§2.2). Let's now return to the question of precisely what the threads are.

There are two things that go into understanding the threads. First, we must understand the nature of the threads. Threads of an actual tapestry are collections of fibers bound into thin strands. What sort of thing are "phenomenal threads"? Second, we need to understand which specific threads form the tapestry of *our* world.

Let's start with the nature of the phenomenal threads. In "Idealism without God" (Yetter-Chappell 2018a), I described reality as a vast unity of consciousness "binding together sensory impressions of every point-from-a-perspective." Following this, we might—at first pass—think of sensory threads as phenomenology as-of a point, had from a given perspective. But we saw in §2.1 that this was too simplistic. An ordinary wool thread is not a single, primitive strand of fiber, but is constructed out of many strands of fiber, twisted and bound into whole. Likewise, the tapestry of reality is not woven directly out of bits of phenomenology. Rather, bits of phenomenology indexed to a perspective are property-bound into the "threads" out of which reality is constructed. The sensory impression as-of a point, experienced from a perspective, is more akin to a single strand of fiber, out of which a wool thread is spun.

I think this is a good first pass. (Though this goes against the tapestry analogy, in that is not a single thread that extends from one end of our universe to the other. In some respects, a mosaic would be a better analogy—where each tile is composed out of a multitude of different indexed perspectives.) But we don't have to think of the phenomenal fibers specifically as sensory impressions as-of *points* from a perspective.[29] We could carve the world up into a 1×1×1 cm grid, or a 1×1×1 m grid, or ... in any arbitrary way we like. There is no privileged scale. Whatever scale we pick, the resulting phenomenal tapestry will be qualitatively identical. It's like taking a picture and putting it through a puzzle-making machine: the machine could carve the picture up into big or small pieces, but the resulting image will be the same.[30] (Note that by thinking of phenomenal strands as sensory

---

[29] Perhaps you think that phenomenology doesn't occur in point-sized increments, or that there's no single smallest unit of phenomenology across modalities.

[30] As noted earlier, I am not interested in questions of fundamentality. We could take phenomenal threads to be fundamental, or not. The sort of structure I'm interested in is independent of fundamentality.

THE PHENOMENAL TAPESTRY   53

impressions *as-of points* from a perspective, I am not presupposing an understanding of space prior to the phenomenal tapestry. The world is merely constructed out of experiences *as-of* points—this does not presuppose that there *are* such points independently.)

Now that we have a sense of the nature of the threads that compose our phenomenal tapestry, let's turn to the question of *which* threads form the tapestry of our world.

The goal of this book is to present an idealist account of the nature of the world we live in and how we relate to this world. The task of this chapter is to give an idealist account of physical reality. To do this, we want to be able to give an account that will capture both our intuitions about the world we inhabit, and what we learn about the world from scientific inquiry. We want this account to both (a) yield plausible verdicts about what there positively is in the world, and also (b) not entail that the world contains things which it intuitively lacks.

Given that this is the task, we should take the world (our beliefs about what it is and isn't like) as our guide for constructing the tapestry. I will not argue that any idealist world *must* include or omit certain things from reality. I will simply aim to capture *an* idealist world: one that best corresponds to what we take to be true of our world.

So what sorts of threads are necessary to comprise a world like ours? Our world is rich. I have certain perceptions from my human vantage-point at my desk in Miami. But intuitively, my perceptions of the world aren't privileged in accurately capturing reality. The perspectives of all other human beings are equally well suited to grasping reality, as are those of all other actually existing animals. But even this is not sufficient to capture reality in its totality. The perspectives that each such creature *could have* had, were they in different locations, equally seem to capture facets of reality. The perspectives of all creatures that *might have* evolved, or might come into being in the future, seem equally well to count. It might seem that an infinite number of perspectives will have to be included in the tapestry![31]

We might construct the tapestry as follows:[32]

---

[31] Whether or not reality includes an infinite number of perspectives is a question to which we will return in §2.3.1. There I'll argue that it doesn't. Or, at least, we needn't accept that it does.

[32] While it is only correct to describe these as steps for *constructing* the tapestry if one accepts a bottom-up approach on which the threads are fundamental, the core idea is compatible with a top-down view of the tapestry. Given a top-down approach, step 6 might be rewritten as: the tapestry has as aspects threads that are qualitatively akin to these threads, related by spatial, temporal, and binding relations.

54 THE VIEW FROM EVERYWHERE

1. Make an enormous list of all the veridical perceptual experiences that might be had from all possible perspectives. (Many of the items on the list will be merely possible experiences.)

2. Enumerate the perspectives, while keeping track of the experiences attached to each perspective. This should be done in a Ramsified way that simply keeps track of the content and relations had from each perspective (as opposed to specifying *whose* perspective it is): #ps1,#lo1 [blue expanse above green circle], #ps2,#lo1 [yellow expanse above red circle], . . . #ps1,#lo2 [blue expanse above green ellipse]. . . .

3. Reify the experiences from (1), so that there is an actual experience qualitatively identical to each item on the list.

4. Index the experiences in (3) to the perspectives in (2).

5. A relevant bundle of property-bound indexed experiences constitutes a thread. For example, a thread corresponding to a patch of sky might be constructed out of: bluishness from #ps1#lo1, yellowishness from #ps2#lo1, bluishness and polarized light orientation x from #ps3#lo2, and so forth.

6. These threads are woven into the tapestry of reality via the unifying relations discussed in section 2.2.

7. (You may rest.)

(Steps (4)–(6) are not so different from what happens in our brains facilitating binocular vision. Recall that indices do not provide additional phenomenal *content*. Rather, they structure the content that is present. My right eye does not provide a "right-eye feel" to my visual experience. But my brain must keep track of which visual inputs are coming from which eye (indexing) in order to construct a coherent image. These component pieces are then property-bound into the world as we experience it.)

The first thing to note is that, while (1) appeals to the experiences that possible observers would have from different perspectives, I am not *defining* the experiences that make up the tapestry in terms of the experiences that perceivers would have from different perspectives. Step (1) is not intended to give a definition of the perspectives that make up reality, but rather as a *heuristic* to give a sense of the richness/variety of the threads that constitute reality—a way of capturing our independent intuitions about the richness of our world. Another useful heuristic is to consider all the experiences making up God's conscious experiences of our world.

One could never hope (sitting in an armchair) to give a definition of the phenomenal experiences that make up reality. We have to go out into the world to find out what's there. And no matter how much empirical investigation I carry out from my human perspective, I would never come to a complete list of the threads that comprise reality. So the best we can do—the only reasonable thing we can do—is to appeal to the threads that intuitively seem like they should count as objective parts of reality, while excluding those that don't.

The second thing to note is that our heuristic for determining what sorts of experiences make up reality appeals to *perceptual experiences*. The hallucinations, mental imagery, thoughts, dreams, desires, and so on that experiencers might have do not contribute to the fabric of our physical reality. Omitting these experiences from the tapestry might seem to be something that requires justification. But this simply follows from taking our beliefs about the physical world we live in as a guide. The bugs you seem to feel crawling on your skin, that no one else can detect, intuitively aren't part of physical reality; nor is the ocean scene you imagine as you meditate. While there presumably is *a* possible idealist world in which these things are parts of reality, a world that omits them seems more plausibly to capture *our* world.

One might likewise worry about restricting the experiences the tapestry is constructed out of to *veridical* perceptual experiences. If perceptions are veridical only when they accurately capture the way the world is, and the way the world is, in turn, is characterized in terms of experiences that are veridical, we're left without a way of specifying which the veridical experiences *are*. This is correct. But I don't think this should worry us. Again, I am not aiming to *define* the threads that make up the tapestry in terms of their being veridical—which would be circular—but only to *characterize* the threads that are relevant. Insofar as we have an independent grasp on what is meant by a veridical perceptual experience, there is nothing problematic about this. While philosophers may like to think that theories are needed to fill in an understanding of what is meant by an illusory experience, I take it that ordinary folk have a perfectly good understanding that would allow them to understand step (1) of the tapestry construction guidance just fine!

Still, while it is sufficient for my purposes to appeal to an intuitive grasp of what the physical world is like, we plausibly can offer a more systematic account of which experiences are world-revealing. There is, after all, *something* that our intuitions are responding to. Katalin Farkas (2013) and Howard Robinson (2022) have argued that the structural organization of

56 THE VIEW FROM EVERYWHERE

experiences determines whether we take the experiences to correspond to objective features of the world, or to merely be states internal to the experiencer.[33] Experiences that we take to be world-revealing are, roughly, Farkas (2013, 109) puts it, "organised into a systematic, cross-modally coherent and predictable order." The campfire not only binds together a predictable set of experiences from across sensory modalities—heat, warm glow, smoky smells, crackling sounds—but these sounds change together in predictable ways. The intensities of all the sensations increase as you get closer, decrease as you step further back, and collectively cease when you pour water on the fire. By contrast, pains, itches, afterimages, vertigo, anxiety, hallucinations, and wonderings all lack this cross-modal coherence.

Other intuitive restrictions on world-revealing experiences might include that features of the physical world (a) exhibit temporal coherence; (b) are publicly accessible; and (c) seem to occur in space.[34]

(a) Temporal coherence: Beyond momentary cross-modal coherence, reality has temporal coherence. Suppose you're in the kitchen pouring yourself a cup of tea, and then find yourself on a beach in a swimsuit, and then are giving a philosophy lecture (fully clothed), and then are in a garden, with no coherent narrative connecting each moment's experience to the last. The appropriate conclusion is either that you've gone mad (and become disconnected from reality) or that you are dreaming. Reality is not disjoint in this way. Experiences that reflect reality have a temporal coherence and stability.

(b) Public accessibility: If only a single creature has some experience, it doesn't intuitively seem to be an experience of something real. Of course, not all experiencers are capable of experiencing all features of the physical world. I can't perceive the ultraviolet patterning on flowers. But if only a single bee were to have such an experience, while other bees with similar perceptual systems did not, we would take this to be a reflection of some quirk of the bee, rather than a reflection of reality.

(c) Spatiality: Experiences that reveal the physical world also plausibly must be presented as occurring within space. Even if humans all experienced anxiety when standing unsupported at a tall height, and this

---

[33] Robinson traces the view back to Hume and subsequently Ayer.
[34] I do not mean to imply that this is an exhaustive list.

THE PHENOMENAL TAPESTRY 57

anxiety gradually lessened the further from the edge they stepped, anxiety would still not intuitively be a feature of the physical world.

So while we carried out step (1) by appeal to an intuitive understanding of what constitutes the veridical perceptual experiences, it is also plausible that a more systematic account of these experiences can be given. But this still doesn't settle precisely what experiences are included. Two sets of questions still need to be addressed. First, how extensive is perception? When we look at a plate, tipped at an angle, is circularity part of what I perceive from this perspective, or merely ellipticality? Do I see a duck and a rabbit in the duckrabbit image, or merely lines of a certain shape? Second, which perspectives count? I've said that "all possible perspectives" count. But what is meant by *possible*?

In §2.3.1, I'll address the question of which perspectives are possible. In §2.3.2, I'll return to the question of which experiences count as perceptual in the relevant sense.

2.3.1 How "Thick" Is the Tapestry?

The tapestry contains experiences qualitatively identical to every possible perceptual experience that might be had from every possible perspective. What is the relevant notion of possibility? Are the relevant perspectives those that are physically possible, metaphysically possible, or something else? And once we've determined what sort of possibility is relevant, how numerous should we expect these possibilities to be? Which sort of possibility is relevant will have implications not only for how "thick" the tapestry is, but for whether we can account for features of reality that are imperceptible.

There are elements of reality that are thought to be imperceptible—not just imperceptible by humans, but imperceptible by any physically possible creature. One challenge for the idealist is to explain how an account on which reality is composed out of perceptions (or experiences qualitatively akin to perceptions) can accommodate the existence of such imperceptible objects. Black holes are a classic example of apparently imperceptible objects. The event horizon of a black hole is so dense—the gravitational field so strong— that nothing, not even light, can escape it. Given that no light, no information, can escape from the black hole, it seems impossible for any observer to see past the event horizon. If objects are constructed out of experiences as of

58   THE VIEW FROM EVERYWHERE

perceptions of those objects, it might seem that there is nothing that a black hole could *be*.

The example of black holes is a curious one. In 2019, the Event Horizon Telescope (EHT)—actually a global network of radio telescopes—constructed images of two black holes. While nothing can emerge from the black hole's event horizon, black holes are encircled by a glowing disk of gases. The event horizon casts a shadow across this glowing disk. The images taken by EHT show not only the glowing disk, but the shadow of the event horizon (Landau 2019). If, as I argue in Yetter-Chappell (2018b), we can literally see objects through their shadows, it turns out that we can see black holes.[35] Black holes are not even nomically imperceptible.

But let's set this response aside. Perhaps you reject my argument that we can see through shadows, or perhaps there are other apparently imperceptible phenomena, for which the shadow reply isn't available. If science implies such entities exist, it is open to us to embrace a broader set of possible experiences to make up the tapestry. The tapestry could include experiences such that it's physically impossible to have them from the perspectives they're indexed to.

Recall that the tapestry is not constructed out of experiences of perceiving subjects, but out of experiences *qualitatively akin to* those that would be had were a subject to be perceiving the world from that perspective. The perceptual experiences in step (1) of our tapestry construction needn't be physically possible. And it's metaphysically possible (even if not physically) that there be perceptions of the event horizon.[36] These physically impossible (but metaphysically possible) perceptions can be reified and partially constitute the tapestry.

What might the content of such experiences be? One way to think about this would be to imagine God (by some nonphysical means) transferring information out of a black hole to an experiencer. Alternatively, we could make sense of the idea of black hole–ish experiences as the experiences that God would have of a black hole.[37]

---

[35] At the very least, a creature with a perceptual system like the EHT would be able to see black holes.

[36] Note that there's nothing physically impossible about an experience qualitatively akin to the experience God would have of the event horizon. What's physically impossible, if anything, is such an experience constituting a *perception* of the event horizon.

[37] While I have no insight into what the particular content of such experiences would be like, astrophysicists have constructed models of what it would be like to fall into a black hole or to watch an object fall into a black hole (from a perspective outside). (See, e.g., Andrew Hamilton's Black Hole Simulator [Nadis 2011].) Of course, such models at best tell us about what an object falling into a

THE PHENOMENAL TAPESTRY   59

The heuristic model I appealed to earlier to distinguish what experiences are veridical (and so constitute the tapestry) is of no use when it comes to physically imperceptible objects. No heuristic can guide me in determining which black hole–ish experiences are veridical. I do not have any independent grasp on what it is for an experience of a black hole to be veridical. This might seem to introduce circularity worries. But I think this is a feature, not a problem.

It is open to the idealist to hold that there is a *fact of the matter* about what experiences constitute such physically imperceptible objects, much as there can be a fact of the matter, for a Berkeleyan, as to what constitutes God's experiences of black holes.[38] The lack of a heuristic to guide us simply means that we cannot *know* what these aspects of reality are like, beyond the effects they have on us. But this is precisely as it should be! We surely cannot know anything about the natures of physically imperceptible objects. So while heuristic guidance breaks down, it breaks down precisely where our sphere of knowledge breaks down.

How one makes sense of the specific case of black holes may depend one's view of spacetime. Inasmuch as a black hole is a particular contour of spacetime, the apparent imperceptibility of black holes is an instance of the apparent imperceptibility of spacetime itself. Whether this is a challenge or not depends on your view of spacetime. For a relationalist, the imperceptibility of spacetime poses no problem, as there is no thing to perceive. There are merely the experience-structuring relations. We perceive the effects of the black hole's massive gravity on other perceptible objects, and this is all that there is to perceiving a black hole. For a substantivalist idealist there is a challenge posed by space being imperceptible. To address this, we need an idealist-friendly account of substantivalist space, one that makes space suitably phenomenal. This is a challenge to which we'll return in Chapter 5. There, I'll flesh out different ways an idealist could be a substantivalist about space. For instance, one could hold that space is intrinsically experiential, though not all creatures have perceptual systems capable of experiencing it. A suitably attuned perceiver (e.g., God) would experience space as a three-dimensional expanse of some particular phenomenal quality. Such a creature

---

black hole would look like, not what the black hole itself looks like. God's experiences of the black hole itself might be radically different.

[38] What is God's experience like? I cannot hazard to guess, beyond the fact that it presumably has cross-modal and temporal coherence, and seems to be laid out in space.

60 THE VIEW FROM EVERYWHERE

would experience gravity's warping of space as warping of this phenomenal expanse. This might be something like God's experience of the nature of a black hole.

The general lesson to take from putative cases of imperceptible facets of reality is that idealists can appeal to physically impossible (but metaphysically possible) perceptions to make sense of their content. But this itself magnifies a challenge we've already encountered. We already had a huge number of perspectives bound into the threads of reality. And now we're adding more, more, seemingly without end! For while there may be limits on the possible experiences of actual perceivers, there are no clear limits on the possible experiences of merely metaphysically possible experiencers. It might seem that this will commit us to there being an infinite number of experiences composing our world.

Fortunately, it does not entail this. If there are physically imperceptible objects—objects not merely imperceptible by humans, but by all physically possible creatures—the idealist is committed to there being *some* physically impossible (but metaphysically possible) experiences in the tapestry.[39] But it doesn't follow that *all* metaphysically possible experiences are in the tapestry.

To see why, consider an analogy to dualism. Let's assume that—thanks to the combinatorial potential of physical reality—there could emerge an infinite number of physical systems, which give rise to consciousness. Accepting this does not commit the dualist to embracing an infinite number of potential phenomenal experiences, as bridging laws might connect different physical systems to the same phenomenal experience. For instance, a human, a bee, and a Martian might all have the very same phenomenal experience, despite very different neural correlates. The bridging laws might be such that neural correlates h, b, and m all generate experience Q. Thus, the number of experiences that can be generated could well be finite. There might simply be a finite number of nomologically possible experiences, even if there is an infinite number of physical arrangements that could be connected up to these experiences. Similarly, the fact that there could be an infinite number of physical perceptual systems doesn't entail that the idealist must embrace an infinite number of phenomenal threads. The nomologically possible

---

[39] More carefully, the idealist is committed to some of the experiences that make up the tapestry being *qualitatively identical to* experiences that it would be physically impossible for any finite creature in the tapestry to have as veridical perceptions.

THE PHENOMENAL TAPESTRY   61

experiences might simply be limited. Why couldn't there be more types of experiences? *There simply aren't any more to be had.*

We should all grant that there are worlds with alien properties (relative to our world), and worlds such that our world contains properties alien to them. Likewise, we should think that there are idealist worlds where the tapestry is thicker than ours—containing perspectives that our world does not. And we should think that there are idealist worlds whose tapestries are thinner—containing fewer perspectives. What would happen if a new creature, with a new sort of perceptual apparatus, evolved in one of these worlds? Would the tapestry of the world then expand? No. The experiences that comprise the tapestry are the only experiences to which a new type of experiencer could be hooked up. There simply *aren't* more experiences that they could be hooked up to.

So how thick is *our* tapestry? We should obviously expect there to be phenomenal threads we're unaware of, much as a physicalist should expect there to be physical entities they're as yet unaware of. But this doesn't mean that we should expect the number of threads to be endless, any more than a physicalist should expect the number of physical entities to be endless. The idealist's reality is constructed out of experiences qualitatively akin to those of all veridical perceptual experiences that might be had from every possible perspective. The relevant class of possible experiences here is broader than the physically possible experiences (as the physical world might include physically imperceptible entities). But it needn't include *all* metaphysical possible experiences.

The point is easy to appreciate when it comes to theistic idealism. The theistic idealist can take our physical world to include experiences that outstrip those had by finite physical creatures, without being committed to its including all metaphysically possible experiences. God's experiences of our world can outstrip our own without including all possible experiences. Likewise, for the nontheistic idealist, what's part of our physical world is God-minus's experiences of our world. There simply is a fact of the matter about what is included in this. While there *could have been* a world with ghosts or with alien properties, our world does not seem to be one. Such worlds would include phenomenal threads that our world does not. We do not need an independent theory or account that predicts the precise "thickness" of our world. It is a contingent matter (and, as such, may admit of some arbitrariness). The aim is to capture what we take to be true of *our* world. For this, the tapestry is thick enough; no more, no less.

2.3.2 Cognitive Phenomenology and Reality

Let's return to the question of what sorts of experiences count as perceptual in the relevant sense to make up the tapestry of reality. My interest here is not in the nature of perception or how to draw the line between perceptual and cognitive states, per se, but in *what experiences intuitively make up the tapestry of our (physical) world.* It may be that this follows a joint in nature between perception and cognition. Or it may be that the experiences suitable for comprising the tapestry are more restricted than veridical perceptions. Regardless, we need to answer questions like "is duckishness part of the tapestry, or does the tapestry merely include patterns of lines (which would be appropriately judged to look like a duck)"?

First, note that cognitive phenomenology generally does not seem to be a part of the tapestry of the physical world. Cognitive phenomenology is intuitively private—not part of the publicly accessible world. My thoughts, beliefs, and desires are accessible to me alone, much as are my mental imagery, dreams, and hallucinations. Moreover, much of our cognitive phenomenology is non-spatial, whereas the physical world is spatially laid out. While our auditory, olfactory, and gustatory perceptual experiences are not as obviously spatial as our visual and tactile experiences, even they plausibly present sounds as coming from *over there*, smells as *here*, and tastes as *within my mouth.* By contrast, my thoughts, beliefs, and desires aren't presented as having spatial locations. For these reasons, I think that the threads of the tapestry should be taken to be constructions of *sensory phenomenology.* (Again, I take it there could be *an* idealist world that violates this restriction and includes cognitive phenomenology. But such a world seems less plausibly to be *our* world.)

But while most cognitive phenomenology is private and non-spatial, this is arguably not essential to cognitive phenomenology. Consider perception-as. I might see a shaped greenish patch (simply experiencing the low-level sensory qualities), or I might see the shaped greenish patch *as a leaf.* I might (overhearing a conversation in Urdu) hear a string of sounds and inflection; while a friend hears it *as a meaningful conversation.* You might simply smell an unfamiliar smell, while a Jahai speaker might smell it *as a very ltpit bearcat.* Are these instances of perceiving-as a part of the tapestry?[40] Perception-as is plausibly understood as involving cognitive phenomenology as a sort of

---

[40] The Jahai have basic olfactory concepts analogous to our colors concepts (Majid et al. 2018).

THE PHENOMENAL TAPESTRY   63

"overlay" modifying our low-level sensory phenomenology (Montague 2017). But the leafishness of a leaf is publicly accessible (at least to one who possesses the right concepts). And it's arguable that the leafishness of a perceived leaf is spatially laid out. So the case presented above for excluding cognitive phenomenology from the tapestry doesn't seem to extend to perceptions-as.

Nevertheless, I think the most plausible way to construct the tapestry of physical reality is to omit these perceptions-as, constructing it solely from low-level sensory phenomenology. The physical world clearly contains objects that have low-level properties such that it's correct for me to judge of them that they are iPhones, diapers, and birdbaths. But to build the perception of the iPhone *as an iPhone* into the tapestry into the tapestry on top of this, we would need to build *iPhoneness* into the fabric of reality as a primitive property. And this strikes me as bonkers.[41]

While my exclusion of cognitive phenomenology and perceptions-as from the tapestry is not essential to idealism, it will play an important role in the account of illusions developed in Chapter 4.

2.4 Conclusion

In Chapter 1, we gave a rough characterization of nontheistic idealism as Berkeley's God, *minus*: minus beliefs, desires, will . . . minus everything but his vast collection of sensory experience and the relations that structure these experiences. In this chapter, we've given a more precise characterization of the contents and structure of the physical world. For the nontheistic idealist, physical reality is like a tapestry, weaving threads of phenomenology into a world of structured color, warmth, sound, and taste.

If physical reality is akin to a tapestry, it is not one woven out of wool thread and structured via over-under relations. This chapter has sought to give a concrete idealist account of the nature and structure of the physical world by answering the questions: (i) What exactly are the threads that make

---

[41] The cognitive phenomenology interpretation of perceiving-as is not the only candidate option. One might, alternatively, hold that perceptions-as are best understood as *sensory* experiences of high-level properties (e.g., Siegel 2006). Regardless, insofar as something more than low-level sensory phenomenology is required, it seems to me that this is not be a part of the tapestry. While the tapestry contains things that it would be correct for us to judge to be diapers, it does not contain primitive *diaperish* phenomenology—either cognitive phenomenological properties or high-level sensory properties.

64   THE VIEW FROM EVERYWHERE

up the tapestry of physical reality? And (ii) what exactly are the relations that structure these "threads"?

The physical world is far richer than the experiences of any finite observer reveal. It includes not just the greenness of trees that I observe, but the redness that my inverted twin would observe. But, though no color inverts actually inhabit our world, merely possible experiences are not a part of the tapestry. Rather, the tapestry is composed out of *actual experiences qualitatively identical to* all possible veridical perceptual experiences. These experiences are akin to the fibers that make up a thread of wool in an ordinary tapestry. These experiences correspond to experiences that would be had from all possible perspectives. Threads are bundles of such phenomenal fibers, *indexed to perspectives*. So a thread of phenomenology corresponding to a plate might include circularity (from one perspective) and ellipticality (from another); a bath might include warmth (from one perspective) and hotness (from another).

These threads of indexed phenomenology are woven into a world via the same relations that structure our own experiences of the world. The unity of consciousness explains why we have *an* experience at a moment (rather than a disjoint collection of experiences). For the nontheistic idealist, it explains why the tapestry is *a* tapestry—*a* world—rather than a heap of disconnected phenomenal threads. Property binding explains why we perceive the greenness of the leaf as bound up with the teardrop shape. And for the nontheistic idealist, it explains why the greenness of the leaf *really is* bound up with the leaf's shape. The phenomenal spatial and temporal relations that structure our experiences of the world also provide the spatial and temporal structure *of the physical world itself.* The reality of the world is not disconnected from the appearance. It is composed of threads of such experience.

We've looked at what the physical world is like. Now let's turn to creatures like us. How do we fit into this tapestry of experience?

3

Idealism and the Mind-Body Problem

The previous chapters developed an idealist account of physical reality—an account according to which the quarks, molecules, houses, trees, planets, and stars of our universe are aspects of a vast, impersonal phenomenal unity. But I haven't said anything about how conscious subjects like *us* fit into this world. Are you just another aspect of the phenomenal tapestry? If not, how do you relate to it?

Our brains clearly are just one more aspect of the tapestry, alongside our bodies and houses. But how do ordinary conscious subjects like us relate to the tapestry?[1] Where do *our* experiences and thoughts fit in to this picture? In short, what does the mind-body problem look like within an idealistic framework?

While idealism is often presented alongside physicalism and dualism as a candidate position on the mind-body problem, this is a mistake. Idealism is a view about the nature of physical reality. (Physical reality is fundamentally experiential.) While this clearly entails realism about experiences, idealism per se does not tell us anything about the relationship between our minds and our bodies, or our experiences and physical reality (cf. Robinson 2009). In fact, I'll argue that analogues of all the familiar positions on the mind-body problem can exist within an idealistic framework, and that all the familiar debates reemerge within this context—albeit with a few noteworthy differences.

Section 3.1 surveys the candidate positions on the mind-body problem, given idealism about physical reality. Section 3.2 considers the physical correlates of consciousness, outlining traditional "local" versions of each

---

[1] I'm inclined toward a bundle theory of subjects, on which we are simply unified collections of thoughts and experiences. For this reason, I'll focus on the relation of our experiences to the tapestry. But the nontheistic idealist can also embrace a thick conception of subjects, on which they are additions to our ontology over and above the phenomenal tapestry. This would stick closer to the Berkeleyan view of subjects as spirits.

The View from Everywhere. Helen Yetter-Chappell, Oxford University Press. © Oxford University Press 2025. DOI: 10.1093/9780197795057.003.0003

66 THE VIEW FROM EVERYWHERE

mind-body position (on which consciousness is grounded in or caused by states of the subject's brain) and "extended" versions (on which consciousness is grounded in or caused by states of the subject and their broader environment).[2] The latter views are a version of what Andy Clark (2009) dubs the "extended conscious mind thesis" (ECM). But they go beyond standard ECM, in that—for the idealist—it is not merely the *vehicles* of subjects' conscious experiences that extend into the world, but the *content* of their experiences. As we'll see in the next chapter, embracing such a view has important implications for the nature of perception. Finally, §3.3 considers which of these candidate solutions to the mind-body problem the idealist should embrace, arguing for an extended non-reductive view.

3.1 The Options

To begin, let's restrict our consideration to non-perceptual experiences: bodily sensations, thoughts, mental images, hallucinations, and so forth. (The reason for this initial restriction will become clear as we go on.) Assuming realism about these experiences, there are three ways these experiences could relate to the tapestry (physical reality): (i) they could reduce to other elements of the tapestry; (ii) they could be sui generis parts of the tapestry; or (iii) they could be sui generis parts of reality that are distinct from the tapestry—that is, they could be *real*, but not part of the *physical* world.

3.1.1 Reductionism

Suppose my non-perceptual experiences reduce to other elements of the tapestry. Given the undeniable empirical connection between our experiences and our brain states, this view is most naturally fleshed out as one on which our non-perceptual experiences reduce to brain states, where brain states are understood as aspects of the phenomenal tapestry.[3] So my pain isn't a sui

---

[2] Following Wilson (2014, 539) I will use small-g "grounded"—here and throughout the chapter—as a generic term that encapsulates identity, constitution, functional realization, big-G Grounding, etc.

[3] Though it would also be open to the idealist to hold that, rather than reducing to brain states, at least some non-perceptual experiences reduce to aspects of our body. Pain would be a natural state to hold this of. On such a view, the pain in my wrist reduces to other (not intrinsically hurty) aspects of my wrist. Such a view has the advantage of vindicating our pretheoretic intuitions about pain. But

IDEALISM AND THE MIND-BODY PROBLEM 67

generis part of the tapestry, but it reduces to (e.g.) the shape of the neural networks, the flash of electrical signals, the zoominess of neurotransmitters crossing synaptic gaps, and so on. The experiences that constitute the brain are clearly mind-bogglingly complex—even more so than for other physical objects—woven out of an unfathomable number of phenomenal threads. But what is crucial to this view is that *pain* isn't an additional thread. Pain *reduces to* other (non-pain) phenomenal threads.

This should look familiar. Pain reduces to other (non-pain) aspects of brain-states . . . just as it does for standard reductive physicalists and constitutive panpsychists. Perhaps pain reduces to a macroscopic brain structure like C-fibers firing (CFF) or to a functional state of the brain (where these are understood as fundamentally phenomenal). Or perhaps pain reduces to features of collections of fundamental particles (again understood as fundamentally phenomenal). Insofar as my pain reduces to macroscopic features/ states of my brain, the view is akin to reductive physicalism (within an idealistic physical world). And insofar as it reduces to features of microphysical entities, it is akin to constitutive panpsychism.[4]

This may seem curious. Standardly, the distinction between physicalism and constitutive panpsychism is not merely one of scale. This follows from the fact that we are taking for granted that reality—at every scale—is phenomenal, and are thus partially collapsing the standard distinction between physicalists and constitutive panpsychists.

I'll argue in §3.2.4 that reductive idealism faces serious challenges. But it is (at least prima facie) an option.

3.1.2 Immanent Non-Reductionism

Likewise, if pain is a sui generis part of the tapestry, it is plausibly a sui generis aspect of brains, given the undeniably empirical correlations between brain states and experiences.[5] On such a view, in addition to the shape of

---

it looks far less plausible when it comes to thoughts or hallucinations. So such a view would presumably need to reduce these to brain states.

[4] But see §3.2.4, where I'll explore a different dimension along which reductive idealism can be akin to physicalism or panpsychism.

[5] Though as before, it would also be open to an idealist to hold that the pain that you feel as being in your wrist is a sui generis aspect of *your wrist*—albeit one that you are aware of only in that your brain functions in a certain way. On such a view, pain would be a state of your *body* that you perceive directly in the manner described in the next chapter.

68   THE VIEW FROM EVERYWHERE

the neural networks, the flash of electrical signals, and the zoominess of neurotransmitters crossing synaptic gaps, there is *primitive hurtiness* bound up as part of your brain.

This also looks familiar. In surveying the terrain of possible panpsychist solutions to the combination problem, Chalmers (2016, 195) proposes identity panpsychism, which holds that "macroexperiences are identical to microexperiences: experiences had by fundamental physical entities." For the identity panpsychist, pain is a primitive aspect of the physical world. More specifically, it is a primitive aspect of some fundamental physical particle in my brain.

An idealist who thinks that pain is a sui generis part of the tapestry might hold that this is property-bound with the other features of some fundamental particle in my brain, giving a direct analogue of Chalmers's identity panpsychist. (So there's a quark somewhere in the brain that has hurtiness as one of the phenomenal threads it comprises.) But they could also hold that the property binding relation binds my pain to macroscopic features of my brain. (So hurtiness is a primitive feature of, say, CFF, bound together with grayness and zoominess.) What's distinctive to this view is that my non-perceptual experiences are both (i) primitive and (ii) part of the tapestry of physical reality. I'll call this form of non-reductive idealism *immanent* nonreductionism, to reflect that my primitive non-perceptual phenomenology is *present within* the tapestry.[6]

3.1.3 Transcendent Non-Reductionism

Finally, my non-perceptual experiences could be sui generis parts of reality, but *not* part of the tapestry. Nontheistic idealism identifies *physical* reality with the phenomenal tapestry. According to this variant of non-reductive idealism, physical reality is not the totality of reality. There is more to reality *as a whole* than tapestry. I'll call this *transcendent* non-reductionism to indicate that our primitive non-perceptual phenomenology exists outside of physical reality.

---

[6] Embracing immanent nonreductionism would entail that—contrary to §2.3.2—cognitive phenomenology is part of the tapestry. But rather than being bound up with objects outside of us, it is bound up with our brains. When I look at the duckrabbit image, seeing it as a duck, the cognitive phenomenology of duckishness is a part of the tapestry. But it is not a part of the image, rather it is a part of my brain. Likewise, my hallucinations and other non-perceptual phenomenology are all part of the tapestry, as they are all parts of my brain.

IDEALISM AND THE MIND-BODY PROBLEM 69

This leads to the question of what the relationship is between the tapestry and these additional primitive aspects of reality. Again, it would be ridiculous to deny the tight connection between our brains and our experiences. There is (at the very least) a causal relationship between my brain-state and my feeling of pain. This should again look familiar: it's precisely the dualist and emergent panpsychists' view of the relationship between experiences and brain states. The transcendent non-reductive idealist can follow these familiar positions in embracing psycho-physical bridging laws—where these are understood as relating aspects of the tapestry with primitive non-perceptual experiences that are not part of the tapestry.

Transcendent non-reductive view can look like dualism or emergentist panpsychism depending on the scale that's relevant to the neural correlates of our experiences. Insofar as macroscopic bits of the brain (e.g., macro-level features, such as CFF) are among the neural correlates, the resulting view looks akin to dualism: my c-fibers fire within the phenomenal tapestry. Thanks to the bridging laws, an experience of pain is generated, which is not phenomenally unified with the tapestry, but is phenomenally unified with *me*. Insofar as microscopic bits of the brain (e.g., the phenomenology comprising quarks) are among the neural correlates, the resulting view is akin to emergent panpsychism: out of suitable quark phenomenology emerges (via the bridging laws) a new experience of pain, which is not phenomenally unified with the tapestry, but, again, is phenomenally unified with *me*.

What does this mean for the relation between your experiences and your brain? There are two views one could adopt. First, we could hold that brains have a physical aspect (which is part of the tapestry) and a nonphysical aspect (which is not part of the tapestry). Alternatively, we could hold that our pains are not parts of our brains, but are merely causally related to them.[7] Effectively, this is a matter about how to delineate our *brains*. How we answer this question seems rather arbitrary to me.

Curiously, though the transcendent non-reductive view is monistic, in the sense that there is only one *type* of stuff, it is dualistic (or, perhaps, multiplicitous) in that (a) there is more than one phenomenal *unity*, and that (b) in virtue of this, physical reality does not exhaust reality.

---

[7] The details of the causal relationship are a separate question. At the very least, brain activity is causally responsible for our experiences. Whether there is any causation the other direction is not entailed by anything said here. The candidate options will again be familiar from the literature on dualism, with epiphenomenalist, interactionist, and overdeterminist options.

3.2 Local vs. Extended

Thus far, I've narrowed our focus to considering non-perceptual mental states. Now let's broaden it, to consider our conscious experiences more generally.

Standard positions on the mind-body problem—what Rowlands (2010) labels as "Cartesian cognitive science"—take for granted that our brains are the sole physical entities directly relevant to our experiences. Our mental states are either grounded in or caused by our brain states. The world affects our experiences only indirectly, by affecting our brains. Granting this assumption yields positions closely mirroring their standard non-idealist counterparts.[8] But we could also take a broader swath of the world to be relevant to our experiences. And doing so has the potential to yield a novel theory of perception with important epistemic benefits.

So let's explore what happens when we take a broader swath of the physical world to be relevant to our experiences, beginning with the transcendent non-reductive view.

3.2.1 Transcendent Non-Reductionism: Local vs. Extended

Property dualism posits bridging laws, relating physical states to conscious experiences. Traditional property dualism presumes that these laws are "local."

> *Local bridging laws:* intrinsic features of the brain are the sole physical items referenced in the bridging laws.

Whether I'm hallucinating an elephant, having a veridical perception of an elephant, or feeling pain, my brain is the sole physical entity of relevance to the existence of my phenomenology. A transcendent non-reductive idealist analogue of this view would posit local bridging laws, ensuring that whenever the brain-bits of the tapestry are in thus-and-so state, an appropriate experience is generated (separate from the tapestry).

---

[8] I.e., materialistic physicalism, dualism, and panpsychism.

But they could also embrace an alternative "extended" account of the bridging laws, on which laws concern not only the intrinsic features of the agent's brain, but their circumstances more broadly.

Extended bridging laws: the agent's brain and broader physical environment are both items referenced in the bridging laws.

There are doubtless many different ways such a view could be fleshed out. Here, I'll outline the sort of bridging laws that strike me as the best motivated and most philosophically fruitful. Much of Chapters 4 and 6 will be devoted to making the case for the value of positing such bridging laws.

Let's consider an example to illustrate the two sorts of bridging laws. Let EFF (short for E-fibers firing) stand for the state that my brain is in when I have a visual experience of an elephant. On the familiar local account of bridging laws, there is a law such that whenever my brain is in EFF, elephanty phenomenology is generated. This works in the same manner, regardless of whether the experience is a veridical perception or a hallucination. Perhaps the experience will only *count as a perception* if certain additional conditions are met (e.g., if there's an appropriate causal connection between the elephant-bit of the tapestry and the brain-bit). But the *phenomenology*—both its qualitative nature and its numerical relation to the tapestry—is unaffected by this. In all instances, this bridging law can be thought of as a *law of generation*: a law that accounts for the generation of new phenomenology, numerically distinct from that of the tapestry. (The area in the dotted line signifies the physical relata of the bridging laws.)

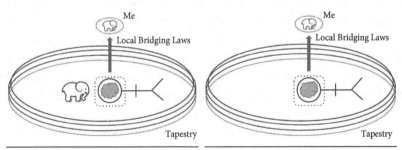

Veridical perception with local bridging laws　　　　Hallucination with local bridging laws

By contrast, on an extended account of bridging laws, the physical relata includes not just the physical state of the agent's brain (the brain-bits of the tapestry), but the agent's physical environment more broadly. When no elephant is appropriately causally connected to the agent, these laws function as laws of generation: generating new phenomenology that is phenomenally unified with my mind, but not with the tapestry. But when there is an elephant standing an appropriate causal relation to the agent, these laws function very differently. Rather than generating new phenomenology, the laws function to *pull bits of the tapestry's phenomenology into the agent's mind*. So some of the bits of phenomenology that make up the elephant's body simultaneously parts of two phenomenal unities: the tapestry of physical reality and the perceiving agent's mind. In such contexts, we can think of the laws as *laws of expansion:* "expanding" our minds to literally overlap with physical reality.[9] Thus, the extended bridging laws do more than generating phenomenology; they also affect the phenomenal unity relations: determining which bits of phenomenology are unified to form my mind.

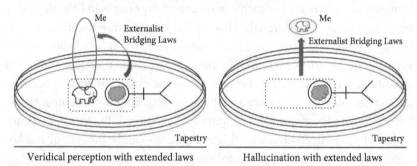

Veridical perception with extended laws | Hallucination with extended laws

On the extended account of bridging laws that I have in mind, some (but not all) of my experiences literally overlap with the tapestry. My perceptual experiences will involve overlap with the tapestry; my hallucinations, dreams, imaginings, cognitive phenomenology, and so on will involve the generation of new phenomenology, distinct from the tapestry. This generated phenomenology and the bits of the tapestry that I overlap with are bound together by the unity of consciousness relation into *my total experience* at a moment.

I'll argue in Chapter 4 that an extended account of bridging laws makes possible a view of perception that robustly captures the motivations for naïve realism. I'll also consider whether standard materialistic dualists can embrace such an account of the bridging laws. (They can, but—unfortunately

---

[9] Such bridging laws entail that "being phenomenally unified with" is not transitive—a claim that I'll defend in Chapter 4.

IDEALISM AND THE MIND-BODY PROBLEM   73

for naïve realism—doing so does not yield the same epistemic benefits.) Chapter 6 will explore the benefits that arise from this theory of perception.

3.2.2 Immanent Non-Reductionism: Local vs. Extended

A similar distinction can be drawn between different variants of the immanent non-reductive view. According to the immanent nonreductionist, my experiences are primitive aspects of the tapestry. While my experience of pain is a part of the tapestry, it doesn't reduce to any non-hurty elements of the tapestry. Rather, hurtiness is a primitive aspect of (say) my brain, in addition to my brain's grayness, the zoominess of neurotransmitters crossing synaptic gaps, and so on.

On a local interpretation of immanent non-reductionism, all my experiences are aspects of my brain, numerically distinct from other bits of the tapestry. Whether I am hallucinating an elephant or seeing one, there is elephanty phenomenology bound up with the other phenomenology comprising my brain. And this elephanty phenomenology is numerically distinct from the elephanty phenomenology that comprises the elephant.

On an extended interpretation of this view, when I hallucinate an elephant, there is primitive elephanty phenomenology bound up with my brain, and it is this phenomenology that I'm aware of. By contrast, when I *see* an elephant, the primitive elephanty phenomenology I'm aware of is (part of) the phenomenology that constitutes the elephant. What would account for this difference? In both cases, the phenomenology is already *there*, present within the tapestry, but the environment determines *which* aspect of the environment I'm aware of. How could this be?

It seems to me that the answer requires an analogue of the transcendent bridging laws. But, for the immanent idealist, the laws never generate phenomenology; they simply govern its fusion. They determine whether the phenomenology that is fused into me is *brain-based* elephant phenomenology or *elephant-based* elephant phenomenology. To use our previous terminology, rather than ever being laws of generation, they are laws of expansion and contraction.

It makes sense that there would be such laws. Just settling which phenomenology exists doesn't settle which phenomenal *unities* exist. One natural way of understanding the phenomenal unity that corresponds to me is to take it to unify a certain subset of the phenomenology that composes my brain. This is the answer that the local view offers. But it is not the only possible unity that would correspond to my perspective. Another possibility is that

I am a unified fusion of brainy phenomenology and phenomenology from my perceptual environment. This is the extended answer. Which of these views is true seems like a substantial question. It's also a question that can't be settled by appeal to physical truths, and so requires something more—which is why we need to appeal to laws of fusion—to understand the view.

3.2.3 Reductionism: Local vs. Extended

This same distinction can also be drawn within the reductive view. A local interpretation of reductionism will reduce our phenomenal experiences to brainy-phenomenology (e.g., reducing your pain experience to CFF-phenomenology). An extended interpretation will still reduce our phenomenology to elements of the phenomenal tapestry, but (in perception) the relevant reduction base will include things outside of our brains. So for the externalist reductionist, your perception of an elephant might reduce to a subset of the phenomenology that constitutes the elephant (e.g., its form-from-perspective, its grayness-from-perspective), whereas for the local reductionist, the perception of an elephant reduces to brainy-phenomenology. The image below depicts the externalist and local reductionists' understanding of perceptual phenomenology.

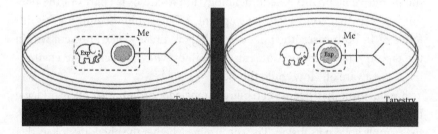

This mirrors the distinction between standard materialistic views and those that embrace the Extended Conscious Mind thesis (ECM) (Clark 2009). On the standard (local) materialist picture, conscious experiences are wholly grounded in brain states.[10] By contrast, ECM holds that the physical basis for conscious experiences extends outside of our brains: "the local material vehicles of some of our conscious experiences might include more

---

[10] As before, I use small "g" grounded here as a catch-all for identity, constitution, supervenience, big-G Grounding, etc.

than the whirrings and grindings of the brain/CNS" (Clark 2009, 976).[11] But idealist external reductionism goes beyond ECM. For on this view, it is not merely the *vehicles* of some conscious experiences that extend outside of the brain, but the very *contents* of the experiences. The *actual elephant phenomenology* that I'm experiencing when I see an elephant is a part of the elephant before me.

I think that, contrary to first appearances, idealist reductionism is not a tenable view. But before I present the challenges to this view, let's explore it in a bit more detail.

There are interesting questions about the relationship between the extended and local variants of reductionism, and the nature of subjects for the reductionist. To start: when the externalist and local reductionists each describe the worlds they take us to inhabit, how do these worlds differ? Insofar as we're realists about phenomenology—as everyone ought to be, but idealists surely are committed to!—there must be a difference between the two worlds. There must be a fact of the matter about what phenomenology there is and what phenomenal unities there are. For non-reductionists, differences in bridging laws and laws of phenomenal fusion accounted for these differences. How can reductionists about the mind account for the difference? When we consider two possible worlds—one where local reductionism is true and one where externalist reductionism is true—what is the difference between these worlds?

There are two ways we might make sense of the respect in which the extended and local reductionists disagree: (i) the extended reductionist has a different (broader) reductive base than the local reductionist, or (ii) the reductive bases are the same but the extended reductionist has a different (broader) view of the phenomenal unities that constitute subjects.

Start with the reading on which there is a dispute about the reductive base of our phenomenal experiences. One might think that extended reductionists can agree with local reductionists that EFF is the reductive base of elephant perceptions in hallucinatory cases, and that they simply need a different account of the reductive base in perception. But this clearly cannot be right. If EFF only grounds elephanty phenomenology sometimes, there must be more to elephanty phenomenology than EFF. But this is just to say

---

[11] This goes beyond the tenets of the (mere) extended mind hypothesis (Clark and Chalmers 1998), which holds an analogous claim about the physical basis of some (perhaps non-conscious) mental states (e.g., dispositional states). Clark himself rejects this more radical view.

76 THE VIEW FROM EVERYWHERE

that reductionism is false. So the extended view needs a different account of the reductive base for hallucination as well as perception.

More promisingly, the extended reductionist could hold that EFF *in isolation* never constitutes elephanty phenomenology. In the hallucinatory case, the reductive base isn't EFF, but EFF-in-absence-of-causally-related-elephant. In the perceptual case, the reductive base of elephanty phenomenology is the phenomenology that comprises the elephant. Thus, whereas for local reductionists, the reductive base of elephanty phenomenology is simply EFF, for the externalist reductionist, it's the disjunctive (EFF-in-absence-of-causally-related-elephant) OR (elephant). But this only makes sense of the disagreement between the local and extended views *if there's a fact of the matter* about whether EFF or EFF-in-absence-of-causally-related-elephant grounds elephanty phenomenology. And insofar as elephanty phenomenology is nothing over and above its reductive base, it's not clear that there is any substantive fact of the matter.

A more promising way to make sense of the disagreement has extended and local reductive idealists agreeing about the physical state of the world, the phenomenology that comprises the world, and what experiences are grounded in what physical states. In particular, they agree that EFF (simpliciter) grounds elephanty phenomenology. The disagreement is over how the phenomenal unity relations carve things up—in this case, over whether EFF-grounded elephanty phenomenology is essentially a part of the *conscious subject's* phenomenology. As the local reductionist sees it, ordinary conscious subjects are phenomenal unities wholly comprised by (a subset of) brain phenomenology. As the extended reductionist sees it, conscious subjects can include phenomenology grounded in the brain or other phenomenology from the causal environment.

Suppose you currently seem to be seeing two elephants. As it happens, one is a real elephant that you perceive; the other is a hallucination. There are (let's ridiculously suppose) two elephant-fibers in your brain, both of which are firing. According to the local reductionist, both instances of EFF are bound together to form your current experience. Although the extended reductionist agrees that both instances of EFF comprise elephanty phenomenology, both bits of phenomenology are not unified with you. Rather, one instance of EFF (hallucinated elephant) is bound together with *the look of the elephant before you* (perceived elephant) to form your current experience.

While this way of making sense of the disagreement between local and extended reductionists strikes me as more plausible than our earlier attempts, it also raises the question of how a reductionist ought to make sense of phenomenal unity. One possible answer is that there is a primitive phenomenal unity relation, which is connected to the workings of the tapestry in a law-like way. This would yield a curious view, on which our *phenomenology* reduces to bits of the tapestry, but *we* are primitive unities constructed out of this phenomenology. Although reductionistic about phenomenology, it would be possible for there to be zombie worlds, of a sort: worlds that are physically just like our own world, where *the world* is constituted by all the same phenomenology as our own, but where there is no phenomenal unity (and hence no subject of experience) associated with your brain.

For a more thoroughly reductive view, it could be held that the phenomenal unity relation itself reduces to other relations present within the tapestry. In this case, the dispute between local and extended reductionism would boil down to a disagreement over the reductive base of the unity of consciousness. But as before, it's not clear that the reductionist can take there to be a substantive fact of the matter about this.

3.2.4 Is Idealist Reductionism Tenable?

Why would one embrace reductive idealism? Given that the view is idealistic, it already accepts that (at least some) phenomenology is fundamental. Still, by reducing (all or some of some of) our phenomenology to other elements of the tapestry, we reduce the number of primitive phenomenal experiences making up reality. We could eliminate primitive bodily sensations, hallucinations, and thought-phenomenology to give a sparser view. But while this provides some reason to entertain idealist reductionism, the view faces serious challenges. Along the way, I'll argue that these challenges also illuminate a new challenge for materialist reductionism.

First, reductionism entails that one and the same phenomenal property is (in some instances) fundamental, and (in other instances) reduces to distinct phenomenal components. The gray elephant phenomenology of my hallucination reduces to brainy-phenomenology, whereas the gray elephant phenomenology that partially constitutes the elephant is a primitive aspect of reality.[12] Phenomenal properties are real. (We are idealists, after all.) And one and the same phenomenal property—phenomenology like thus-and-so—is

---

[12] This is true even on a local interpretation where my perceptual experiences are "inside the head."

78 THE VIEW FROM EVERYWHERE

sometimes primitive and at other times reduces to brainy phenomenology. This metaphysical disjunctivism is unpalatable, to say the least.

The reductionist could perhaps insist that phenomenology of the elephant also further reduces (e.g., to quark phenomenology). But it's difficult to see how the grayness of the elephant and the grayness of my hallucination could have reductive bases that are anything alike. The resulting reductive base is still hopelessly disjunctive.

Second, it's far from clear that the reduction this view relies on is intelligible. Galen Strawson (2006) objects to physicalism[13] on grounds that it's unintelligible how one could wring experientiality from non-experiential building-blocks. While this specific problem is alleviated by reductive idealism, a related brute emergence problem emerges, which is far worse than the original.

The reductive materialist maintains that experiences emerge from wholly non-experiential material building-blocks, appropriately arranged. Such brute emergence, Strawson argues, is no more intelligible than space emerging from non-spatial building blocks (arranged via non-spatial relations). This would not even be intelligible within "God's physics" and, as such, requires a miracle in each instance. By contrast, idealist reductionism about the mind doesn't try to wring experientiality from non-experiential building-blocks. The building-blocks themselves are thoroughly experiential. We can now wrap our minds around the nature of the building-blocks. This might seem to alleviate Strawson's brute emergence worries. But instead of rendering the emergence of our phenomenology more intelligible, it makes the unintelligibility of reductionism all the clearer.

If C-fibers are fundamentally phenomenal, their nature is graspable by us. But far from rendering it intelligible how pain could reduce to CFF, it seems *manifestly* incoherent that my experience of pain be reduced to the bundle of sensory experiences that constitute this brain state. If idealism is true, we can literally wrap our minds around the nature of our brain states. And when we do so, all we find are sensory impressions (e.g., of the visual experiences of brain activity seen through an fMRI or neurons seen through a microscope) that clearly don't amount to the hurtiness of pain. Furthermore, we not only grasp the experiences that make up our brain states, but also *the relations between them* that unify them: the relations that structure reality are the very relations that structure our minds, and we are aware of these relations insofar

---

[13] "PhysicSalism" in Strawson's terminology.

as we're aware of our experiences as *being bound* together. In spite of this, the reduction of pain to CFF (or any other non-hurty state) appears manifestly incoherent. It's as if we grasped the nature of hydrogen and of oxygen, and of the covalent bonds that bind them into H_2O molecules, . . . and yet found it incoherent that water could reduce to hydrogen and oxygen molecules.

This poses a challenge not just to reductive idealists, but to traditional materialist reductionists as well. For *if materialist reductionism is to fare better than idealist reductionism, there must be something about the nature of the mind-independent that renders it particularly suitable for constituting our phenomenal experiences.* And, Strawson (2006) would put it, that just seems *silly*.

But perhaps this is too quick. Idealism entails that we fully grasp the *sort* of thing that our brains (as aspects of the physical world) are: experiences. But it does not entail that we grasp the *specific* phenomenal experiences that comprise our brains or any aspect of physical reality. Far from this, as I'll argue in Chapter 4, we only grasp a minuscule portion of the threads of the physical world. Given this ignorance, why think that we're in any position to say whether pain can reduce to CFF phenomenology?

Think about the experiences we can have (mediated by scientific instruments) of our brain states. These clearly do not give a reductive base for the feeling of pain. Add to these the experiences other animals could have, by way of these instruments. While I don't know what any of these experiences are like, it seems clear that none of these help us to form an intelligible reductive base. Imagine a virus-sized organism traveling through the brain, perceiving through alien sensory organs as it goes. None of these seem to help either. While I can't truly wrap my mind around any of these non-human experiences, it does seem clear that the feeling of pain doesn't reduce to any collection of such experiences. They're simply the *wrong kind of thing*. In each case, we have (what we might call) an *extrospective experience*—an experience of perceiving the brain state, as opposed to embodying it. And such extrospective experiences simply don't seem to be the right sort of thing to constitute the what-it's-likes of subjects.[14]

In this respect, reductive idealism differs from constitutive panpsychism and is more akin to traditional physicalism. According to the panpsychist, it is not the "extrospective" experiences of the fundamental particles

---

[14] Cf. Leibniz's mill (*Monadology* §17). Rendering the mill identical to the experiences observers have when walking inside of it doesn't make it intelligible how the mill feels.

80 THE VIEW FROM EVERYWHERE

that constitutes our experiences, but their intrinsic (phenomenal) natures. A reductive idealist could propose adding such experiences to the tapestry, bringing them closer to panpsychism. The most straightforward way to do this would be to posit that pain itself is a primitive aspect of CFF (thus moving away from reductive idealism and toward immanent non-reductive idealism). But they could also hold that there are intrinsic phenomenal properties of C-fibers, which are not themselves pain, but intelligibly combine to constitute pain. This would remain a version of reductive idealism, but one that is more akin to constitutive panpsychism than to physicalism. (While I am skeptical that this approach could successfully account for the rich variety of experiences that creatures like us have—at least, without a similarly enormous reductive base—there is no *new* challenge here, only the familiar challenge of the combination problem.)

So idealist reductionism—whether local or extended—faces at least two serious objections: first, the problem of offering an unpalatably disjunctive account of reality, and second, the challenge of the manifest incoherence of reducing phenomenology to extrospective experiences. The latter of these could be solved by moving away from merely "extrospective" experiences, and toward an analogue of constitutive panpsychism—but only if the constitutive panpsychist has a solution to the combination problem. And the disjunctivism remains.

3.3 Which Way to Turn?

Idealism does not constitute a position on the mind-body problem (cf. Kastrup (2018).[15] We've seen that the familiar positions on the mind-body problem re-emerge within an idealistic context, yielding analogues of physicalism and constitutive panpsychism (reductive idealism), identity

---

[15] Bernardo Kastrup (2017a, 2018) has argued that idealism not only presents a solution to the "hard problem" of consciousness, it circumvents the problem altogether. On Kastrup's view, we are all "dissociated alters" (à la Dissociative Identity Disorder) of a cosmic consciousness. Our physical bodies and brains are the "revealed appearances" of these alters (2018, 145). And the physical world, more generally, is the "extrinsic appearance of phenomenality surrounding—but outside—our respective alter" (2017b, 24). Why is it that my brain doing this feels this way? Kastrup's answer is that the feeling causes there to be a "revealed experience" of a brain doing this thing. We don't have to explain why or how the brain generates the experience. It doesn't. The generation is the other way around. While this avoids the challenge of explaining how my brain gives rise to consciousness, we face an analogous problem going the other direction: why should my hurty experience give rise to a brain with CFF? Why should my hurty experience give rise to any "revealed experiences" at all

panpsychism (immanent non-reductive idealism), dualism, and emergent panpsychism (transcendent non-reductive idealism). Which way should an idealist turn? Among philosophers of mind who take the physical world to be material, there is no agreement as to how to solve the mind-body problem. Does the situation look any clearer within an idealistic framework?

In many respects, the debates between these positions in the idealistic context will look very familiar. Mary in an idealist world, knowing all the facts about brains and surface-reflectance properties (cashed out in phenomenal terms), will be precisely as surprised when she finally *has* a phenomenally red experience as her materialist counterpart. Responses to the knowledge argument—for instance, on grounds that our intuitions about Mary are unreliable, or that Mary comes to learn a previously known fact in a new way— are precisely as good when made by the reductive idealist as when made by their materialist counterparts.

Likewise, it's just as conceivable that there be creatures physically just like us, but with no phenomenal experiences of their own in an idealist world as in a materialist world. The idealist zombie world, of course, cannot be conceived of as a world physically like our own, but with *no phenomenology*, since, for the idealist, the physical world is constructed out of phenomenology. But it is perfectly intelligible to imagine an idealist world with trees, stars, buildings, computers, cars, bodies, brains, instances of toe-stubbings and C-fibers firing, and hollering . . . but where there is no phenomenology of *pain*, and/or no phenomenal unity associated with the brains of the toe-stubbing bodies. And this would equally well work to yield the first premise of the zombie argument as the traditional conception of a zombie world. For if such a world is possible, it follows that being physically just like our world (in the idealist's sense of being physically like our world) isn't sufficient for being phenomenally just like our world. In particular, it isn't sufficient to explain the conscious experiences *of* the toe-stubbing creatures. And the potential

---

(beyond the pain itself)? Kastrup holds that "the revealed side of nature [is] grounded in its concealed side" (2018, 147). But, paralleling the zombie argument, it seems conceivable that there be a world that appears just as our world does, populated by ghosts rather than embodied minds. So it doesn't seem necessary that brains be generated. If the relationship is metaphysically contingent, we need to explain why it obtains in our world. The obvious answer would be, following the dualist and the emergent panpsychist, to appeal to some sort of generative laws. These would need to be fleshed out, and fleshed out in a way that gives us not just our brains, but the whole manifest world. My point is not that Kastrup's view fails, but that the very same issues that arise for the physicalist, the dualist, the panpsychist, and my nontheistic idealist also arise when conceptualizing the world as Kastrup does. The account may prove interesting and illuminating. But we haven't circumvented the mind-body problem; rather, we've flipped it upside down.

82 THE VIEW FROM EVERYWHERE

responses to the zombie argument made by traditional physicalists will be just as available to idealist reductionists: bases for rejecting the zombie intuition, and for rejecting the move from conceivability to possibility.

This is obviously not the place to try to offer a general adjudication over the relationship between mind and body (though my own sympathies lie with the dualists [Yetter-Chappell 2019, 2022]). But we have also seen that—though much is unchanged about the mind-body debate—there are some respects in which things look different from within an idealist metaphysics. First, reductive idealists (as idealists) must be realists about phenomenology. And their reductionistic view of our experiences entails a bizarre disjunctivism in the natures of qualitatively identical bits of phenomenology: phenomenal greenness being at once primitive (in the tree's leaves) and reducing to brain-phenomenology (in my hallucinations). Second, while the knowledge argument and zombie argument look similar regardless of the metaphysical nature of the physical world, the explanatory gap looks far more problematic within an idealistic context. If materialism about the physical world is true, we can't really wrap our minds around the *nature* of C-fibers. We can understand how they function within the nervous system and their low-level structure, but that is all. And what we do grasp about them leaves us with a *mystery*: *why* should CFF feel like pain? Why should it feel like anything at all to have CFF? By contrast, if we live in an idealist world, we can grasp the very nature of CFF. The sensory impressions we have when we look at nerve tissue under a microscope or look at fMRIs is a part of what our neural states *are* (along with the sensory impressions that would be had of these things from many other perspectives we are not privy to). But these "extrospective" experiences that make up C-fibers for the reductive idealist are *manifestly* incapable of explaining why CFF feels painful. We can, if idealism is true, grasp the kind of thing that our neural states are. And when we do so, rather than finding a solution to the explanatory gap, or even an enduring mystery, we find *clarity* that what reductive idealists would reduce pain to cannot really be what pain amounts to.

So we should reject reductive idealism, and embrace either transcendent or immanent non-reductive idealism (the idealistic analogues of dualism or nonconstitutive panpsychism). On these views, our experiences are sui generis parts of reality.[16] For the immanent nonreductionist, these sui generis experiences are parts of the tapestry of physical reality: my

---

[16] On local views, *all* of our experiences; on externalist views, only our *non-perceptual* experiences.

pain upon stubbing my toe is a part of my brain state, bound up with the gray, squishiness, and neurotransmitter-zoominess. The transcendent nonreductionist agrees that your pain is a sui generis part of reality but does not take it to be bound up with the tapestry of *physical reality*. Physical reality includes brains and bodies and trees and stars, and these are structured complexes of phenomenology. But the phenomenology that makes them up is what I've called "extrospective" phenomenology. And there is more to reality, as a whole, than this.

While the transcendent and immanent positions are both plausible ones for the idealist to take, I'm inclined to favor transcendent non-reductive idealism. It seems characteristic of the physical world that its constituents are accessible from multiple perspectives. Unlike my wincing, my cursing, and my C-fibers firing, the pain I feel is private: it is only accessible to me. As such, it seems most natural to think that it is only a part of me—phenomenally unified with my mind, but not with the tapestry of physical reality.

I've argued that each candidate position on the mind-body problem comes in a traditional "local" variety (which takes our brains to be the sole bit of the world of relevance to our experiences) and an extended variety (which takes a broader swath of reality to be of relevance, including our perceptual environment). Much of the remainder of this book will be spent arguing that idealism holds distinctive benefits when held in conjunction with extended nonreductionism. In the next chapter, I'll develop an idealist theory of perception that is available if we embrace extended non-reductive idealism. Chapter 6 will make the case for the distinctive epistemic benefits of this combination of views, arguing that the total worldview on offer is superior to materialistic alternatives.

4
Perception

In the last chapter, I argued that idealists should embrace a non-reductive account of our minds, on which our non-perceptual experiences are sui generis and distinct from the phenomenal tapestry that constitutes the physical world. I called this transcendent non-reductive idealism, to distinguish it from the "immanent" view on which our experiences are sui generis aspects of the phenomenal tapestry. For simplicity, in this chapter, I'll simply refer to this view as non-reductive idealism.

Psychophysical bridging laws account for the relation between the physical world (understood as a phenomenal tapestry) and the sui generis phenomenology of our pains, hallucinations, and so forth. The previous chapter distinguished two ways of understanding these bridging laws: local and extended. The local view follows traditional dualism in taking all bridging laws to be "laws of generation." Whether I'm imagining, hallucinating, or veridically perceiving an elephant, my brain is the sole physical entity of relevance to the existence of the phenomenology I'm experiencing. The bridging laws ensure that whenever my brain is doing something like it is now, a relevant sui generis experience is *generated*—where this experience is not phenomenally unified with the tapestry. The extended view takes a more expansive view of what features of the physical world form the physical base of the bridging laws. Not only is the brain of relevance, but also the perceptual environment that the brain is situated within—including the presence or absence of an elephant in an appropriate causal relation to the brain.

In this chapter, I present the case for an externalist account of bridging laws, arguing that doing so affords us an attractive theory of perception that puts us in literal and direct epistemic contact with reality. Given an externalist account of the bridging laws, idealists can account for our having contact with reality that is as direct as that which we have to our own minds—for, in perception, the external world literally overlaps with and is a part of our minds.

The View from Everywhere. Helen Yetter-Chappell, Oxford University Press. © Oxford University Press 2025. DOI: 10.1093/9780197795057.003.0004

PERCEPTION   85

§4.1 develops this theory of perception, which I dub "naïve idealism." Veridical perception involves an overlap between my mind and the physical world I perceive, whereas in hallucination, my experiences are localized to my mind. If veridical perception involves literal contact between my mind and the world, there is a huge epistemic gulf between veridical perception and other sensory states. Section 4.2 considers the extent of our overlap with reality, assessing how much of what we take ourselves to perceive involves such overlap, and how much is constructed by our minds. Section 4.3 draws on this discussion, putting it to work developing a neo-Berkeleyan account of illusions. We'll return to the nature of perception in Chapter 6, where I'll argue that naïve idealism is *uniquely* poised to capture the virtues more familiarly claimed by naïve realism.

4.1 Naïve Idealism

On the extended account of bridging laws, the physical base of the bridging laws extends outside of the agent's brain to the agent's perceptual environment. So the physical base of my hallucination is very different from that of my veridical perception, even if I have a qualitatively indistinguishable experience as of a tree in both cases.[1] When no tree is appropriately causally connected to me, the laws generate new phenomenology that is phenomenally unified with my mind, but not with the tapestry. Whereas when I am appropriately causally related to a tree, the laws function to pull bits of the tree—strands of the phenomenology comprising it—into my mind.

Thus in veridical perception, the objects of perception are literally part of my mind. When I perceive the world around me, my mind overlaps with—and is partially constituted by—aspects of the tapestry of physical reality. The idea of overlapping with physical reality is not merely a metaphor. When I perceive the greenness of the palm tree outside my window, the palm's greenness (that "fiber" of the tapestry) is literally a part of my mind, in precisely the same way that my pains and worries are. The greenness of the palm is simultaneously part of (at least) two phenomenal unities: the phenomenal unity that is physical reality, and the phenomenal unity that is my mind.

---

[1] In the former case, the physical base is my brain-state together with no tree causally related to me; in the latter, it's the brain-state together with the tree I'm causally related to.

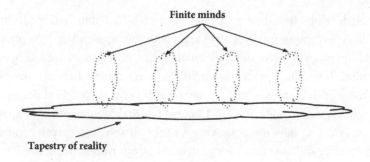

Of course, as I look at the palm, I am not aware of all aspects of it. I do not perceive the palm's back-side, its chemical structure, or the redness of the leaves (which would be perceived by my inverted-twin). But these are (plausibly) genuine components of the palm, which make up parts of its nature, and which other observers (situated from different vantage points, or with different perceptual systems) could perceive. In perception, my mind does not overlap with the palm tree bit in its entirety, but only with a subset of its phenomenal fibers. Nevertheless, just as seeing a man's face and arms is sufficient for seeing the man, so too I see the palm by directly experiencing the fibers that are accessible to me.

By contrast, my non-perceptual mental states—feelings of anxiety, pains, mental imagery, beliefs, hallucinations—do not put me in direct contact with external reality. These non-perceptual mental phenomena are part of my unity of consciousness but are not a part of the tapestry of physical reality. My total phenomenal experience at any given moment may be comprised of fibers of the tapestry together with distinct non-tapestry phenomenology. Suppose that I simultaneously see a bird fly across my window, hear my son calling for me, feel an ache in my wrist, and contemplate the next sentence I'm going to write. This visual, auditory, interoceptive, and cognitive phenomenology form a unified conscious experience. But only some features of the experience—the visual and auditory—also comprise reality. Were I to hallucinate a bloody dagger hanging in front of my computer screen, the aspects of my total phenomenal experience corresponding to the computer would be elements of physical reality, whereas the bits of phenomenology corresponding to the (apparent) bloody dagger would be bound up in my unity of consciousness, but not the phenomenal unity that is physical reality. This is what distinguishes perceptual from non-perceptual mental phenomena. In perception, and only in perception, physical reality is a constituent of my experiences and my mind. So what fundamentally distinguishes hallucination from perception is not the *phenomenal character* of the experience or the intrinsic metaphysical nature of the mental state, but *whether or not the experience is numerically identical with an aspect of the tapestry.* And because the tapestry of reality is governed by laws that account for its regularity, physical reality (and the experiences we have which overlap with it) will also exhibit a regularity that hallucinations do not.

This means that, for the naïve idealist, there is a sharp boundary between perceptual and non-perceptual experiences. We may not be able to *identify* where this boundary lies. But this does not pose a metaphysical problem for the idealist. The precise location of the line between perceptual and non-perceptual experiences may be surprising. Can we see by way of glasses? Telescopes? Optical microscopes? Electron microscopes? What about mirrors? Shadow? Videos? Naïve idealism does not commit us on these issues.

For the naïve idealist, there simply is a fact of the matter as to what experiences make up the tapestry, and a fact of the matter as to what it takes to overlap with these threads. There is a world out there, and *it* supplies the dividing line between veridicality and non-veridicality. And there simply is a fact of the matter about the *relationship* between my mind and the external world, determined by the psychophysical bridging laws. Answers about the specific phenomenal contents of reality (and my relation to specific contents) are provided by *the world* and not by the naïve idealist theory—much as facts about the number of planets are supplied by the world and not our theory of the nature of reality.

In (Yetter-Chappell 2018b) I suggested an analogy to the Extended Mind Hypothesis that treated sensory "mediators" like mirrors and shadows as extended sense organs. The argument proceeded as a continuum of cases, pushing the line for what counts as seeing further and further; arguing that at each step of the way, there's no principled basis for drawing a line between perception and not-perception. For the naïve idealist, there is a line. And the line is given by the psychophysical bridging laws. If they function to expand my mind such that I overlap with a bit of reality as a result, we get perception. If not, not.

We don't have infallible insight into the bridging laws. We can't know for sure whether their base is functional or physical. We can't know for sure whether they render earthworms conscious. And we can't know for sure whether they treat mirrors and microscopes as extended sense-organs. But we can know that there must be a fact of the matter. And we can offer arguments as to what seems most elegant and most plausible. I won't endeavor to do so

88 THE VIEW FROM EVERYWHERE

in this book. The point is simply that idealism is compatible with a plurality of answers to these issues.

So this is the theory of perception in a nutshell. The aspects of reality that we perceive are bound by the unity of consciousness relation into two distinct phenomenal unities: the tapestry of reality, and the mind of the perceiver. My non-perceptual mental states are only bound into a single unity: that of my mind. The fundamental difference between hallucinations and veridical perceptions is not the qualitative nature of the experienced items, but whether the items are phenomenally bound to the tapestry as well as to a finite observer's mind.

This picture of perception will be complicated in section §4.2.3, where I'll suggest a second, looser notion of veridical perception that doesn't require overlap with the tapestry—but merely accurate, appropriately caused experiences (which could overlap with the tapestry or be distinct). But the distinctive epistemic benefits described in Chapter 6 will only apply to the veridical perceptions of the narrower sort.

This account of veridical perception raises several questions: (1) (How) can our minds overlap with the tapestry of reality? Such an overlap would entail that the unity of consciousness relation is intransitive, since if the relation were transitive, any overlap of my mind with the tapestry would entail that all of my mind was unified with the tapestry. But many—including Dainton (2000) and Bayne (2010), whose theories of the unity of consciousness I've appealed to—take the unity of consciousness to be transitive. (2) My perceptual system systematically puts me in touch with only a single index of the tapestry. So I systematically only have access to the greenness of leaves and granny smith apples, the redness of fire trucks and blood, and so on. By contrast, the fire truck systematically appears green to my inverted twin. How and why is this?

I'll address these issues in the remainder of this section. Section 4.1.1 addresses the (in)transitivity of the unity of consciousness. Section 4.1.2 looks at the systematicity of the aspects of the tapestry which we have access to. Following this, §4.2 discusses the extent of our overlap with the tapestry, laying the groundwork for §4.3, in which I develop an idealist account of illusions.

4.1.1 Transitivity

For my account of perception to be viable, it's crucial that the unity of consciousness not be transitive—that it be possible for our minds to overlap

PERCEPTION   89

with the tapestry, without thereby collapsing our individual minds and the tapestry into a single unity. Is this intransitivity plausible? We saw in Chapter 2 that several writers on the unity of consciousness think not. Dainton (2000) and Bayne (2010) both offer qualified arguments that the unity of consciousness—at least in the case of synchronic unity—is transitive. Fortunately, I think there are compelling reasons to reject these arguments.[2]

Let's begin with Dainton's case for transitivity. Recall that Dainton views the unity of consciousness as a primitive co-consciousness relation, via which the experiences we are having at a given moment are "fused" into a single experience. Dainton writes that when two experiences e1 and e2 are co-conscious,

> the two are wholly joined, there is no "distance" separating them at all. Since e1 and e2 are parts of a single experience in this way, how could it be possible for another experience e3 to be co-conscious with e2 without also being co-conscious with e1? (Dainton 2000, 105)

The implication here is that this is not possible. It's worth noting here that when two experiences e1 and e2 are co-conscious, it is not (on Dainton's view) like candles melting down and fusing into a single candle. Each of e1 and e2 *retains* its own distinct nature and identity.[3] The sense of fusing that Dainton has in mind in the above quote is clearly something less radical. He continues:

> Given that e1 and e2 are fused, any experience that is co-conscious with e2 will automatically and necessarily be co-conscious with e1 as well. Since the same applies to any combination of simultaneous experiences, partial unity is an impossibility. (Dainton 2000, 105)

While evocative, this seems to me to be no more than an assertion that the relation is transitive: co-consciousness fuses, and the right sort of fusing to think in terms of is one that is transitive. It is fine if this is Dainton's intuition, but to make trouble for my account of perception, we would need an

---

[2] See also Luke Roelofs (2019, 2016), who defends the possibility of experience-sharing.
[3] Earlier in the paragraph, Dainton (105) writes: "The two are not mixed or blended together, they retain their own distinctive phenomenal characteristics."

90　THE VIEW FROM EVERYWHERE

argument that we *must* think of fusion in this way. And there are other co-herent ways of thinking about fusion that don't entail transitivity.

If you're puzzled, here's an analogy to help make sense of the idea: we might think of our body parts as—in a sense—being fused into a single, discrete organism, via a "co-body" relation. Typically whenever body part 1 (bp1) is fused with bp2, and bp2 is fused with bp3, bp1 will also be fused with bp3—these will both be part of the same body and organism. It seems reasonable to imagine someone asserting:

> Given that bp1 and bp2 are fused, any body part that part of the same body as bp2 will automatically and necessarily be in the same body as bp1 as well. Since the same applies to any combination of body parts, partial unity is an impossibility.

But the typical order of things can break down. Imagine two conjoined twins who share a liver but are otherwise distinct. It seems perfectly reasonable to think of the liver as being part of both twins, while denying that all other body parts are shared. I'm not arguing that we *must* think of the twins in this way. The point is that it's coherent and highly intuitive to think of them as separate—but overlapping—beings. It is, at the very least, intelligible to think of the co-body relation as non-transitive.

It seems similarly intelligible to think of the co-consciousness relation as non-transitive. I don't mean to claim that we *must* treat the co-consciousness relation in an analogous fashion to the co-body relation. But the point is that the coherence of the co-body relation being non-transitive shows that we need more than a *mere assertion* that the co-consciousness relation must be transitive.

So the *very idea* of co-consciousness does not entail transitivity. Beyond this, the motivation for taking it to be transitive is undercut by the fact that Dainton doesn't take it to be universally true that co-consciousness is transitive. Dainton takes the *same* primitive relation of co-consciousness to be at work in both synchronic and diachronic unity, but the relation to only be transitive in the case of synchronic unity. (Clearly, diachronic unity isn't transitive, or else our experiences from across time would all be co-conscious!) So, co-consciousness is not *essentially* transitive. It is, perhaps, more like the co-body relation, which in many cases appears transitive but is not essentially so.

Dainton argues that the fact that all failures of transitivity that we're aware of occur diachronically is telling, and that the "failure of transitivity is essentially bound up with the way we experience time" (2000, 169). It may be that the failure of transitivity is essential to our experience of time; but it does not follow that our experience of time is essential to breakdowns in transitivity. Once we accept that the co-consciousness relation is *not*, by its very nature, transitive, further insistence that only the cases that are intuitive to us are possible seems more like an imposition of our own imaginative limitations on reality.

So I don't see a good case for thinking that synchronic unity *must* be transitive. Dainton has already acknowledged that the relationship is not essentially transitive. And insofar as one finds the picture of reality and perception that I outline in this book *intelligible* (even if you think it's false), this itself provides evidence that synchronic unity is not transitive: it illuminates a case that we can wrap our minds around, in which transitivity at-a-moment fails.

Like Dainton, Bayne takes the unity of consciousness to be transitive when (but only when) applied to simultaneous experiences.[4] It's worth noting that while Bayne explicitly sets out to defend transitivity, he really seems to have in mind a more specific target: rejection of partial unity, where "partial unity" involves a breakdown in transitivity *within a single subject*. Naïve idealism does not require the possibility of transitivity failing within a subject. Rather, it requires the possibility of overlapping subjects/unities. Insofar as this narrower target is Bayne's true interest, it may be that he would not object to transitivity of the sort that I require. (I make no claims regarding the possibility of intransitivity within subjects. For instance, it would be compatible with everything I've written to individuate subjects in part on the basis of transitivity holding within them.)

With this in mind, let's treat Bayne's arguments as objections to overlapping phenomenal unities, more generally, and see whether they present a case that is troubling for my purposes. Bayne offers two arguments in support of transitivity. The first is closely related to Dainton's argument. Bayne writes:

> One might argue that partial unity is incoherent on the grounds that there is no consistent assignment of partially unified states to subjects of experience. Suppose that e 1 and e 2 are both unified with e 3 but not with each

---

[4] Though he tempers this, concluding that the "prudent position . . . is to retain partial unity as a potential model of consciousness, albeit one that is surrounded by a significant degree of suspicion" (Bayne 2010, 44).

92 THE VIEW FROM EVERYWHERE

other. One might reason as follows. Both e 1 and e 3 must be assigned to the same subject for they are phenomenally unified, and as phenomenally unified states they are subsumed by a single experiential state. Precisely the same considerations suggest that e 2 and e 3 must also belong to the same subject. But, so the argument goes, e 1 and e 2 cannot belong to the same subject of experience, for they are not phenomenally unified with each other. . . . The key move in the argument is obviously the final one: the assumption that simultaneous experiences that belong to the same subject must be phenomenally unified. (Bayne 2010, 38–39)

The problem is that this argument takes for granted that there cannot be overlapping subjects. If subjects can overlap, e 1 and e 2 can be phenomenally unified (say, in my mind), and e 2 and e 3 can be unified (in the tapestry) without e 1 and e 3 being unified. But whether or not there can be overlapping subjects is precisely what's at issue, and so cannot be taken for granted.[5] Bayne sets this argument aside and turns to another. (Note: the text in brackets is my recreation of Bayne's anti-partial unity argument as an argument against *overlapping* unities.)

(1) If partial unity [overlapping unities] were possible then there would be something distinctive it is like to be a partially unified subject [a subject who overlaps with another subject]. . . .

(2) We are unable to project ourselves into a partially unified phenomenal perspective [a perspective of an overlapping unity].

(3) If there were such a thing as a partially unified phenomenal perspective [a perspective of an overlapping unity] then we should be able to project ourselves into it.

(C) Thus, partial unity [overlapping unity] is impossible.

When fleshed out in terms of overlapping unities, this argument clearly fails. There is something it's like to be an overlapping subject. But it isn't distinctive; nor need it be. This can be seen by considering counterfactual circumstances in which your mind is (or isn't) overlapping with another mind. Consider a case in which part of your mind overlaps with mine. We both share the (numerically same) experience e. Experience e is a point of overlap between our minds—perhaps analogously to the conjoined twins

---

[5] Assuming each subject corresponds to a single unity of consciousness.

PERCEPTION 93

who share a liver. Now consider a case in which you have experience e, but my mind does not overlap with yours. What it's like to be you is the same in both circumstances, regardless of what's going on with me. Or alternatively, consider the case of you and the tapestry. When you have a perceptual experience of a tree, your mind overlaps with the tapestry. Had you hallucinated a qualitatively identical tree, what it was like to be you would have been precisely the same. So there is nothing *distinctive* it is like to be a subject whose mind overlaps with another. And this is precisely as it should be. What it's like to be a given subject has to do with features intrinsic to that subject, and not with what other subjects are doing (S. Hurley 2003, 73–74).[6]

What of the second premise? We can certainly project ourselves into this overlapping perspective, in the sense of imagining being *one* of the overlapping subjects (one side of the overlap). But there is no thing it's like to be both sides of the overlap: there are two such things. There's what it's like to be you and what it's like to be me; what it's like to be you, and what it's like to be the tapestry. So we can't have *an* imagination that captures the essence of overlap cases. But that doesn't in any way indicate that such cases are impossible.

So this argument too fails to make a compelling case for transitivity—in particular, it seems to leave the possibility of overlapping unities untouched.

As I noted in §2.2, both Dainton's fusion model and Bayne's subsumption model can naturally accommodate the idea of phenomenal unities as having experiential parts. It's easy to see how two phenomenal unities made up out of experiential parts can have experiential parts that *overlap*. But since I've argued that the phenomenal tapestry is also compatible with theories of

---

[6] Bayne considers a similar response from Susan Hurley (1998), which relies on subjects who have "phenomenal duplicate" experiences: experiences with exactly the same phenomenal character. Bayne objects to this argument on the grounds that—given his preferred "tripartite" method of individuating phenomenal experiences—phenomenal duplication is impossible. But, at least when considering overlapping subjects, phenomenal duplication isn't necessary to make the case. We can just as well appeal to counterfactuals involving precisely the same phenomenal experiences, as above. Further, the tripartite conception of experiences is one that begs the question against the possibility of overlapping phenomenal unities. On this way of individuating experiences, "experiences are to be individuated in terms of subjects of experience, times, and phenomenal properties" (Bayne 2010, 24). This builds subjects into the individuation conditions for experiences. On the face of it, this renders overlapping phenomenal unities impossible. (To not be impossible, we would have to allow some experiences to be individuated by reference to multiple subjects. This would have the bizarre consequence that if you and I shared a visual experience, and then I close my eyes, you suddenly have a new visual experience. So the identity of my experiences would be affected by what's going on in your head. This would have the bizarre effect within the tapestry of changing the experiences making up the tapestry whenever subjects began or stopped perceiving facets of it. So it's obvious that the idealist should reject such an conception of experience.)

94 THE VIEW FROM EVERYWHERE

unity on which there are No Experiential Parts (NEP), it's worth pausing to
see whether the same is true for NEP theories of unity.

Michael Tye (2003) defends both a NEP view and the non-transitivity of
phenomenal unity.

First, let's consider Tye's argument for the non-transitivity of phenomenal
unity. Tye thinks that when a split-brain subject is receiving different inputs
to the two hemispheres, each hemisphere corresponds to a separate phenomenal unity. He considers a case in which (i) the left visual field is red; (ii)
the right visual field is green; and (iii) the subject is poked in the neck. Due to
the underlying neurophysiology, the redness is relayed only to the right hemisphere, the greenness is relayed only to the left hemisphere, and the poke to
the neck is relayed to both hemispheres. In this case, according to Tye, there
are two multimodal experiences: E1 (the experience of the redness and neck
prick) and E2 (the experience of the greenness and neck prick). Neither of
these multi-modal experiences decomposes into further experiences.

> The pricking is phenomenally unified with redness by their entering
> into the same phenomenal content—the phenomenal content of E1. The
> pricking is phenomenally unified with greenness in a like manner, but this
> time the common content is the phenomenal content of E2. Since [subject]
> S has no experience whose phenomenal content has entering into it both
> greenness and redness, the two colors are not phenomenally unified. (Tye
> 2003, 131)

Note that Tye does not argue that *the experience of* the neck prick is simultaneously part of two phenomenal unities, but that *the neck prick itself* is *experienced as* part of two unities. There is no neck-prick experience that exists
independently of phenomenal unities.

As this suggests, if we embrace a NEP account of phenomenal unity, phenomenal overlap cannot be understood as involving a single *experience* that
is simultaneously part of two different unities. Rather, there is a single "element," which is simultaneously a part of two phenomenal unities. Insofar as
it is an element of each phenomenal unity, it is phenomenal—but considered
in isolation, it is not (for NEP) an experiential unit.[7]

---

[7] For Tye, this is bound up with his position as a strong representationalist. Tye takes phenomenal character to be one and the same as representational content of a certain sort. So phenomenal
unity E1 is a representational state: a state that simultaneously represents redness and the neck prick.

PERCEPTION 95

The difference between NEP and EP when it comes to transitivity amounts to whether the points of overlap are themselves discrete experiences, or are merely aspects of experiences (things that are phenomenal within the context of a broader unit, but are not themselves experiences). What would NEP mean for naïve idealism? A natural way of fleshing the view out would have it that the tapestry as a whole is metaphysically fundamental. While the whole is an experience, it cannot be broken down into smaller *experiential* units. The greenness of the grass is an aspect of the phenomenal tapestry. But there is not a *discrete experience* of phenomenal greenness that is an element of the tapestry. We can *consider* the grass's greenness in isolation, but that does not show that the grass's greenness is itself an experience, like an experiential Lego-block out of which we build the whole. When I overlap with the greenness of the grass, I am not overlapping with something that is an experience in its own right, but with something that is an aspect of an experience. But insofar as the greenness is a part of the tapestry, it is an experience, and insofar as it is a part of *me*, it is an experience.

Insofar as we think of the tapestry as metaphysically fundamental, this would mean that there can be partial overlap among fundamentals.[8] This might sound strange, but I'm not sure if it's problematic.[9] Even if the tapestry is fundamental, it has complexity and structure. This aspect of the tapestry is on fire; that aspect is suffering torrential rains. Why couldn't one difference be that one aspect is shared with another phenomenal unity? This doesn't violate the idea that the aspects are not *experiential* in isolation. We're not taking an aspect *out* of the unity; we're putting it *into* another one.[10]

Phenomenal unity E2 is a representational state that simultaneously represents greenness and the neck prick. But neither the redness, greenness, nor the neck prick are themselves phenomenal/experiential items. But the representationalist basis of Tye's position isn't essential to NEP or to its position on transitivity. Since strong representationalism is in tension with idealism, I focus here on a more neutral form of NEP.

[8] At least, there can be things that partially overlap with fundamentals.

[9] Nor am I sure it's unproblematic. I remain noncommittal.

[10] Note, though, that there is a form of phenomenal holism that is in tension with this sort of phenomenal overlap: the view that *necessarily*, every aspect of a phenomenal experience can *only* exist within the context of the particular whole it's a part of. Such holism would preclude any aspect of the tapestry existing as part of anything other than the tapestry. I don't see this as a problem. While there are good empirical reasons for embracing a modest form of contingent holism (Chudnoff 2013), they do not give us any reason to embrace the strong necessitation holism that is in tension with naïve idealism. Two things jump out about clear-cut cases of phenomenal holism (e.g., the Müller-Lyer illusion, the color tile illusion, the McGurk effect). First, many involve cognitive phenomenology, which I argued in §2.3.2 is not part of the tapestry of reality. Second, the examples all arise from the "hidden assumptions" that our brains rely on to make sense of the world, given limited or conflicting

96 THE VIEW FROM EVERYWHERE

If there is a problem with partial overlap of fundamentals, this would mean that NEP is incompatible with the extended *transcendent* non-reductive idealism that I've proposed. But it would arguably still be compatible with an *immanent* form of externalist non-reductive idealism. On this view, our experiences are wholly present within the tapestry. My pains, hallucinations, and cognitive phenomenology are all aspects of my brain. So while I overlap with the phenomenal tapestry, I do so by being a partial subset of the tapestry, as opposed to by merely *partially* overlapping with it. The phenomenal unity of my mind is an aspect of the tapestry. It's an aspect that has a further sort of unity to it, beyond the unity possessed by random spatial regions. But I see no reason why this should be incompatible with NEP or the fundamentality of the tapestry. This view is, perhaps, a variant of Philip Goff's (2017) cosmopsychist view of subjects and their relations to the universe.

4.1.2 Bridging Laws and Indices

Now let's turn to the question of the systematicity of our access to reality. Let's grant the naïve idealist picture of reality and perception: physical reality is a multifaceted phenomenal unity, binding together phenomenal experiences as-of all possible perspectives. Perception involves an overlap between ordinary minds and this vast phenomenal unity of reality. It is striking that— though reality includes a multitude of different perspectives—each ordinary mind can only come to overlap with a tiny subset of these. The granny smith apple in my fruit bowl is phenomenally green; it is also phenomenally red. But when I look at the apple, I systematically overlap with the apple's greenness (not its redness), whereas my inverted twin systematically taps into the redness (not the greenness). How and why is this?

information. In §4.2 we'll take an in-depth exploration of hidden assumptions, and the extent to which they can facilitate contact with reality. The thing to note here is that these hidden assumptions are all contingent. The mere fact that *my* experiences of the lines in the Müller-Lyer are affected by the addition of arrows gives us no reason to think that the experiences of a ghost or an angel or God-minus would. So the plausible empirical case for holism in human experience does not illustrate that holism is a *necessary* feature of experience. Even if my experiences must be assessed holistically, there's no reason to expect the same to be true of the tapestry. And even in cases where aspects of experiences are dependent on the whole, it's far from clear that there cannot be qualitatively identical aspects embedded within different phenomenal wholes. (E.g., in the Müller-Lyer illusion, the line with the wings extending out appears longer than the line with the wings extending in. But for any length the line could seem to be, I could perfectly well have an experience as-of a line *that length*, without wings.) Hence, even if the phenomenal character of some aspects of the tapestry were dependent on the phenomenal character of the broader tapestry, it's not obvious the same phenomenology couldn't *also* be had as part of a different phenomenal unity (e.g., us).

PERCEPTION 97

Recall that the phenomenal fibers of reality are indexed to perspectives. I proposed that there are two features that go into a perspective: the as-though spatial location (lo) and the as-though perceptual system (ps). Each phenomenal strand is indexed to a lo and a ps hashtag, and these indexed phenomenal strands compose the phenomenal threads out of which reality is woven. The granny smith apple is composed (among other things) of greenishness$_{\#ps1,\#lo[\ ]}$, reddishness$_{\#ps2,\#lo[\ ]}$.

The nonreductive idealist, like the dualist, takes there to be bridging laws that account for the phenomenal experiences of ordinary minds. But unlike traditional dualists, idealists can embrace externalist bridging laws that function as laws of phenomenal fusion: pulling existing bits of the phenomenal tapestry into one's mind, rather than generating new phenomenology.

Let's start by thinking about how standard (local) dualist bridging laws function. I look at an apple and (say) my G-fibers start firing (GFF). The bridging laws ensure that a certain experience is generated: a greenish experience. Every instance of GFF (in me) generates a greenish experience. Likewise, every instance of GFF in my inverted twin would generate a reddish experience.

The situation is very similar for the nonreductive idealist's externalist bridging laws. To account for the systematicity of our experiences, we simply need to posit that each bridging law systematically attaches to a particular #ps. Stipulate that ps1 corresponds to the perceptual system of normal human beings, and ps2 corresponds to the perceptual system of color inverted humans. My brain and that of my inverted twin are physically identical. What differs between us is the bridging laws. In my case, the bridging laws systematically relate me to ps1, and in my inverted twin's case, to ps2. This means that when we look at the granny smith, I overlap with greenishness$_{\#ps1,\#lo[\ ]}$, while my i-twin overlaps with reddishness$_{\#ps2,\#lo[\ ]}$. And this is systematic across all our experiences. So when we look at grass, I overlap with greenishness$_{\#ps1,\#lo[\ ]}$ (and my i-twin overlaps with reddishness$_{\#ps2,\#lo[\ ]}$), and when we look at a fire truck, I overlap with reddishness$_{\#ps1,\#lo[\ ]}$ (and my i-twin with greenishness$_{\#ps2,\#lo[\ ]}$).

Of course, there's no reason bridging laws *have* to be systematic in this way, either for the nonreductive idealist or for the traditional dualist. Perhaps every time there's a geomagnetic reversal, the bridging laws shift over to connect you to different facets of reality (or to generate a different phenomenal experience). But the contingency of the bridging laws is not unique to idealism. It's also something that I've argued is a virtue, as it accurately captures

98 THE VIEW FROM EVERYWHERE

logical space (Yetter-Chappell 2022). (Surely such shifts are *possible*, even if we don't think they're *actual!*) In actuality, we presume, the bridging laws are systematic in the manner described. And the interplay between bridging laws and indices is how idealists can account for this.

4.2 How Much Do We Overlap with the Tapestry?

If naïve idealism is correct, when we perceive the world, our minds overlap with—and are partially constituted by—bits of the tapestry of physical reality. We systematically overlap only with certain aspects of reality. But how extensive is this overlap?

As I look into my living room, I see a black cat sleeping on a tan sofa, blocks and magnatiles scattered across the floor, and square floor tiles receding into the kitchen. I've already argued that perceptions-as are not a component of external reality. The *cattishness* and *sofaishness* of the scene are not elements of the tapestry, which I tap into, but rather are a part of the cognitive overlay of my mind. How much of the rest of my experience overlaps with the tapestry?

Gazing at my living room, I don't seem to be presented with two-dimensional objects, despite the fact that all information about this scene is recovered from a two-dimensional projection on my retina. I do not experience my living room as a collection of visible *surfaces*. The blocks I see scattered about the floor appear (in a sense) to be cubes—although I cannot directly observe the back-side of these objects. Does my mind overlap with the entire three-dimensional shape of the blocks? Or just with the surface facing me? Do I overlap with the triangularity of the partially obscured magnatile?

These three-dimensional shapes and partially occluded shapes are clearly a part of *physical reality*. We can see this in a variety of ways: (a) These things would be a part of the overall experience of Berkeley's God. (b) I can perceive these features of reality directly via tactile perception. (c) The tapestry contains perspectives on these objects as-though from all possible spatial locations—related as in Pelczar's Sphinx example—where these overlapping experiences are property bound into individual objects. So the question is not whether physical reality contains these features, but whether *ordinary perceivers overlap with* properties like three-dimensionality in visual perception.

For each feature that our perceptual experiences seem to include, we can ask three questions:

(i)   Is the feature a part of the tapestry?
(ii) Do I veridically perceive the feature?
(iii) Does my perception of the feature involve my overlapping with the tapestry?

It is open to us to deny (iii), even if we answer (i) and (ii) affirmatively, although this would require us to tell two stories about veridical perception: some, but not all, veridical perceptions involve the phenomenal overlap described in §4.1. We would then have to tell a separate story about what veridical perception consists in for cases of veridical perception without literal contact with reality.

How we answer these questions will vary depending on the feature in question. In what follows, I will explain what I take to be the best way to make sense the extent of our overlap with the tapestry. An account of illusions will emerge from this discussion in the next section. (Note that the basic metaphysical picture and the naïve idealist's theory of perception do not require agreement with what I say in §§4.2–4.3. It is open to the idealist to hold that we overlap with reality in a far more minimal way. The view developed here is what strikes me as the most plausible way of making sense of illusions and our relation to reality.)

If perception were simply a matter of subjects letting information about the world pass through a window into our minds, determining the extent of our overlap with the tapestry would be a straightforward task. But it isn't. Perception involves the filtering and active processing of inputs from the external world by our minds. Consider visual perception. All the visual information I take in about the world comes to me by way of a two-dimensional projection onto my retina. My brain must somehow transform this two-dimensional image into my (apparently) three-dimensional visual experience of my living room. But the information contained in this retinal image is not itself sufficient to reconstruct a three-dimensional world, depth, constancy of shape/color/size, or many other features that we seem to perceive. Visual perception faces an underconstrained inverse problem. We face the same sort of problem in perception of distance and auditory perception. To solve these inverse problems, our brain must rely on background priors or "hidden assumptions" that select from among the possible interpretations

100 THE VIEW FROM EVERYWHERE

of the limited information that reaches our brains (Palmer 1999; Cusimano, Traer, and McDermott 2017).

But—as we have seen in the cases of hallucination and cognitive phenomenology—experiences that have *our minds* as their source are intuitively *not* respects in which we overlap with reality. So the question before us is whether this active filtering of perceptual inputs puts us in contact with the external world, or whether it contributes to our experiences in a manner akin to hallucination and cognitive phenomenology.

I'll begin by describing two extreme positions on whether hidden assumptions facilitate our contact with reality. On the first view, *No Hidden Assumptions* put us in contact with reality. Insofar as an experience is influenced in any way by my mind, it fails to put me in contact with reality. If this is right, we only overlap with the tapestry in extremely minimal respects. On the second view, *Any Hidden Assumption* our minds might make puts us in contact with reality. I'll argue, contra Louise Antony (2011), that there is a coherent middle ground between these positions—at least if you're an idealist. I'll propose two possible restrictions on what hidden assumptions relate us to reality (§4.2.2). I'll then use these restrictions to answer the questions we started with of three dimensionality, occlusion, and objects' back-sides (§4.2.3), and extend this to offer an account of illusion (§4.3).

4.2.1 Two Extremes

No Hidden Assumptions
At one extreme, we might hold that the only respects in which our experiences are truly open to reality are those for which hidden assumptions play no role. Perhaps our perceptions of lines, (inconstant) colors, and pitch are respects in which we overlap with reality. But any aspect experience that is not *fully* derived from our causal connection with the world fails to put us in contact with the world. On such a view, we would only *overlap* with the tapestry in very minimal respects, if at all. But we might still say—in a less epistemically powerful way—that we veridically perceive more than this. For example, accurate hidden assumptions might play a role in *generating* phenomenology that accurately reflects the tapestry (and hence is veridical in a loose sense), while not putting us in literal contact with the world.

PERCEPTION 101

There is some intuitive plausibility to holding that we are open to the world only insofar as *the world itself* is responsible for our experiences. Imagine a person who lives in a very regular, predictable world, but whose eyes have been destroyed. Thanks to robust and well-calibrated hidden assumptions, this individual's brain generates visual experiences that broadly mirror their environment. We would not take this individual to have veridical perceptions, even if their experiences are qualitatively identical to those of a sighted individual. And the reason is because *the world* is not causally responsible for their experiences.

On the other hand, this view entails that we are only open to the world in the narrowest of ways. We intuitively take ourselves to have veridical perceptions of trees, sky, depth, shape—we take (or might take) these veridical experiences to put us in contact with reality. According to No Hidden Assumptions, all this is mistaken. Again, we might construct a weaker sort of veridical perception, which does not entail this sort of openness to the world. But as we will see in Chapter 6, narrowing of the extent to which we overlap with reality entails a corresponding narrowing of the distinctive advantages of naïve idealism.

Any Hidden Assumptions

At the other extreme, we might hold that *any* hidden assumptions can put you in contact with reality. Louise Antony (2011, 33–34) endorses this position:

> Instead of taking the facts about the constructive character of visual perception to defeat the claim that perception is *ever* "open," take them instead to support the claim that perception is *always* open. . . . What vision science tells us is that the character of falsidical experiences is determined by objective features of the environment to exactly the same degree as is the character of veridical experience. In both cases, the input to the experience is fully determined by the properties of external objects responsible for structuring the light that hits our retina, and in receiving these data, we are fully open to those properties.

Such a view would entail that phenomenology arising from any possible hidden assumption is both (i) a part of the tapestry and (ii) a respect in which we overlap with the tapestry.

102   THE VIEW FROM EVERYWHERE

4.2.2 A Middle Ground

There's a sense in which the no hidden assumptions view and Antony's any hidden assumption view are in agreement: both take it to be impossible to carve off a subset of "good" hidden assumptions that successfully put us into contact with reality. The lesson each position draws from this is different: the former view concluding that hidden assumptions can never facilitate contact with reality, and the latter that any old hidden assumption can.

While I agree with much of Antony's "any hidden assumption" argument, I think the resulting view is too liberal. Suppose phenomenology arising from any possible hidden assumption is veridical. This will include the "bentishness" of the straight stick in the water . . . but also far more bizarre things. While *our* hidden assumptions may be ones that generate consistent results, there is nothing to say that this must be true of *all possible* hidden assumptions. Imagine a creature for whom the entire left half of their visual field was a giant blind spot, which the creature's visual system deftly filled in with its best guess: the assumption that the left half of the visual field was a mirror image of the right half. Call this the Mirror Image Blind-Spot (MIBS) case. On the "any hidden assumption" view, this creature would have veridical visual experiences. This seems clearly mistaken.

Beyond this intuitive wrongness, embracing MIBS as putting us into contact with reality would have bizarre and disastrous consequences for the idealist. Insofar as veridical perception involves overlap with the tapestry of physical reality, *physical reality would have to include this mirror image phenomenology*—as well as any other phenomenology that might be generated by similarly bizarre assumptions. We lose any grip on reality being as it seems. We would have to accept that reality includes *all possible* phenomenology (of dragons, bubbles, blue expanses . . . anything that a perceptual system could fill in).

What we'd intuitively like is a way to walk the middle road rejected by No Hidden Assumption and Any Hidden Assumption. We'd like a way to accept that some hidden assumptions facilitate contact with the tapestry, and others don't. I think reflection on the mirror image blind-spot case can help us to find such a middle road.

Suppose the MIBS creature looks at my desk. The teacup in the right visual field is duplicated on the left; the right half of my computer screen is duplicated on the left, giving garbled palindromes of text. In reality, there is no teacup to the left of my computer, and I do not write in palindromes. The

PERCEPTION   103

tapestry includes no such phenomenology. So this creature clearly cannot be overlapping with reality in having these perceptions. This gives us our first restriction:

Veridicality: Hidden assumptions can facilitate contact with reality only if qualitatively identical experience is part of the tapestry.

Recall that the task of this book has been to show how there could be an idealist world that corresponds to the world we take ourselves to inhabit. I have not *defined* the world as built up out of all possible veridical phenomenology—which would here be circular—but have used the totality of veridical perceptual experiences *heuristic* to capture the world we take ourselves to inhabit. As discussed in §2.3.1, there are other ways of systematizing this heuristic. As Farkas (2013) puts it, we take things to be part of the physical world when they are "organized into a systematic, cross-modally coherent and predictable order."

The veridicality restriction does not give us practical guidance for determining when a phenomenal experience of mine overlaps with the tapestry. But taken together with Farkas's (2013) and Robinson's (2022) characterization of world-suggestive experiences, we have a plausible basis for taking some possible experiences to fail the veridicality constraint. In particular, whenever there is a lack of cross-modal coherence in our experiences, we can infer that one or more modality is not putting us into contact with reality.[11]

This is—at least to an extent—in tension with Antony's argument against the coherence of identifying a subset of hidden assumptions as the accurate ones. Antony (2011, 32–33) writes:

The idea that we get things *right* perceptually when the hidden assumptions are correct, and wrong when the hidden assumptions are false, encourages the thought that, in the case of illusion, there is some *better way things could look*—indeed that things don't look the way they *ought* to. But if the vision science is correct, this makes no sense. It's not just that our perceptual states are the only way they can be, given the perceptual machinery with which we are equipped, and the circumstances in which we find ourselves. The

---

[11] Of course, there could be idealist worlds that include all sorts of bizarre things. I am not claiming that it would be impossible for there to be a world that includes cross-modally incoherent phenomenology. The claim is, rather, that *given that we are trying to capture a world like we take ours to be*, it seems most plausible to think that our world doesn't have this phenomenology in it.

104 THE VIEW FROM EVERYWHERE

point is that, if the empirical story is even roughly right, *all* perception is artificial.

How big *should* the moon look? How *should* the relative sizes of the subjects in the Ames room appear? How *should* the tiles in a color tile illusion look? How *should* a white wall with shadows cast across it look? There is not *an* answer to these questions. For Antony, "all perception is artificial." There is no "right way" for the world to look.

By contrast, I've argued that I can only be in contact with the tapestry if there's an experience qualitatively identical to my own, which is part of the tapestry—that is, I can only be in contact with the tapestry if my hidden assumptions are accurate (i.e., reflect the tapestry). But this is not to say that there is *one* privileged way that reality should look. Nor is it to deny that (in Antony's sense) perception is artificial. There are many possible experiences that can put one in touch with reality—as many as there are phenomenal fibers to reality. But that doesn't mean that *all possible experiences* put one in touch with reality—as there are some experiences that simply reality doesn't include. And we can embrace perception as essentially mediated by hidden assumptions (and hence as artificial) without accepting that *any* hidden assumption will do.

I think it's far easier to insist that there are right ways for things to look within an idealist context than a materialist one. For the materialist, the world itself is not a world of phenomenal appearances, but of mind-independent things. How these things appear to us is arbitrary. Appearances essentially result from the combination of world *plus mind*. And it's difficult to see what basis there could be for insisting that some minds do a better job—a "more accurate" job—of combining with the world than others. (If nothing is like an idea but an idea, the materialist's world isn't like *any* of these appearances!) By contrast, the idealist's world is constructed out of phenomenal appearances. When my mind presents me with an appearance, it's either there, as part of reality, or it isn't.

Our first restriction concerns the phenomenology that results from hidden assumptions: only phenomenology qualitatively identical to bits of the tapestry could possibly overlap with the tapestry. But it seems to me that *how* the hidden assumptions work is also crucial to answering the question of whether they afford us contact with the world. Hallucinations are not just epistemically defective, in that they present us with appearances that don't correspond to reality. Even *veridical* hallucinations are epistemically defective

PERCEPTION   105

and fail to put us in contact with reality. Likewise, the problem with MIBS is not just that the blind spot is being filled in with something bizarre—something that doesn't correspond to anything in reality—it's *how* the phenomenology gets produced: it's the fact that the agent's mind is generating phenomenology.

Consider the far less bizarre case of our own blind spots. Each of our eyes has a "blind spot" where the optic nerve exits the retina. Since there are no photoreceptors at this point, our eye takes in no information about the corresponding region of our environment. But even if you close one eye and fixate your gaze, so that your brain receives no external input about a region of the world, there is no hole in your phenomenology. Your brain assumes that what's in this location is, in some important respect, similar to the environment around it. Information about the surrounding environment together with these hidden assumptions lead your brain to fill in the gap—despite receiving no input about the gap itself. Unlike the MIBS case, the assumptions that our brains make to fill in the gap are generally reliable. But the source of the phenomenology is the same: the perceiving agent. Now imagine that the blind spot slowly grows, filling up more and more of the agent's visual field, until the whole visual field is blind spot. The result is a paradigmatic case of hallucination. Even if the hidden assumptions miraculously continue to generate phenomenology that corresponds to bits of the phenomenal tapestry, the result is no less hallucinatory. This brings us to our second restriction on hidden assumptions:

> *No Generation:* Hidden assumptions can facilitate contact with reality only if they function to select from possible options that the informational input underdetermines, without adding experiential content.

Hallucinations and the filling in of blind spots are importantly similar, in that both involve our minds *generating* phenomenology. That which has my mind as its source is intuitively not a part of the external world. What sets apart the hidden assumptions that fill in blind spots from hidden assumptions that more plausibly can put us in contact with reality is whether the hidden assumptions "create something from nothing" (something from mere assumptions) or whether the hidden assumptions take concrete inputs that have more than one possible interpretation and select from among the possible interpretations to present to consciousness. In the cases where hidden assumptions plausibly facilitate contact with reality, the interpretation that

106 THE VIEW FROM EVERYWHERE

is presented to consciousness is an interpretation *of* inputs from the external world, not a fabrication of the subject's mind.

I propose that hidden assumptions facilitate contact with reality only when they (i) function to select from possible options that the informational input underdetermines, and (ii) the selected option is in fact present within the tapestry.

The big challenge to this view is whether there is really a sharp line between selection and generation. There is presumably a sharp line dividing veridical experiences from nonveridical ones.[12] If perceptual experiences are only veridical when hidden assumptions *select* from among candidate interpretations of sensory inputs, there must be a corresponding sharp line between selection and generation. But is there? Consider a case similar to that of blind spot filling, but where my brain receives a tiny bit of information about the environment—say, whether it's bright or dark. There are perhaps an infinite number of possible experiences that could go with such a coarse-grained input. Some phenomenology results, thanks to hidden assumptions and this coarse-grained input—perhaps using other visual inputs from outside of this quasi-blind region as a guide. Did my brain *generate* the phenomenology to fill this quasi-blind spot? Or did it *select* from among an infinite number of possible interpretations of the very coarse-grained visual inputs it took in? We could construct a continuum of cases like this, going from clear-cut cases of generation to clear-cut cases of selection. Where do we draw the line?

While I agree that such a continuum of cases can be described, I don't think that it has to worry us. Given the naïve idealist metaphysical framework, there simply *is* a sharp line between perception and hallucination: the one involves overlap with features of reality; the other does not. While we can construct sorites-like cases ranging from generation to selection, the sorites principle that an incremental difference never makes a difference is simply false within the context of such a metaphysics. Somewhere, there is a tiny difference that makes a difference—whether we can identify it or not— for somewhere, there is a step that makes the difference between selection and generation, a step that makes the difference between overlapping with the tapestry and not.

---

[12] This could be denied within a different metaphysical framework. But according to naïve idealism, veridical perception alone involves overlap with reality, and overlap with reality is an all-or-nothing thing. So a sharp distinction between veridical perception and hallucination is essential to naïve idealism.

PERCEPTION   107

Beyond this, it's worth keeping in mind that the idealist needn't treat all features of one's visual experience in a uniform way. Your current visual experience could be a patchwork of elements, some of which are aspects of the tapestry, and some of which are not. I might overlap with the burgundy color that's right before my eyes, but not with the burgundy of the patch in my blind spot. Likewise, if darkness is the only input from the environment that my brain is receiving (and hidden assumptions are responsible for selecting from among interpretation of this input), I might overlap with the darkishness of the tapestry, but not its other features. But there is—there must be—for the idealist a fact of the matter about this overlap.

4.2.3 Hidden Assumptions in Practice

I've proposed that hidden assumptions facilitate contact with reality only when they function to select from possible options that the informational input underdetermines, and the selected option is in fact present within the tapestry.

Let's see how these two restrictions function in practice. We began this section with three questions we might ask about features that our perceptual experiences seem to include: (i) Is the feature a part of the tapestry? (ii) Do I veridically perceive the feature? And (iii) does my perception of the feature involve my overlapping with the tapestry? Where (iii) is answered in the affirmative, we will have a particularly robust epistemic access to the world— discussed in detail in Chapter 6. When it is denied, we will not have literal contact with reality, and any epistemic access to the world will be more akin to that which sense-datum theory or representationalism delivers.

In this section, we'll consider how to answer these questions in the following cases: the three-dimensionality of objects, the back-sides of objects, and shapes that are partially occluded. In the following section, we'll consider the implications for illusions.

Three-Dimensionality

All my visual experiences are reconstructed from two-dimensional images projected on my retina. Nevertheless, when I look at a ball, it *looks* three-dimensional. One might insist that this is just a judgment. But I think there is more to it than this—that the *sensory phenomenology* of looking at the ball

108   THE VIEW FROM EVERYWHERE

with stereoscopic vision is different from looking at the ball with one eye closed. (Try sword-fighting while wearing an eye patch, if you doubt this.)

Is this sensory phenomenology a part of the tapestry? The *ball* certainly is three-dimensional, as is obvious from our tactile experiences. It seems most plausible to me that the three-dimensional sensory *look* of the ball is also a part of the tapestry. It seems possible that there be a creature with eyes distributed in a 3-d array—like numbers on a clock surrounding the object at the center—for whom the three-dimensionality of objects would be fully determined by the environmental inputs. Their phenomenology clearly satisfies the constraints on hidden assumptions, and would be part of the tapestry. And our sensory experiences of three-dimensionality seem like an aspect of this creature's. So it seems most natural to me to think that our experiences of three-dimensionality likewise are part of the tapestry.

Given this, our visual perceptions of three-dimensionality satisfy the Veridicality constraint. But do these perceptions involve our overlapping with the three-dimensionality of the ball in the tapestry? Do they *select* from possible options that the informational input underdetermines, or do they *generate* new experiential content? As I've noted, for the idealist there simply is a fact of the matter about whether hidden assumptions involve selection or generation—though we may not be in an epistemic position to know where the boundary lies. An idealist could interpret this case in either way: as generation (and so not overlap) or as selection. I'm inclined to think that this is a case of our brains selecting from among candidate interpretations presented by the world. If this is right, we overlap with the three-dimensionality of objects we perceive visually. The answers to our three starting questions are: (i) yes; (ii) yes; and (iii) yes.

Even if we think of this as a case of phenomenology generation, and so answer (iii) negatively, we can still answer (ii) affirmatively. We will simply need an alternate account of veridicality. We might say that a subject S veridically perceives (loosely) when either (i) S's mind overlaps with the objects of perception, or (ii) S generates phenomenology qualitatively identical to an aspect of the tapestry, where this generation is the result of an appropriate, well-calibrated connection with the object of perception. What an "appropriate, well-calibrated connection with the object of perception" amounts to would need to be fleshed out, but would surely involve a causal connection from the object of perception to subject's mind, and reliance on well-calibrated hidden assumptions to generate the phenomenology.

Back-Sides

We clearly don't see objects' back-sides. My experiences don't even *seem* to present me with the back-side of the ball. And yet, we have experiences that seem predicated on certain assumptions about the back-sides of objects. The ball looks spherical to me. And it could not be spherical were its back-side not shaped in a certain way. So we might ask: is the sphericality a part of the tapestry? Is it something I veridically perceive? And is it a respect in which I overlap with the tapestry?

The ball's sphericality is obviously a part of the tapestry. The reasons are analogous to those given above for three-dimensionality. So the ball has a back-side. And this back-side has a certain curvature. But I do not overlap with this curvature. At best, I perceive the ball *as* a sphere. And since I'm inclined to think of perceiving-as as involving cognitive, rather than sensory, phenomenology (as discussed in §2.3.2), I think that seeing the ball *as a sphere* involves a sort of judgment of sphericality.[13] This judgment is not a perception, nor is it a respect in which I overlap with the tapestry. So we can answer (i) yes; (ii) no; (iii) no.

Occlusion

Likewise, there are objects in the tapestry that are partially occluded from one vantage point. Consider the triangular magnatile, partially covered by a square.

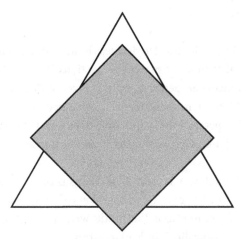

---

[13] It is difficult to see what kind of *purely sensory* phenomenology could make the difference between a ball perceived *as a sphere* and a simple perception of a ball.

110 THE VIEW FROM EVERYWHERE

There is a triangular magnatile in the tapestry. But in perceiving this partially occluded triangle, I do not see three lines, intersecting to form a closed figure. When I look at the tiles, the occluded tile may be *perceived-as* a triangle. But as with the sphericality of the ball, this strikes me as best understood as involving cognitive phenomenology—which I have argued is not part of the phenomenal tapestry. So although there is a triangle within the tapestry, I do not overlap with its triangularity. We can again answer (i) yes; (ii) no; (iii) no.

4.3 Illusion

We have already developed accounts of veridical perception and of hallucination. But how are we to make sense of illusions? As Berkeley's Hylas puts it:

> Since, according to you, men judge of the reality of things by their senses, how can a man be mistaken in thinking the moon a plain lucid surface, about a foot in diameter; or a square tower, seen at a distance, round; or an oar, with one end in the water, crooked? (3D, 181)

Berkeley's own answer was that illusions don't involve mistaken perceptions, but mistaken *judgments* about the experiences we would have under different conditions.

> He is not mistaken with regard to the ideas he actually perceives, but in the inference he makes from his present perceptions. Thus, in the case of the oar, what he immediately perceives by sight is certainly crooked; and so far he is in the right. But if he thence conclude that upon taking the oar out of the water he shall perceive the same crookedness; or that it would affect his touch as crooked things are wont to do: in that he is mistaken. (3D, 181)

I think that the Berkeleyan account of illusions is broadly right for many—but not all—illusions. The previous discussions of cognitive phenomenology and of the hidden assumptions that underwrite perception can provide a nuanced account of how illusions lead us astray.

There are three ways in which illusions idealists can make sense of illusions: (i) they can be purely cognitive, as Berkeley argues; (ii) they can violate the Veridicality restriction; or (iii) they can violate the No Generation

PERCEPTION 111

restriction (and so be more akin to hallucination). My aim is *not* to take a firm stand on how each specific illusion should be understood, but to give an indication of the resources available to idealists in making sense of illusions. Depending on one's views about perceiving-as and the contents of the tapestry, different illusions may warrant different treatment; and some illusions may be best explained by a conjunction of the three mechanisms.

Cognitive Phenomenology and Illusion

In the previous section, I argued that the sphericality of balls and the triangularity of partially occluded triangles are present within the tapestry but are not directly perceived by us. I propose that our awareness of these features comes from the "cognitive overlay" that our mind supplies to our perceptions. In the partially occluded triangle, I see three wedges arranged in a particular way around a square, and *my mind* supplies a conceptualization of this *as* a triangle behind a square. I do not have a sensory experience of the triangle. I *judge* that there is a triangle, and this judgment affects the overall phenomenology. This is similar to the Berkeleyan account of illusion, and is, I think, the correct account of many illusions.

Take the Müller-Lyer illusion. In looking at the illusion, I see one line *as* longer than the other. As before, I take the best explanation of this to be that my total experience includes more than merely sensory phenomenology—it includes a sort of cognitive overlay of conceptualization *as* longer. And this cognitive overlay is not a part of the tapestry. The world includes a raw, sensory way that the Müller-Lyer lines look. This way of looking *isn't* illusory. In grasping it, we are grasping a way that the world truly is. But this way of looking is such that we conceptualize the lengths of the lines as being different. While the raw-look is a part of the tapestry, the conceptualization is not. So insofar as this case is genuinely illusory (i.e., involves misperception), it is because of the cognitive component of our experience.

The same is true for perceptions (as) of "impossible objects." There is nothing impossible about the experience of seeing the Penrose triangle. (I cannot have impossible experiences—such a thing would be impossible!) What is impossible is that there be a triangle that is a closed, three-dimensional figure, structured as the Penrose triangle appears to be. Clearly the *judgment* that such a triangle is possible would be mistaken. But there is an earlier step where a mistake can be attributed: insofar as I have an experience in which I see the Penrose triangle *as* a closed, three-dimensional figure, this experience involves an internal tension, which is not present in

112 THE VIEW FROM EVERYWHERE

reality itself. But as with the Müller-Lyer illusion, my raw sensory experience itself does not generate this tension. The tension comes from the cognitive overlay: seeing the triangle *as* a closed three-dimensional figure. The raw look itself is no more illusory than the world itself is.

This offers a compelling idealist account of many illusions. Since raw sensory phenomenology doesn't include comparisons, it is particularly attractive in cases where comparison plays a role. The world includes the raw way which the color tiles look in the color tile illusion . . . but doesn't include perceptions of colors *as* different. In the Ebbinghaus illusion, the world includes two circles, each surrounded by a ring of circles . . . but it doesn't include one circle *as* looking larger than the other.

Veridicality and Illusion

But the idealist also has the resources to offer a further account of illusion, on which our perceptions themselves are mistaken. As I've argued, hidden assumptions can only facilitate contact with reality when a qualitatively identical experience is a part of the phenomenal tapestry. And this, arguably, is not always the case.

The "bent" stick in water is plausibly such a case. When I look at the stick, I have a sensory impression of bentness. The idealist could hold—as Berkeley does—that this bentness is a genuine part of the phenomenal tapestry, and the problem is simply the judgment that the stick will look bent when I pull it out of the water (or feel bent when I touch it). But given the Veridicality constraint, it is also open to the idealist to hold that the bentish appearance is simply not a part of the tapestry. My perception doesn't capture a genuine way the world is. This is all the more plausible given the intuitive requirement that the experiences making up physical reality exhibit cross-modal coherence. Since, in this case, our visual experience does not cohere with our tactile experience, we have grounds for inferring that one or more modality is not putting us into contact with reality. And since our tactile experiences remain stable as the stick is pulled out of the water, it seems plausible that it's the visual experiences that are failing to capture reality.

The apparent motion of movies and alternating lights plausibly fit in this category. Suppose you see a road sign "CAUTION: ROAD WORK AHEAD" that seems to move across a board of lights. The words appear to move, but there is no actual motion here. There is simply a series of lights flashing on and off. One could hold that the raw sensory phenomenology is of immobile

PERCEPTION   113

lights flashing off and on, but that my cognitive phenomenology projects motion onto this. But given that we perceive alternating lights as moving when they alter at a rate of 100 ms (Palmer 1999, 472)—which is briefer than the amount of time required to form a conscious percept—it seems far more plausible that the motion phenomenology is itself part of the sensory phenomenology. My mind is selecting from among possible interpretations of the visual data, and selecting something that—plausibly—is not present within reality itself.

Illusions of Generation

There are also "illusions" that involve the generation of sensory phenomenology that is not a part of the tapestry. So-called blind spot illusions are cases where one eye is closed, and a stimulus is positioned in the open eye's blind spot, causing the stimulus to "disappear"—the gap in visual inputs filled in by a uniform expanse of the surrounding background. This involves the *generation* of phenomenology, as opposed to the selection of an interpretation of stimulus taken in from the world. Thus, blind spot "illusions" are more akin to a hallucination than to standard illusions. Unlike traditional illusions in which I misperceive some stimulus, there is no stimulus that I misrepresent. There is simply an *absence* that I fill in.

4.3.1 Afterimages

How to understand afterimages is a murkier issue. Arguments can be made for classing them with hallucinations or with veridical perceptions.

There are two sorts of afterimages, with distinct empirical bases. Positive afterimages are those in which the colors of the original experience are preserved—as when you look at a bright light, and then away. The standard understanding of these afterimages is that they involve a sort of retinal inertia, where the cells in the retina don't instantly respond to a change in stimulus but continue firing for a period. I look at the sun at t_1, look away, and see an afterimage at t_2.

Arguably, this can be understood on the same model as what's happening when a star gives off light at t_1, which reaches our eyes at $t_{gazillion}$. I see the star. But I see the t_1-star, not the $t_{gazillion}$-star (now a black hole). Similarly, given this understanding of positive afterimages, I continue to see the sun at t_2. But

114   THE VIEW FROM EVERYWHERE

I see the t_1-sun, not the t_2-sun.[14] Given this model, my mind overlaps with the tapestry at t_2, but with a part of the tapestry that is now past. I am literally in contact with the tapestry's past. Alternatively, we might understand the continued firing of cells in the retina (once the sun is no longer in view) as a sort of generation, and think of this on the model of our blind spot, as something that does not put us in contact with reality.

Curiously, for the idealist, which of these two interpretations is the correct one is a matter of substance—not something we can dismiss as two equally good ways of conceptualizing the phenomenon—for they make a meaningful difference to the metaphysics, to whether or not we overlap with reality in experiencing positive blind spots. I'm inclined to think that the overlap-with-past model is the correct one. All perception takes time, and there seems no principled reason for insisting that the time taken by my visual system must be x, rather than x + 1 (cf. Yetter-Chappell 2018b).[15]

Negative afterimages pose an even more interesting case. Negative afterimages are those for which the colors are inverted from the original experience. Staring at the Union Jack for a minute, then looking away at a white wall, you seem to see the same pattern with the colors flipped: yellow in place of blue, green in place of red, black in place of white. This is standardly explained in terms of fatigue and post-inhibition activity of opponent-process cells. Opponent-process cells are photoreceptors that are simultaneously activated by one sort of light and inhibited by complementary light. One is activated by red light, and inactivated by green (R+G−); one is activated by green light and inactivated by red (G+R−). There are similar pairs for blue and yellow, and for white (all wavelengths) and black (absence of light). After an intense period of firing, as you stare at the original image, the R+G− cells become fatigued, such that they will fire less strongly in response to white light. The complementary cells (G+R−) become more active and *more* likely to fire, as a result of being inhibited while you stared at the flag. So when you

---

[14] The only difference between these two cases is where in the causal chain the information about the past is preserved. In the case of the star, it is in the light traveling out from the star. In the case of the afterimage, it is in the continued firing of cells in the retina.

[15] There are other empirical models of positive afterimages, the veracity of which would change how to make sense of them within the idealist framework. Holcombe et al. (2004) argue that "positive afterimages are not caused by continuing activity at a peripheral level, but rather reflect the persistence of a visual representation in the absence of evidence that the world has changed." If this is right, afterimages seem more akin to blind spot filling. But rather than filling in an absence using information from the surrounding region of space, our mind fills in an absence with information about an adjacent moment in time.

PERCEPTION 115

look at the white wall, balance of these cells firing in this region of the retina is thrown off. You see green (Palmer 1999, 119).

What should the idealist make of such afterimages? The wall is white. (I veridically perceive it when it looks white.) But phenomenal green, yellow, red, and blue are also genuine aspects of the wall. Creatures who are only able to see visible light in one fraction of (what for us is the) visible spectrum, still see the wall, even if they don't see it in its entirety—much as I can veridically see the wall, despite not seeing the ultraviolet light that it reflects. So a creature who only can see red wavelengths of light still sees the wall. And it would seem arbitrary to privilege the whiteish look over the red.

One way of making sense of afterimages would be that, in experiencing the afterimage, I am veridically perceiving different aspects of the wall in different regions of my visual field. The afterimage is a veridical perception, arising from my "tapping into" different threads of the tapestry in different regions of my visual field. I mostly see the whiteness of the wall. But in the afterimage region, I see the wall's redness. (In effect, prolonged exposure to the original image has temporarily altered my perceptual system, and which threads of the tapestry I can relate to.) On the other hand, the lack of coherence across a single visual field might be seen as a problem. Perhaps any one sort of perceptual system can tap into reality, but there needs to be *consistency* within the system in order to do so. The whiteness of the wall can be seen, or the redness. But if a checkerboard of redness and whiteness is seen— with color boundaries supplied by my mind—this is a case of *generation*.

We could also take an intermediary position. In the flag afterimage, you are overlapping with the yellowness, greenness, and blackness of the wall. But you are also experiencing something that is not a part of reality, namely the *contrasts* between different regions of the wall. Your sensory experience includes not just the whiteness of the background and the greenness of different regions, but a *border* between the white and the green. This is an aspect of the sensory phenomenology of the afterimage, not merely a matter of how you conceptualize the image of the Union Jack. And this border is a figment of your perceptual system, rather than a feature of the tapestry. Thus, the *form* of the figure and the *borders* are akin to hallucinations, while the *color-appearance* of each region is veridically perceived. But while the wall has phenomenal redness, blueness, and so forth as constituents, there is no *single* perspective from which the wall is all these colors. In the afterimage, we effectively have a disjoint visual system, which taps into different threads of the tapestry in different regions. Thus, were I to judge that the wall is

116 THE VIEW FROM EVERYWHERE

multicolored *in the normal sense* (i.e., from a single perspective), I would be judging incorrectly, in spite of the fact that I am genuinely perceiving many colors of the wall.

I take no stand on how idealists ought to make sense of afterimages. But the range of options is itself interesting. And for the idealist, which of these options is true is a substantive matter.

4.4 Conclusion

We have seen that combining idealism with the externalist account of bridging laws proposed in Chapter 3 yields an attractive theory of perception on which we stand in literal and direct epistemic contact with reality. In perception, the external world literally overlaps with and is a part of our minds, affording us the same access to distal objects of perception that we have to our own thoughts and bodily sensations. On this "naïve idealist" view, the acquaintance we have with the world in perception is no different in kind from introspective acquaintance. The difference lies in whether the mental item we're acquainted with is *merely* a part of my mind, or whether it is additionally a part of the phenomenal tapestry of reality. Likewise, the difference between hallucinations and veridical perceptions is not the qualitative nature of the experienced items, but whether the items are phenomenally bound to the tapestry as well as to a finite observer's mind.

This chapter also developed an idealist account of illusion, arguing that the idealist has resources to account for illusions that extend beyond those appealed to by Berkeley. Berkeley takes all illusions to be rooted in mistaken judgments. This is one possible explanation the idealist can appeal to. But the idealist can also hold that for some illusions, the sensory appearances simply don't correspond to a genuine way the world is, and so cannot involve overlap with the tapestry. For example, in the case of the "bent" stick in water, the bentish appearance is simply not a part of reality, and so not a respect in which I am in contact with reality.

According to the idealist, ours is a world of color, sound, and warmth; a world that truly *is* as our seems to be. The theory of veridical perception developed in this chapter is one on which we have an intimate connection to reality. We can directly grasp the nature and character of reality. This is an epistemic benefit more familiarly claimed by naïve realism. We'll return to the nature of perception in Chapter 6, where I'll argue that idealists are *uniquely* poised to capture the benefits claimed by naïve realism. There I'll argue that we can only account for direct epistemic contact with reality if reality is fundamentally experiential. Naïve realists can, at best, get us direct-contact-in-name-only: a sort of contact that derives from word play of how we carve off "experiences" and "subjects of experience"—not something that gives us true metaphysical contact with the objects of our perceptions. Idealism alone can account for the compelling common-sense world we started with in Chapter 1.

The remaining task is to make good on the claim that idealism is compatible with our scientific worldview: that the idealist can account for the structure of reality that empirical investigation reveals, and that it can give a plausible account of spacetime and natural laws.

5

Science, Structure, and Spacetime

Let's turn to the compatibility of idealism with our scientific worldview. There seems to be a widespread belief among philosophers that idealism is anti-scientific. I know of nowhere where this is explicitly argued. But a common response to hearing that one is working on a book developing an idealist metaphysics is some variant on an incredulous: *But isn't the world made of atoms? But what about the laws of physics? But . . . don't you believe in science?* I suspect some of this incredulity comes from a failure to appreciate that idealism *does not do away with the physical world*, but merely characterizes the metaphysical *nature* of the physical world. Nevertheless, there are real questions in this vicinity. And the compatibility of idealism with mainstream interpretations of science (and its underlying norms) is the source of the most serious challenges to idealism.

In §5.1, I'll consider the compatibility of idealism with different philosophical accounts of laws of nature—arguing that nontheistic accounts of laws are metaphysically neutral. In §5.2, I consider the relation between the micro- and macro-levels of reality—between the green leaves that we're directly acquainted with and the cells and atoms that make them up. Section 5.3 turns to the charge that idealism is excessively profligate. While idealism is undeniably quantitatively profligate, I argue that this is not actually a vice. And while a profligacy of laws would be a vice, idealism is not guilty of it. Finally, §5.4 considers the nature of space and time within an idealist context, arguing that idealism is compatible with both relationalism and substantivalism, and offering a few speculative remarks on the intuitive appeal of an idealistic spacetime.

The View from Everywhere. Helen Yetter-Chappell, Oxford University Press. © Oxford University Press 2025. DOI: 10.1093/9780197795057.003.0005

SCIENCE, STRUCTURE, AND SPACETIME 119

5.1 The Neutrality of Laws

The idealism developed in this book is neo-Berkeleyan, in the sense that it embraces a physical world that is independent of *our* minds, but is grounded in structured phenomenology. It departs from Berkeley in eschewing God as the metaphysical ground for reality. We saw in Chapter 1 that God performs a number of central roles in Berkeley's metaphysics, including accounting for (i) the persistence of reality and (ii) the phenomenological difference between ideas of imagination and those of sense, and (iii) underwriting Berkeley's understanding of laws of nature.

We've seen that the nontheistic idealist can offer a broadly Berkeleyan account of (i) and (ii). But without God, we must give a very different answer to (iii). For Berkeley,

THE SET RULES OR ESTABLISHED METHODS WHEREIN THE MIND WE DEPEND ON EXCITES IN US THE IDEAS OF SENSE, ARE CALLED THE LAWS OF NATURE; and these we learn by experience, which teaches us that such and such ideas are attended with such and such other ideas, in the ordinary course of things. (Principles 30)

Without God—without a *rational agent*, whose mind grounds reality—we cannot take laws of nature to be *rules* "by which the unseen Author of nature actuates the universe" (D2, 151). Divine agency is central to Berkley's conception of laws of nature. Without this, we will have to look elsewhere.

Fortunately, we are not alone in this quest. We are in good company with all those materialists who seek to give a nontheistic account of the regularities of nature. In fact, we need look no further than existing materialistic accounts of laws for options.

The literature on the nature of laws is vast. My aim here is neither to offer a complete survey of possible accounts, nor to settle which account is correct. My aim is simply to show that whatever (nontheistic) account a materialist takes of laws, the same account is available to the nontheistic idealist. Laws account for the regularities we find in the physical world. Laws tell us about structure, about relations. The intrinsic nature of the things that are so-structured is neither here nor there.

Let's begin with two familiar realist accounts of laws: regularity theory (of which I'll take Lewis [1986b] as the exemplar) and contingent necessitation

120 THE VIEW FROM EVERYWHERE

relations among universals (of which I'll take Armstrong [1983] as representative).

For the regularity theorist,

> [A]ll there is to the world is a vast mosaic of local matters of particular fact, just one little thing and then another.... We have geometry: a system of external relations of spatio-temporal distance between points. Maybe points of spacetime itself, maybe point-sized bits of matter or aether or fields, maybe both. And at those points we have local qualities: perfectly natural intrinsic properties which need nothing bigger than a point at which to be instantiated. For short: we have an arrangement of qualities. And that is all. There is no difference without difference in the arrangement of qualities. All else supervenes on that. (Lewis 1986b, ix–x)

Laws of nature are merely a special class of contingent generalizations about this "Humean mosaic": the generalizations that achieve the "best combination of simplicity and strength" (Lewis 1986b, 73).

Can the idealist embrace a conception of reality as a Humean mosaic, with laws as the simplest, most explanatory generalizations thereof? Of course. There is nothing about this picture requiring that the mosaic be made of *insensible matter*. The account has all the same virtues (and challenges) if laws are patterns of simple, explanatory regularities among structured phenomenology. Material mosaic or phenomenal tapestry makes no difference.

By contrast, Armstrong (1983, 1982) takes there to be a lawmaker relation N, which (contra Lewis) does not supervene on the arrangement of intrinsic qualities. For this relation to be suitably general as to constitute a law, it must be a relation between event-types, rather than merely token events. Thus, "we are led straight to the notion that the necessitation is based upon, is indeed constituted by, a relation between universals" (Armstrong 1982, 8).

> Suppose it to be a law that Fs are Gs. F-ness and G-ness are taken to be universals. A certain relation, a relation of non-logical or contingent necessitation, holds between F-ness and G-ness. This state of affairs may be symbolized as N(F,G). Although N(F,G) does not obtain of logical necessity, if it does obtain then it entails the corresponding Humean or cosmic uniformity. (Armstrong 1982, 12)

SCIENCE, STRUCTURE, AND SPACETIME 121

As before, there is nothing in this account that renders it dependent on materialism. Berkeley himself may have been a nominalist. But this stems from his denial of abstract general ideas and is not essential to idealism as a positive theory.[1] An idealist could (precisely as well as the materialist) take there to be universals and contingent necessitation relations between these universals, and take this to be what laws of nature consist in.

Both of these accounts of laws face significant, well-known challenges. The regularity theorist seems unable to distinguish laws from mere accidental regularities. Intuitively, there is a difference between (a) a world in which every coin flip has landed heads because there is a law that all coin flips land heads, and (b) one where there are probabilistic laws governing coin flips ... and it just so happens every flip has always landed heads up. But for the regularity theorist, there is just the Humean mosaic, and laws supervene on this. The distribution of intrinsic qualities is the same in (a) and (b). There are not two worlds, but one—and that world is such that "coin flips land heads" is part of the simplest, most informative theory of that world.

The relational view has an answer to this challenge: in world (a) there are relations that do not obtain in world (b). But it is not clear that this account actually *explains* the regularities we find in nature, as opposed to merely redescribing the need for an explanation. As David Lewis (1983, 366) puts it:

> Whatever N may be, I cannot see how it could be absolutely impossible to have N(F,G) and Fa without Ga. (Unless N just is constant conjunction, or constant conjunction plus something else, in which case Armstrong's theory turns into a form of the regularity theory he rejects.) The mystery is somewhat hidden by Armstrong's terminology. He uses "necessitates" as a name for the lawmaking universal N; and who would be surprised to hear that if F "necessitates" G and a has F, then a must have G? But I say that N deserves the name of "necessitation" only if, somehow, it really can enter into the requisite necessary connections. It can't enter into them just by bearing a name, any more than one can have mighty biceps just by being called "Armstrong."

Or as Maudlin (2007), 11) rhetorically puts it:

---

[1] Even if it is a part of Berkeley's positive case for embracing idealism.

122 THE VIEW FROM EVERYWHERE

do we really have a firmer grasp of what a necessitation relation between universals is than we do of what a law is? This is especially troubling since the species of necessitation at issue must again be denominated nomic necessitation.

The challenges faced by nontheistic realist reductions of laws might lead one in any of three directions: (i) we could conclude that *nontheism* is the problem and return to a theistic account of laws (Foster 2004); (ii) we could conclude that *realism* about laws is the problem and embrace anti-realism (Fraassen 1989); or (iii) we could conclude that *reductionism* is the problem and embrace a primitivist account of laws (Maudlin 2007).

Nontheistic idealism is obviously compatible with anti-realism about laws (as well as anti-realism more generally, as we shall see in the next section). But suppose we're inclined toward realism. This leaves us with the primitivist and theistic options.

John Foster (2004) and Howard Robinson (2022) have each argued that the problems facing existing nontheistic reductions of laws should, roughly, lead us back to Berkeley.

As Foster sees it, we have good reason to be realists about laws, but no (nontheistic) account of laws is able to account for laws as something *more than mere regularities, but less then strict necessities.* However, such an account can be given if laws stem from the *personal* agency of a supernatural personal being or group of beings,

> [who] are endowed with a rational mentality and who bring about the regularities deliberately. So to the question "Why are things thus regular?," the answer, in each case, would be "Because this being or these beings have deliberately made them so." (Foster 2004, 121)

These beings "would have to be free in a strong libertarian sense—a sense which logically excludes the possibility of their being causally determined by prior events and conditions" (Foster 2004, 128). In short, we can make sense of the regularities of the universe and their nomic necessity if and only if they stem from the agency of a Divine Lawmaker. We return to our Berkeleyan starting point, with God as the cause of the regularities we find in nature.

Without God—without an all-powerful *personal agent*—this account of laws is not open to us. Of course, nontheistic idealism is not anti-theistic. It is perfectly compatible with the existence of God (as we shall discuss in §6.4.3).

SCIENCE, STRUCTURE, AND SPACETIME   123

But reintroducing God and relying on him to do half of the metaphysical work that he does for Berkeley would leave us with the question: why not leave God's role in Berkeley's metaphysics intact? If God were necessary to account for regularities in the physical world, why not also appeal to him to account for the nature and persistence of the physical world as well? So I'm inclined to see this as a non-starter for the nontheistic idealist.[2]

There are questions as to how much the theistic solution really solves—in particular, questions about *how* God imposes regularities on the universe "as regularities" (Beebee 2009). But since this account of laws is not available to the nontheistic idealist, let's set the success of the theistic account aside.

Interestingly, the same reasoning that leads Foster and Robinson to conclude that laws require a Divine Lawmaker leads Tim Maudlin (2009) to embrace a primitivist conception of laws. Both agree that laws are required to make sense of the regularities of the physical world; both agree that existing reductions of laws fail; both find special difficulty in accounting for laws as something more than mere regularity, but less than logical necessity. But where Foster sees the failure of {realism, nontheism, reductionism} as pushing us to theism, Maudlin takes it to be a basis for rejecting reductionism. If no satisfactory reduction of laws can be given, perhaps we should take laws to be ontological primitives.

> My analysis of laws is no analysis at all. Rather I suggest we accept laws as fundamental entities in our ontology. Or, speaking at the conceptual level, the notion of a law cannot be reduced to other more primitive notions. (Maudlin 2007, 18)
>
> Laws are the patterns that nature respects; to say what is physically possible is to say what the constraint of those patterns allows. (Maudlin 2007, 15)

I find this proposal quite attractive. Inasmuch as proposed reductions of laws face challenges, we should at least be open to the primitivist answer. As Maudlin says:

> Taking laws as primitive may appear to be simple surrender in the face of a philosophical puzzle. But every account must have primitives. The account

---

[2] Although insofar as God's mind is a "black box," it is arguably better to have less work concealed within the black box, rather than more!

124   THE VIEW FROM EVERYWHERE

must be judged on the clarity of the inferences that the primitives warrant and on the degree of systematization they reveal among our pre-analytic inferences. Laws are preferable in point of familiarity to such primitives as necessitation relations among universals. And if we begin by postulating that at each time and place the temporal evolution of the world is governed by certain principles our convictions about possibilities, counterfactuals, and explanations can be regimented and explained. (Maudlin 2007, 15)

Now, is primitivism available to the nontheistic idealist? Of course. There is no reason to think that this primitive could only constrain the unfolding of the universe if the universe is fundamentally material. The idealist's theory of reality can contain physical objects—which are fundamentally collections of structured phenomenology—and primitive laws that govern the unfolding of these physical objects over time.

So where does this leave us? The laws that scientists posit take no stance on the fundamental ontological nature of reality. Standard accounts of these laws are similarly neutral. Regularity theory, necessitation relations among universals, anti-realism, and primitivism are all just as available to the nontheistic idealist as they are to the materialist.[3]

Whatever view of laws the materialist finds compelling, the idealist can answer "I agree."

5.2 The Microphysical Structure of Physical Reality

Thus far, this book has focused on the way the world is at a macroscopic level. Grass is green; snow is cold; tables are solid. But the idealist's worldview need not bottom out there. We have particularly strong reason to believe in the reality of the macro-objects and properties that we're directly acquainted with through our senses. But idealism is also compatible with realism about

---

[3] These accounts of physical regularities are not exhaustive. One could, e.g., hold that physical objects have their dispositions essentially. The idealist might flesh this out by embracing a phenomenal powers view (Mørch 2020, 132). On such a view,

> phenomenal properties . . . have non-Humean causal powers—which is to say that they metaphysically necessitate their effects—in virtue of how they feel, i.e. in virtue of their phenomenal character, as opposed to in virtue of entering into contingent regularities, as per Humean or Lewisian regularity theory, or being constrained by external governing laws, as per Armstrongian realism about laws.

I think such a view gets logical space wrong (Yetter-Chappell 2022). But for those who disagree, this is another option open to the nontheistic idealist.

SCIENCE, STRUCTURE, AND SPACETIME 125

entities that are not directly observable (or even are in-principle unobservable by creatures like us). I'll argue that idealism does not constrict our account of unobservable entities. It is compatible with both realism and anti-realism regarding those features of scientific theories that are not directly observed.[4]

Our understanding of the world has advanced markedly from the time of Berkeley: from the discovery of atoms in the early 1800s to subsequent discoveries of subatomic particles and genes. While we cannot observe any of these with the unaided senses, our best scientific theories posit these entities to make sense of phenomena that we can directly observe— including instrument-mediated experiences, such as those we have by way of microscopes.

When I see a leaf, light reflects off the leaf, casting an image on my retina, and sending a signal to my brain. (Just add bridging laws, and voilà!) I cannot directly differentiate the cells that make up the leaf. But I can do so via an optical microscope. As before, light reflects off the cells. This light is refracted by glass lenses, leading to a larger-than-life image of the cell on my retina. Atoms are too small to be seen directly using visible light. Rather than bouncing light off atoms, we can bounce electrons off atoms. By shooting electrons at an atom from different angles, and measuring where they go, scientists can make inferences about the source of the electron scattering. Electron ptychography records the patterns of electron scattering and uses algorithms to create images of atoms based on this. Visible light bounces off the images . . . and we "see" the atom. At each step, our grasp on the target becomes less direct. But most philosophers and lay people seem to grant the reality of the microphysical particles posited by science.[5] Can idealists agree?

My aim here is to show that idealists can (though don't have to) agree. Idealists, like materialists, can be realists or anti-realists about the entities posited by science. The metaphysical nature of reality does not commit us one way or the other.

---

[4] Provided "realism" is understood—as I've used the term throughout the book—as commitment to existence independent of *our-minds* (i.e., all ordinary minds), as opposed to independent of *mind, per se*. To achieve total mind-independent status, the idealist would have to either deny that experiences require experiencers or reject the equating of experiencers with minds. But it seems to me that independence from our minds is sufficient to capture the force and appeal of realism.

[5] Seventy-two percent of philosophers reported embracing or leaning toward scientific realism according to the 2020 philpapers survey (Bourget and Chalmers 2023). (The survey did not distinguish between different types of scientific realism.)

126 THE VIEW FROM EVERYWHERE

First, start with anti-realism. While there are numerous varieties of scientific anti-realism, the central unifying idea is a lack of belief in the reality of that which is not directly observable. (This could take the form of a positive denial of the reality of such entities, agnosticism about them, or the view that terms for unobservables fail to refer and hence statements putatively "about" them are not truth-evaluable [Chakravartty (2017)].) It is fairly obvious that the idealist could embrace scientific anti-realism. While the motivation for idealism is the reality of the way the world appears to us—the reality of cold snow, green leaves, and solid tables—this motivation does not extend to give us reason to believe in negative-y electrons or double-helixy DNA strands. It is open to the idealist to hold—with Bas Van Fraassen (1980, 12)—that science simply "aims to give us theories which are empirically adequate; and acceptance of a theory involves as belief only that it is empirically adequate." That is, we could hold that science is simply in the business of capturing that which is directly observable, while remaining agnostic about the reality of (physically) unobservable entities. It is open to the idealist to be a fictionalist about scientific theories and the entities that they describe—taking observable reality to function as-if scientific theories were true, without commitment beyond that.

Less obvious is whether idealism is compatible with scientific realism, particularly with the form of scientific realism known as entity realism, which embraces the reality of the unobservable (i.e., not directly observable) entities posited by our best scientific theories. At a first pass, one might object that idealism is incompatible with unobservable entities. Put as a reply to the Berkeleyan: if to be is to be perceived, how can there be something unperceivable?[6] To this the Berkeleyan can respond by drawing a distinction between (a) that which is unobservable by humans with their unaided senses, and (b) that which is unobservable, simpliciter. The Berkeleyan must deny the reality of (b) but faces no challenge accepting the reality of (a) (cf. Pelczar [2022]). For the idealist micro-entity realist, the world contains not only green leaves, but molecules, atoms, electrons, protons, and quarks. Just as leaves are structures of indexed phenomenology, so too are the molecules, atoms, and so on that comprise them. Electron ptychography enables us to construct images of atoms and molecular bonds. While we are not be able to do this without the aid of imaging technology, God (according to the

---

[6] I do not embrace the line that "to be is to be perceived." I would put the point more cautiously as: "If our world is an idealist world, to be physical in our world is to be experiential."

SCIENCE, STRUCTURE, AND SPACETIME   127

Berkeleyan micro-entity realist) would have phenomenology of molecules, atoms ... and quarks within his purview. Likewise, the nontheistic idealist can take such experiences to be part of the tapestry.[7]

But there is a deeper challenge to the idealist in accommodating scientific realism. The physical world doesn't merely *have* leaves, molecules, atoms, and so on. We take leaves to be *made up out of* molecules; these to be *made out of* atoms, these out of electrons, protons, and neutrons; and so on. Can the idealist accept this?

Those with constitutive panpsychist leanings may take this to be unproblematic: any solution to the quality combination problem would likewise answer the question of how leaves' greenness is composed out of micro-experiences. I myself am skeptical that such a solution can be found— particularly if (as for the Russellian panpsychist) all the rich variety of the world's macro-experiences must be composed out of a small handful of simple micro-experiences. I just can't see how green phenomenology could be composed out of non-color phenomenology (as it presumably must be if the same small set of simple microphysical particles compose the totality of the physical world). But a nontheistic idealist wouldn't have to follow the Russellian. They might hold that macro-qualities can reduce to micro-qualities precisely because the set of micro-qualities is suitably rich. If micro-entities are themselves collections of phenomenology, perhaps a small number of micro-entities would contain all the richness needed to yield the vast array of possible macro-experiences that creatures like us are acquainted with. On this proposal, the leaf's greenness is inherited from some sort of proto-green phenomenology: phenomenology that intelligibly combines to form phenomenal greenness.

An idealist could go this way. But I am not inclined to. Even if we can escape the palette problem (Chalmers 2016), we risk undercutting the appeal of idealism. For the idealist, not only are leaves green, but I am in direct contact with this greenness. (This aspect of) their nature is manifest to me. But I'm unaware of micro-phenomenology composing the greenness. So, if this proposal is right, the real nature of the leaf's greenness remains beyond my grasp.[8] Beyond this, if the leaf's greenness reduces to the proto-greenness of

---

[7] And recall from the discussion of black holes in §2.3.1 that we granted that the tapestry needn't be restricted to physically possible perceptions, but could—if needed to account for the reality of physically unobserv*able* phenomena—include metaphysically possible (but physically impossible) perceptions.

[8] This is a variant of the revelation argument that Goff (2015, 2011) has raised against smallist panpsychists and physicalists, and which Cutter (2016) has raised against Goff.

128 THE VIEW FROM EVERYWHERE

cells and atoms, we're left with a disjunctive account of greenness—given the plausible assumption that the phenomenal greenness of my hallucinated tree does not include cell and atom phenomenology.[9]

So I am not inclined to think that the leaf's greenness reduces to microphysics. The greenness of a leaf is not made out of molecules (even if molecules are bits of phenomenology). Greenness is a primitive feature of reality and a primitive aspect of the leaf. While this might seem inelegant, it is actually not in tension with what we learn from science. Science tells us that surface reflectance properties can be explained in terms of the microphysical makeup of objects' surfaces, but it doesn't tell us that *greenness* can be explained in these terms. Science doesn't tell us that *greenness* reduces to molecules. *It simply leaves the greenness out.*

And even if the leaf's greenness doesn't reduce to its microphysical makeup, the relationship between the macro- and micro-levels of reality are not as counterintuitive as might be supposed: the idealist can accept that if we pull out our electron microscopes, we will find that when we zoom in on the leaf, there is nothing but cells. When we zoom in on these, there are molecules, when we zoom in on these: atoms. In this sense, we can grant that *leaves* are made of atoms—even if their greenness isn't. The cells, molecules, and atoms that we find as we zoom further into the leaf are all phenomenal structures. And they are genuine parts of the leaf—even if there is more to the leaf beyond these (i.e., the leaf's irreducible macro-properties).

Furthermore, the idealist can accept that macroscopic entities have the appropriate counterfactual dependency relations on microscopic entities. There is a leaf (and it is green) *because* there are the right sorts of molecules, arranged in the right sorts of ways. These exist *because* there are the right sorts of atoms, arranged in the right sorts of ways. And so on. Were there not atoms, there would not be molecules. Were there not molecules, there would not be cells. Were there not cells, there would not be a green leaf. Appropriate changes at the micro-level bring about corresponding changes at the macro-level.

Why do these dependency relations exist? Much as dualists take the brain to give rise to conscious experience, the idealist (who wishes to accommodate these counterfactual dependencies) should take the micro-level to give

---

[9] One might think of the leaf's greenness as analogous to a pointillist painting—where dots make up the painting, but perhaps are obscured in the experience of it. But insofar as the dots are obscured in the experiencing, it's questionable whether the dots really are part of the *experience* of the painting—even if they are part of the physical painting that causes the experience.

SCIENCE, STRUCTURE, AND SPACETIME   129

rise to the macro-level. In both cases, "giving rise to" is accounted for by phenomenal laws of generation. Just as for the dualist, the micro-level does not metaphysically necessitate the macro. The necessitation is merely nomological. This might seem inelegant, but it should also strike us as natural and empirically unavoidable. Science simply doesn't reveal properties like *greenness* and *warmth*. So of course we should *expect* these to be metaphysically separable from what's revealed by science.

What about dependency relations at other levels, for example, from atoms to molecules? Again, we could accept a law-like relation. But it's also open to the idealist to embrace a reductive account. While our actual experiences of greenness seem to rule out reducing them to non-color experiences, we do not have micro-level experiences. As such, we do not have a positive basis for rejecting constitutive accounts within the micro-domain. (For all I know, from a molecule-level perspective, experiences of molecules transparently reduce to experiences of atoms.) Thus, it's open to the idealist to hold that experiences of molecules are literally composed out of experiences of atoms. These, in turn, are literally composed out of experiences of protons, neutrons, and electrons. And so forth.

The idealist can also accept that the micro-level of reality is essential to our perceptions. For the idealist who embraces micro-entity realism, the microphysical features of the physical world are fundamentally phenomenal, just as the macrophysical ones are. And the microphysical features of reality are part of the causal story that accounts for veridical perception. Were the microphysics not the way that it is, my brain would not be affected in the way that it is, and I would not be put in touch with the macroscopic features that I am.

The extended bridging laws that I proposed in Chapter 3 are such that the physical base of the bridging laws includes both what is happening "inside the head" and also the causal environment that I'm embedded in. These laws function as "laws of expansion"—phenomenally unifying me with perceived elements of the phenomenal tapestry—only when there is an appropriate object in the physical world *that I am appropriately causally related to*. When I veridically perceive the greenness of the leaf, the causal relation between me and the leaf is a part of the explanation for why the bridging laws function as they do: why they function to put me in direct contact with the leaf.[10]

---

[10] This draws an interesting contrast with Chalmers's (2006) presentation of perceptual Eden. As Chalmers describes things:

130   THE VIEW FROM EVERYWHERE

The idealist's world contains *color*. But this is not to deny that the microphysical structure of objects' surfaces affects which wavelengths of light are reflected from them. And it is not to deny that the microphysics of objects' surface structure is part of the causal explanation for how I come to perceive color. The idealist's world contains *warmth*. But this is not to deny that there are also molecules and molecular kinetic energy. And it's not to deny that this is part of the causal explanation for how I come to perceive warmth. The idealist's world contains *sound*. But this is not to deny that there are also vibrations, which cause compression waves to propagate through the air, to my ear. And it's not to deny that this is part of the causal explanation for how I come to perceive sound.

Whereas materialists eliminate color, warmth, and sound from our world[11]—and so have no need to say how they relate to microstructural features of reality—idealists embrace the reality of these appearances. Given that science does not reveal such properties, there is no reason to expect that they would reduce to microphysical features of the world. Indeed, there is every reason to expect that they won't.

So idealists can accept:

(i) that physical reality includes both macro- and microphysical entities (of the sort posited by our scientific theories, but not directly observed),
(ii) that these microphysical entities are parts of macroscopic entities,
(iii) that there are appropriate counterfactual dependency relations between the macro- and micro-levels of reality, and
(iv) that the microphysical entities are a part of the causal explanation for how we come to be acquainted with macrophysical entities.

> When an apple in Eden looked red to us, the apple was gloriously, perfectly, and primitively red. There was no need for a long causal chain from the microphysics of the surface through air and brain to a contingently connected visual experience. Rather, the perfect redness of the apple was simply revealed to us. The qualitative redness in our experience derived entirely from the presentation of perfect redness in the world.
>
> For the nontheistic idealist, when an apple looks red to us, the apple is gloriously, perfectly, and primitively red. The qualitative redness in our experience derived entirely from the presentation of perfect redness in the world. But the causal explanation for how we get to have this direct contact with the redness in the world involves a long causal chain from the microphysics of the surface through air and brain to a contingently connected visual experience.

[11] Here I'm setting aside views like materialist color primitivism, which we'll return to in Chapter 6. There, we'll see that these views are no more elegant than idealism, and face a more significant challenge in accounting for the causal efficacy of appearance properties.

SCIENCE, STRUCTURE, AND SPACETIME   131

Yet a further question remains: how do the micro- and macro-"levels" of reality hang together? On the idealist's picture, greenness does not reduce to microphysical experiences, but is brutely related to them. Is reality just a muddle of micro- and macro-phenomenology all jumbled up? Or is there *structure* to it?

On the view I developed in Chapter 2, reality is highly structured. Bits of phenomenology indexed to a perspective are bonded into the "threads" out of which reality is woven. A leaf might include green$_{[perspective1]}$+ red$_{[perspective2]}$ + . . . I've now argued that it may also include experiences as-of cells, molecules, and atoms. We might here introduce more structure to the tapestry. As we move from fibers to thread to rope, we don't just add more fibers to the mix: we add more internal structure. A thread may be directly made out of fibers. Rope is made out of many threads that have been twisted together. Similarly, one way of thinking about how phenomenology of micro- and macro-perspectives relate would be to take the micro-perspectives to form one thread, and macro-perspectives to form a distinct thread, where these jointly form a rope out of which the tapestry is woven. What is it that functions to "twist" these threads into a rope? What is the relation that supplies this structure? The most plausible candidate seems to me to be the property binding relation. Within the macro-level, I've argued that property binding explains the relation between the greenness and the teardrop shape of the leaf. Assuming entity realism, there is more to the leaf than this: there are cells, there are atoms, there are electrons. And all this is related via property binding relations. Where does the additional structure come from? Consider two different ways we could make a rope:

1. Take a million cotton fibers and twist them all together into one bundle.
2. Take a million cotton fibers. Divide these into ten groups, and twist them into ten threads. Then twist the ten threads into one bundle.

We've used the same materials (cotton fiber) and the same relation (twisting) to relate them. But there's more internal structure to the second rope than to the first. I propose (assuming entity realism) that we think of the tapestry as being something akin to the second: Property-binding weaves phenomenology into micro-entities. Collections of these are bound together with bindings of macro-properties. And this is what ultimately makes up the tapestry.

132 THE VIEW FROM EVERYWHERE

Again, this picture is less elegant than a fully reductionistic one. But this is not because materialists have a brilliant method of reducing greenness to molecular structure—one that is unavailable to the idealist. Rather, it is because they leave greenness out of physical reality. The physicalist's world is indeed simpler. But it is simpler because it *leaves out* the colors, warmth, pitch, smells, and so on that make up the world we take ourselves to inhabit. It's easy to get simplicity by throwing things out. The question—which we'll return to in Chapter 6—is whether materialists have thrown out too much.

Of course, if I'm wrong and the constitutive panpsychists are right, we can have our greenness and reduce it, too. We can have an intelligible world that is also simple and elegant. I find it difficult to see how this could be possible. But perhaps this is a cognitive limitation of mine, and not an indication of the impossibility of such a task. This would leave us with the virtues of idealism (which I'll discuss in the next chapter) and the simplicity of reductionism.

5.3 Profligacy

We've seen that idealists can accept that physical reality includes both the macro-entities and properties that we're directly aware of and the microphysical entities posited by scientists (but not directly observed). The leaf contains green phenomenology [my perspective], red phenomenology [i-twin perspective] . . . cell phenomenology, molecule phenomenology, quark phenomenology. But there is no *essential connection* between the green phenomenology and any of the other constituents of the leaf. There is no reduction from macrophenomenal aspects to micro.

This naturally raises worries of profligacy. The materialist's worldview is simple. It contains a small number of fundamental physical entities, a small number of physical laws, and voilà! The promise of a world like ours. By contrast, idealism may seem unpalatably baroque.

We have already seen that idealist reality requires an enormous number of "phenomenal threads." The vast number of phenomenal threads comprising the tapestry might itself be seen as a cost to the theory.

I don't find quantitative profligacy hugely troubling. To riff on Lewis (1973), "You believe [or should believe] in sensations already. I ask you to believe in more things of that kind, not in things of some new kind."[12] Of

---

[12] As I noted in Yetter-Chappell (2018a), the materialist might take issue with my parallel to

SCIENCE, STRUCTURE, AND SPACETIME   133

course many have disputed Lewis's claim (1973, 87) that there is "no presumption whatever in favour of quantitative parsimony."[13] And depending on how kinds are individuated, one might take the different types of phenomenology to each be different kinds, resulting in qualitative as well as quantitative profligacy.

But for the idealist, there is no way around it: unless the idealist is prepared to privilege certain sorts of phenomenology over others—human phenomenology over nonhuman, actual phenomenology over merely possible, "ideal conditions" phenomenology over all other—they must accept a large quantity of phenomenology. While this profligacy is especially salient for the nontheistic idealist, this is only because the structure of the ontology is transparent. This profligacy is no less essential to any other mind-first metaphysics. If God experiences the totality of reality, we still must either privilege certain sorts of phenomenology over others or grant that God has an enormous number of perspectives and phenomenal experiences in his purview. The phenomenalist does not construct their world out of actual phenomenology, but potentials for phenomenology. The nature of the threads differs, but the number does not. (And, as I'll argue in §6.4.2, this is no less ontologically burdensome.)

Insofar as you think that this qualitative profligacy is a strike against the idealist, you can note this down in your score book to weigh against the virtues of idealism when we get to Chapter 6. For myself, I don't find this sort of profligacy especially troubling. It is true that quantitatively profligate theories *often* are less virtuous than their sparser counterparts. But this doesn't mean that quantitative profligacy itself is the problem. Quantitative profligacy often goes hand-in-hand with arbitrariness. It seems to me that the intuitive appeal of quantitative simplicity can be captured by (i) a prohibition on arbitrary postulates and (ii) the fact that it is often the least arbitrary to posit the smallest number of possible items.

Daniel Nolan (1997) makes the case for quantitative parsimony as a virtue by appeal to concrete examples in the history of science. As he writes, neutrinos were initially posited to make sense of a drop in energy that takes

---

Lewis: unlike concrete worlds, the materialist does not believe in any sensations, if sensations are to be understood as ontological primitives. Nevertheless, insofar as quantitative parsimony is the concern, it doesn't matter what the primitives are only how many there are. The fundamental question is whether a theory positing x things of a single kind k is (all else being equal) superior to one positing 2x things of a single kind k'. (It doesn't matter whether k = k'.)

[13] See, e.g., Nolan (1997); Sendłak (2018).

134 THE VIEW FROM EVERYWHERE

place during Beta-decay, which could not be explained by the particles known to scientists at the time. Pauli and Fermi proposed that a hitherto unknown, neutrally charged particle was emitted during Beta-decay, accounting for this otherwise inexplicable drop in energy.

This seemed a reasonable posit, and it has been confirmed by subsequent experimental results. But, as Nolan notes, at the time of Pauli and Fermi there were

> a plethora of very similar neutrino theories which would also explain the "missing energy." . . . A theory which stated that there were two "neutrinos" emitted every time Beta-decay occurred would also explain the missing mass-energy—each neutrino's mass-energy could amount to half the missing amount. A theory which postulated three "neutrinos" would also work, as would a theory postulating any finite number of neutrinos. . . . Pauli and Fermi did not consider in their papers outlining the new theory the possibility that there may be more than one tiny neutral particle produced in each case of Beta decay. I predict, however, that if someone had seriously suggested a theory which held that there were, say, exactly seventeen million "neutrinos" produced whenever there was Beta decay (or even suggested that there were only two, without further reason), their theory would have received short shrift from the two scientists (and presumably because it would have been needlessly extravagant).

By postulating a single neutrino in each case of Beta decay, rather than remaining agnostic as to the number, Nolan argues that they

> seemed disinclined to consider the more quantitatively extravagant rival theories even as being on a par with their own. They employed (if only implicitly) a principle of quantitative parsimony, and it seems counterintuitive to suppose that they were at fault for doing so. (335)

But we can agree with Nolan that postulating 17 million neutrinos in each case is less plausible and attractive than positing one without appeal to quantitative parsimony. In this case, it seems *arbitrary* to postulate 17 million neutrinos (over 16,978,321 or 649 or 7). Given that finite whole numbers go up (but not down) indefinitely, the least arbitrary number of neutrinos

SCIENCE, STRUCTURE, AND SPACETIME   135

to posit is 1.[14] The prohibition on arbitrary postulates can give us the same result.[15]

By contrast, I have posited numerous phenomenal threads and perspectives precisely to *avoid* arbitrariness. It seems arbitrary to. privilege my perspective, human perspectives, or bright-light perspectives over others. To avoid arbitrary postulates, the idealist must embrace quantitative profligacy. So while quantitatively profligate theories may often be less theoretically virtuous than their sparser competitors, there are grounds for thinking that this is not such a case.

So where does this leave us? I've granted that the idealist must admit a huge quantity of phenomenal experiences in their picture of the actual world[16] but argued that such profligacy is not a significant cost. First, while idealism is less simple than materialism, this is not gratuitous complexity. Rather, idealism embraces the complexity that is required to yield a world that is as our world seems. Second, quantitative profligacy is not a vice, per se. Rather, it's arbitrariness that's the vice. And idealism is not guilty of making arbitrary postulates.

Even so, it must be admitted that the question of profligacy is the biggest challenge to idealism. Perhaps you think that accounting for the world *seeming as it seems* is sufficient, and there is no reason to hold that it *really is* as it seems. And perhaps you just cannot shake the worry that quantitative profligacy is costly, or perhaps you think that there's no sharp line dividing quantitative and qualitative profligacy (Sendłak 2018). If so, idealism comes with costs. But every theory has its costs. It would be a mistake to look at costs in isolation. These costs must be weighed against the distinctive virtues of idealism, which we'll discuss in Chapter 6.

[14] Compare: compositional nihilism (*no* mereological composites) and universalism (*all* mereological composites) are principled options, whereas compositional restrictivism (some, but not all composites are further objects) faces worries of arbitrariness. Likewise, in Parfit's (1984) spectrum case—series of possible individuals physically and psychologically intermediate between Parfit and Greta Garbo—there is *one* principle line that could be drawn between Parfit and not-Parfit: the first step away from Parfit and toward Garbo. As these cases suggest, the first (and last) items in the series seem to be principled stopping points in a way that the intermediary options are not.

[15] By contrast, suppose it were (somehow) possible for neutrinos to come in fractional quantities corresponding to all the real numbers from 0 to 1. There would seem no reason to posit .1 neutrinos over .2, for both are equally arbitrary. Here 1 and 0 are the principled options. Thanks to Richard Chappell for this point.

[16] Though recall from §2.3.1 that this needn't be infinite.

136   THE VIEW FROM EVERYWHERE

5.3.1 Simplicity and the Laws of Nature

Perhaps the profligacy of the phenomenal threads is a cost; perhaps not. Either way, it is an unavoidable feature of a plausible idealism. But one might worry that this proliferation of phenomenal threads will also entail a proliferation of *laws* governing these threads.

Unlike quantitative profligacy, I think this would be a major cost. Fortunately for the idealist, this is *not* an unavoidable feature of idealism. In fact, we already have the tools to see why no such profligacy of laws follows from idealism. But let's start by laying out the case against the idealist.

On the materialist's worldview, the water in my cup is relatively simple: a liquid, made up of H_2O molecules, which are in turn composed of hydrogen and oxygen, which are in turn . . . down to the fundamental particles. When I put the cup in the freezer and the water turns to ice, there's a simple explanation of this phase change in terms of how the H_2O molecules interact. In liquid water, the motion of molecules prevents stable bonds from forming between molecules. But when I put water in the freezer, the kinetic energy of the water molecules decreases, allowing bonds to form. At this point, thanks to the polarity of water molecules, they bond into a hexagonal lattice structure.

The idealist has not done away with hydrogen, oxygen, or hexagonal lattices. We have given an account of the *nature* of these things. But on this account, hydrogen and oxygen are each composed of a multiplicity of phenomenal threads. Because each physical entity is so much more complex, one might worry that we'll need a correspondingly complex set of laws to govern the behavior of these entities. If there are x perspectives on each H_2O molecule, won't there need to be x laws explaining how the polar bonds form? Worse still, if each perspective must be governed by a separate set of laws, what explains the coherence of all the perspectives? It might seem like a miracle that water freezes at 0 degrees Celsius from every perspective. If separate laws govern each phenomenal thread, why expect them to all cohere? Do we need to posit meta-laws accounting for the convergence of the laws, in addition to all the first-order laws?

The same challenge arises not just at the micro-level, but at all levels of reality. I see a tennis ball fly over the net, arching downward, following a parabolic path. From my perspective, the ball is yellow. From my i-twin's perspective, the ball is blue. Don't we now need two laws (or at least two

SCIENCE, STRUCTURE, AND SPACETIME   137

applications of laws): one to explain why the yellow ball takes a parabolic path, and one to explain why the blue ball does?

No.

One way to secure this result would be to take the laws to apply to structural features that are shared by all the relevant threads of the tapestry. The yellowness of the tennis ball (from my perspective) is not what causes its parabolic path over the net, nor is its blueness from my i-twin's perspective, nor even the heavy *feel* of the ball, but rather, some more general structural property that is shared in common by all the diverse perspectives on the tennis ball. On this view, the physical laws are suitably general as to apply to each thread of the tapestry, affecting it in the appropriate manner.

For those with Humean inclinations, this strikes me as a plausible and elegant response to the problem. If laws simply are a special class of regularities, embodying both simplicity and predictive strength, this sort of generalization is precisely what one would expect. But if one is inclined to a more robust view of laws, it strikes me as in tension with the unity of the idealist's world. While this picture does away with the proliferation of laws, it retains the proliferation of *applications* of laws: the explanation for the yellowish trajectory and the explanation for the bluish trajectory are the same in kind, but they are distinct instances and are explained separately. The relevant structural features of the ball are possessed by the ball-from-my-perspective and by the ball-from-i-twin-perspective, and by . . . This might seem to result in too many applications of laws, too many forces hitting the ball over the net.

But we do not *need* one force to act on the ball-from-my-perspective and another force to act on the ball-from-i-twin-perspective. There aren't two balls (or a million). There is one ball. And an appreciation of this can help us to see a truly elegant solution to the challenge of proliferation of laws.

Recall, the idealist's reality isn't merely a collection of colors, shapes, and textures, any more than a sweater is merely a pilé of yarn. A tennis ball isn't simply {yellow, blue, . . ., sphericality}. A water molecule isn't a collection of disjoint sensory phenomenology. Reality—and all the objects within it—has *structure*. This structure is given by the relations that bind the phenomenal fibers into threads and threads into our world. We delved into this structure in detail in Chapter 2. Most crucial for purposes of this challenge, the *objects* that populate reality are structured in a particularly intimate way, through property binding. The property binding relation *literally fuses* experiences (indexed to perspectives) together into objects. There is not a yellow ball and

138 THE VIEW FROM EVERYWHERE

a blue ball that are superimposed on one another—each distinct and able to be acted on independently. Rather, there is one, unified phenomenal entity.

The analogy of the tapestry is again illustrative. An ordinary wool tapestry has structure binding all the threads together. Because of this, when we lift one thread, all the adjoining threads are lifted along with it. You don't need a separate force to act on each separate thread, *because the threads are not separate*. They are bound into a tapestry. Pick up any thread you like, and you lift them all. This same insight also explains why we can have a simple collection of laws governing the unfolding of the phenomenal tapestry: in reality, the phenomenal threads are already *structured* into objects. Affect one phenomenal thread and you affect all the threads it's property-bound with.

When I imagine a Japanese flag, and imagine drawing a line bisecting the circle, I *thereby* have imagined a line bisecting the red. I don't need to imagine two separate lines: one to bisect the circle, and one to bisect the red. The circle and the red aren't disjoint threads that can be acted on independently. Why? They are *property-bound* into a single phenomenal entity. This is just what it is to be property-bound. Once we fully appreciate what it is for the features of the tapestry to be property-bound, it's easy to see why we don't need—and, indeed, don't have room for—multiple separate laws acting on the separate threads of the tapestry. Within the tapestry, it is not just redness (from my perspective) and circularity that are property-bound, but greenness (from my i-twin's perspective) and all the other myriad perspectives. Thus, drawing a line through a Japanese flag in the tapestry not only results in a line being drawn through the circle and the redness, but also the greenness, the blueness, the %?&@-ness. Just as picking up one fiber of a wool tapestry causes all the other threads to come along ... similarly, a single law attaching to a single fiber of the phenomenal tapestry entails that all the other fibers unfold accordingly.

If I drop my pencil and it falls to the earth at 9.8 m/s^2, not only does the yellow (from my perspective) fall; the purple (i-twin's perspective) falls at the same rate. Why? There aren't two separate entities. The yellowness and the purpleness have been fused into a single object. We don't need one description of the laws of physics as they apply to the aspects of the world perceived by humans, and another as applied to the aspects of world perceived by i-twins, and another. . . . Any one of these will do. The rest comes along for free, as there aren't a multitude of disjoint worlds, but a single world. There's not a pile of threads, each of which needs to be picked up separately, but a tapestry, which can be picked up by lifting any single thread.

SCIENCE, STRUCTURE, AND SPACETIME 139

This is true not just at the macro-level of reality, but at the micro-level as well. When water cools and the molecules arrange themselves into a solid crystalline structure, this doesn't just involve phenomenology as-from a single perspective shifting. We don't need one strong force to hold together the quark experiences that make up a proton from *this* perspective, and another strong force to hold together the quark experiences from *that* perspective. While there are a multitude of phenomenal experiences indexed to perspectives, they have been fused into precisely the number of quarks that materialists take there to be. And only one force is needed to act on them.

So the idealist only needs very simple physical laws, governing the behavior of a single fiber of reality. The structure of reality is sufficient to ensure that all other aspects of reality behave accordingly. The laws need be no more complex than those appealed to by materialists.

One interesting feature of this approach is that—much as there's no privileged set of logical primitives[17]—there is no privileged iteration of the laws.[18] Pick up any single thread of the tapestry, and the rest come along for free. This is just as one would expect: there is no one privileged, glowing set of experiences, and no privileged fiber that the laws most fundamentally relate to. Reality is a structured complex unifying *all* these perspectives. What we need from the physical laws is an explanation of the unfolding of this multifaceted reality. And, thanks to the structure of reality, we can get this with laws that apply to any of its facets.

5.4 Spacetime

The phenomenal tapestry as I've described it is made up of phenomenal threads and relations among these threads. These include spatial relations and temporal relations. This might seem to imply a relationalist understanding of spacetime. But much as with the nature of physical laws, idealism is neutral when it comes to the nature of spacetime. It is compatible with both relationalism and substantivalism.[19]

---

[17] $\wedge$ can be defined in terms of $\neg$ and $\vee$, or $\vee$ can be defined in terms of $\neg$ and $\wedge$, and so on.
[18] But abstracting from what each candidate set of laws has in common may yield something like the structuralist laws that we started with.
[19] As well as anti-realism.

140   THE VIEW FROM EVERYWHERE

5.4.1 Relationalism

For the relationalist idealist, there just are phenomenal threads, standing in spatial and temporal relations. Space and time simply are the orderings of phenomenal threads in accordance with these relations. One might wonder whether this offers a genuinely *idealist* account of spacetime. The idealist's reply is: yes. On this view, all that exists is phenomenology and phenomenal relations. In virtue of what are these spatial and temporal relations *phenomenal*? In virtue of being the sorts of relations that relate phenomenology; in virtue of being relations whose nature is to structure phenomenology.

Consider two analogies: first, there is nothing anti-idealistic about phenomenal binding or the unity of consciousness. Why? In positing phenomenal bonding, the idealist is not arguing that there is an extra element to reality over and above phenomenology. They are simply positing that experiences cohere and relate to one another in certain ways. And while these relations are not themselves phenomenology, they are introspectively accessible by us insofar as their entire nature is the way that they affect phenomenology. Likewise, phenomenal spatial and temporal relations are just more relations that structure our phenomenology. And in that they affect our phenomenology, they are introspectively accessible. There is nothing anti-idealistic about them.

Second, we might flip the question around and ask the materialist relationalist: in virtue of what are your spatial and temporal relations materialistic? Aren't you abandoning your commitment to monism, to everything being material, by embracing such relations? The answer is obvious: there is nothing problematic about the materialist's appeal to spatial and temporal relations. For the materialist, these are just relations among material entities, and that is good enough. The same reply is available for the idealist: spatial and temporal relations just are the sorts of things that relate phenomenology. For an idealistic account of spacetime, that is good enough.[20]

---

[20] One question we might ask is whether the materialist and the idealist are appealing to the same relations. Perhaps the relations are neutral. This seems extremely plausible for temporal relations. Phenomenology, by contrast, is generally held not to exist in (material) space—though it undeniably has spatial features of its own.

SCIENCE, STRUCTURE, AND SPACETIME 141

5.4.2 Substantivalism

For the substantivalist idealist, there is an absolute spacetime that exists independently of the (phenomenal) objects within it. As before, one might object that qualia don't exist within space. But this only follows given a materialist understanding of space. It doesn't make sense to think of qualia as existing within a *physical* space. But the substantivalist idealist understands spacetime differently: as the sort of four-dimensional array that houses phenomenal properties.

There are two ways the idealist might make sense of this. First, they might hold that spacetime itself is not itself experiential, but is *the kind of thing that houses experiences*. On this view, spacetime would be a nonexperiential addition to our ontology—albeit one that is uniquely suited to housing and structuring phenomenology.

But there's also a more radical—and thoroughly idealistic—account open to the substantivalist idealist. On the second version of idealist substantivalism, spacetime itself is intrinsically experiential: a four-dimensional expanse of some specific qualia. (Perhaps it's a four-dimensional expanse of *flow* phenomenology.) We may not directly perceive spacetime.[21] But the phenomenal tapestry is not simply made up out of human-perceptual experiences. Even if humans cannot directly perceive substantival spacetime, it is an aspect of physical reality. And on this radical form of substantivalism, it is an additional phenomenal component of reality. We might call this Radical Idealist Substantivalism (RIS).

The analogy of a tapestry fits neatly with a relationalist view of spacetime. There are (phenomenal) threads, they stand in relations, and this is all we need to get a tapestry (of reality). For RIS, the analogy of a needlepoint might be more apt. Spacetime is itself phenomenal. But it plays the role of the canvas backing of a needlepoint, into which all the phenomenal threads making up familiar objects are woven. Ordinary subjects like us are only aware of the threads making patterns on the needlepoint, and the relations that these threads stand in to one another. But underwriting it all, the structure is "sewn

---

[21] Arguably, we're only directly aware of spatial and temporal *relations*, not of space or time themselves. On the other hand, I don't think this is *obviously* true—at least, not if the world is fundamentally phenomenal. We certainly don't see space or time. But perhaps there are other ways in which we are directly aware of it. I do seem to perceive not just temporal ordering relations, but the flow of time. Arguably, I don't just perceive my right arm as here and my left arm as there, I feel them taking up space. It would be open to the idealist substantivalist to take these to be genuine features of spacetime itself. If so, perhaps we can directly perceive spacetime. I remain agnostic on this point.

142 THE VIEW FROM EVERYWHERE

into" the backing of phenomenal spacetime. Returning to theistic idealism, this canvas backing would be experienced by God. For the nontheistic idealist, it is a constituent of God-minus (the tapestry).

I'm not interested in adjudicating which of these positions is correct. (I take it that the pros and cons of both will look no different within the idealistic context than within a materialistic one.) More interesting are the respects in which thing look *different* if we embrace idealism—a question to which we'll return in §5.4.4.

5.4.3 Temporal Phenomenology

One complication of both Radical Idealist Substantivalism and relationalism is that they presuppose that sensory experiences and relations are sufficient to account for the experienced flow of time. This assumption is not uncontroversial.

Retentionalists about temporal experiences deny that sensory experiences themselves are sufficient for the experienced flow of time. According to retentionalism, sensory experiences themselves are momentary, and packed in one after another. But these momentary sensory experiences do not account for our sense of time—its flow, its duration, its directionality. Rather, temporal experiences are complexes made up out of (a) an experience of the present moment, together with (b) a representation—perhaps memory-imagery—of the immediate past. It's this residual memory impression that accounts for our sense of a past receding from us, and the phenomenal difference between these memory impressions and our present phenomenology that accounts for the apparent primacy of the present. It is obvious that the retentional model of temporal experience cannot apply to the tapestry, as I conceive of it: the phenomenal tapestry is a structure of pure sensory phenomenology. As such, it cannot contain *representations* of the past. Furthermore, the retentionalist takes these momentary experiences to be, as I put it, "packed in one after another." Packed into what? Presumably, packed into *time*. Retentionalism uses time in order to account for the experience of time. As such, we cannot reduce time to a retentionalist experience of time.[22]

---

[22] This is not to say that an idealist cannot embrace retentionalism as the correct account of our temporal experience. We simply cannot use it to construct our account of time itself. Retentionalism is, for instance, compatible with a form of substantivalism that denies that spacetime is experiential, but takes it to be expressly suited to housing and structuring phenomenology.

By contrast, an extensionalist view of temporal experience is well suited to offering an idealist account of time. On the extensional model, experiences don't merely represent the passage of time; rather, they instantiate the unfolding of time. Within the context of the phenomenal tapestry, this means that the phenomenal threads are not momentary bits of phenomenology, but are themselves temporally extended. Perhaps—as on the overlap model (Russell 1915; Foster 1991; Dainton 2000)—what's fundamental is experiences of a brief duration, which overlap to form a phenomenally unified whole. Or perhaps (Tye 2003) what's fundamental simply is a single vast temporally extended experience. Either way, sensory experiences and their relations are sufficient to account for temporal experience, and so are suited to accounting for (objective) time within tapestry.

However, there is a worry about using this model of temporal experience to construct time itself. Extensionalism is often presented as *using* time to represent time. Experiences, for the extensionalist, are essentially temporally extended. There is no such thing as a durationless experience; rather, the smallest temporal unit of experience is what's known as the "specious present": a brief temporally extended period that's (at a minimum) sufficient in duration to yield direct phenomenal access to change and persistence. A natural way to capture this is to hold that the specious present unfolds *in* time. This suggests that there is a separate thing—objective time—within which our experiences unfold. Given this characterization, it seems circular to then use the *experience of time* to characterize objective time itself.

But the idealist can reject this characterization of extensionalism. There are not two separate things—time and the experience of time—where each is defined in terms of the other. There is one thing: there is *time*, which is fundamentally experiential in nature. Time is experiential and experiences are temporal. Experiences don't merely represent the passage of time, nor do they merely occur within an independent objective time. Time is not merely a vehicle via which experiences are presented. Rather, time is part of the *content* of our (and the tapestry's) phenomenology. This is the sense in which the idealist can hold that experiences *instantiate* the unfolding of time.

This is precisely analogous to how RIS and relationalist idealism think of space. Space does not exist independently of experience and experiential relations. There is not some independent space that houses the phenomenology of the tapestry. Rather, space is constituted either by the temporal relations between phenomenal components (relationalism) or by a vast expanse of spatial phenomenology that serves as the needlepoint of reality (RIS).

144 THE VIEW FROM EVERYWHERE

For the idealist, phenomenology constitutes reality. Structured complexes of phenomenology constitute the *tree*, the *space* that the tree exists within, and the *time* through which the tree's branches sway.

5.4.4 Temporal Flow

We've seen that idealism is compatible with both a relationalist and a substantivalist account of time (as well as space). Much as idealism doesn't commit us to a particular account of the nature of laws, it also does not commit us to a particular account of the nature of time. I think this neutrality is a virtue.

But there is one curious respect in which idealism fares differently from materialism when it comes to time, and in which the idealist has the upper hand: Unlike materialist substantivalists, substantivalist idealists can both embrace eternalism *and* accept that time flows.

For the eternalist, all moments in time are equally real. Times are past, present, or future only relative to perspectives. And there is no privileged perspective on which time is *now*—no privileged *now*, that goes marching on into the future. There is just an ordering of times, all equally real, all (correctly) perceived as *now* from the perspective of those existing at that time.

Eternalism may fit neatly within the physicist's view of the world, but it seems at odds with the common-sense *appearance* of the world. Time seems to us to *flow*. *This* time seems to us to be privileged over all other times. Eternalism seems incompatible with these appearances. Further, if no times are privileged and the present does not actually *move* into the future, we need an explanation for the directionality of time. Why doesn't time seem to be symmetrical, as space does?

Eternalists have offered many explanations for the relation between time and our experience thereof. Perhaps the apparent directionality of time is accounted for by the tendency of entropy to increase over time, or by the fact that memories are essentially backward-looking. The idealist can accept these arguments. But they also have additional resources, which are not available to the materialist, as (for the idealist) time and temporal experiences are not disjoint.

Suppose the eternalist embraces Radical Idealist Substantivalism. While there is not a privileged *now* that moves into the future (in the sense of being at this time, then at that time), RIS can hold that time objectively *flows*. Or,

SCIENCE, STRUCTURE, AND SPACETIME 145

more accurately, they can hold that time *is* flow. For RIS, time is one dimension of a four-dimensional phenomenal field. While it's pure speculation to think of this phenomenal expanse as being flow phenomenology, this is something that is an *intelligible* possibility for RIS, in a way that it isn't for materialist substantivalism.

This presupposes that the phenomenology of flow or of movement doesn't require an experience of change in location. And this is surely controversial. But it also seems, to me, correct. The experience of motion tends to go along with actual motion. Actual motion involves something changing location over time. So it's hardly surprising that the experience of motion tends to involve experiencing something *as* changing location. To determine whether this is essential to the phenomenology of motion, we should consider cases where the experience of motion comes apart from actual motion. Vertigo is one such case (of which I unfortunately have vast introspective knowledge). During episodes of vertigo, your environment seems to move in relation to you. But it does not seem to *go* anywhere. You do not seem to change position or rotate in relation to the room. There is the phenomenology of motion—of flow—but no experience as of changes in location or perspective. So it seems to me that there is, at the very least, an aspect of the phenomenology of motion that does not involve apparent changes in location. This primitive motion phenomenology—feeling like there's flow in a direction that we describe as "toward the future"—is what I (completely speculatively) propose could constitute the phenomenology of spacetime.

This doesn't give us a privileged present that moves into the future. What it does do is explain how the apparent flow of time could have its source in the nature of *time itself*, rather than being a feature of *us*.

Likewise, for the idealist, the experienced directionality of time need not be something that our minds generate. It can be part of the experience of time itself (i.e., the experiential field *that constitutes time itself*). Insofar as it makes sense to think of directionality as being something that we can have sensory experiences of, it makes sense for this to be built into the tapestry—or into the substantivalist's phenomenal backing to the needlepoint of reality. Much as the greenness that we perceive when we look at grass is a part of the tapestry, so too the experienced direction and flow of our temporal experiences could be part of RIS time. And insofar as the directionality and flow of our experiences is explained by our sensory experiences and the temporal relations among them, directionality and flow can likewise be part of the tapestry.

146   THE VIEW FROM EVERYWHERE

One final curious point to note is that idealism renders relativity less surprising. For the nontheistic idealist, reality is not just made up out of phenomenology, it's made of phenomenology from perspectives. There is no one privileged perspective on the world. Frames of reference are effectively built into the fabric of reality—with no frame of reference privileged above the others.[23] Thus, it should not be surprising to discover, for instance, that there's no such thing as absolute motion.

5.5 Conclusion

We've seen that science is neutral concerning the metaphysical nature of reality. Idealism does not entail the denial of empirical data; nor need it deny the existence of (humanly) unobservable theoretical posits, such as electrons. In fact, idealism is compatible with both realism and anti-realism regarding these entities. What idealism does is to give an account of the nature of these entities. Whether directly observable by humans or not, all physical entities are fundamentally phenomenal. Science tells us about the *structure* of reality. Idealism tells us about the *nature* of the reality that is so-structured. So it should not be too surprising to find that the two are not in tension.

Perhaps more surprising is the compatibility of idealism with philosophical interpretations of science. But we've seen that each account of laws of nature that is available to materialists is likewise available to idealists. Materialists and idealists simply give differing accounts of the natures of the entities that the laws relate. Likewise, idealism is compatible with both substantivalism and relationalism about space and time. There is no basis to the popular belief that idealism runs contrary to science.

Idealism does posit more quantitative complexity than materialism. But it does so in service to a greater explanatory payoff. We learn about the world through the experiences we have of it: through the way things look, feel, taste, sound, and smell. This includes not only the things we discover directly, but those that we learn about via instruments and experimentation. We can learn about cells via the experiences we have looking through a microscope. We can learn about the structure of atoms via the experiences that we have shooting alpha particles at a thin sheet of gold foil.

---

[23] Though the different perspectives present within the tapestry must respect the invariance of spacetime intervals.

SCIENCE, STRUCTURE, AND SPACETIME   147

For the materialist, our experiences may *reflect* the world we live in, but they do not literally present us with reality. Greenness is not part of the world. Rather, our experience of greenness indicates something about the world, in much the same way that smoke might indicate fire. But what we see is smoke and mirrors. What we experience is indications, reflections of reality. For the idealist, appearances don't merely *reflect* the reality of the world, they *present us with* the reality of the world. The world really does contain color, heat, scent. The apparent greenness of the leaf is a real, primitive aspect of reality.

Because the idealist grants the reality of these appearances, and because human experiences are not ontologically privileged, the idealist has more to incorporate into her worldview than the materialist does. This renders the idealist's reality more complex than the materialist's. But I've argued that this is not a terrible cost. While idealism is not as simple as materialism, it does not contain gratuitous complexity. Rather, idealism embraces the complexity that is required to yield a world that is as our world seems (and no more). And while arbitrariness is a theoretical vice, mere quantitative profligacy is not.

In the final chapter, I'll argue that giving us a world that is as it appears is not merely a *feature* of idealism, but a *virtue*. Science and scientific theory are neutral between idealism and materialism. Other considerations are not.

6

The Virtues of Idealism

This book has differed from other work on idealism in that I have not, to this point, offered an argument for embracing an idealist metaphysics. My focus has been on offering a fleshed-out positive account of an idealist metaphysics—something that I think idealists owe us, and that has not been given adequate attention to date. But why, you may well wonder, should we take this idealist metaphysics seriously? It's all well and good to daydream up alternative metaphysics. But wasn't our old materialist starting point good enough? In the absence of a "master argument"—an argument "refuting realism" (Foster 2008)—why should we bother considering such a radical revision to our view of the nature of reality?

I don't have a refutation of realism in my back pocket. I don't have an argument that you must abandon your materialist ways and embrace a new idealist world order. I don't have such an argument because there *are* no such arguments.[1] The space of possible worlds is vast. Some of these possible worlds are materialist worlds, some presumably are worlds bottoming out in 0s and 1s (Chalmers 2010) or other strange things we cannot even dream of ... and some are idealist worlds. Not all of the idealist worlds will correspond to the world as I've described it. I take it that there are idealist possible worlds far thinner than I take our world to be—e.g., worlds that are phenomenal tapestries of the sort that I've described, but where the tapestry only includes phenomenology as from a human perspective. I take it that there are idealist worlds far thicker than I take ours to be—e.g., worlds that include cognitive phenomenology as part of the fabric of the tapestry. I take it that there are possible worlds in which the tapestry is phenomenally unified with beliefs,

---

[1] This is a bold claim—and one with which other idealist-sympathizers may disagree. Ingenious attempts at such arguments have been devised by philosophers including Berkeley (1996), Foster (1982, 1993, 2008), Pelczar (2015, 2022, 2019)—for phenomenalism, and Builes (2024). I do not think any of these arguments succeeds in their ambitious goal. But it is not my task to refute these arguments here. If you disagree with my assessment, you can take my case for idealism to simply give some positive upshots that come from embracing the inevitable idealistic conclusion.

The View from Everywhere. Helen Yetter-Chappell, Oxford University Press. © Oxford University Press 2025. DOI: 10.1093/9780197795057.003.0006

THE VIRTUES OF IDEALISM 149

desires, complete knowledge, and absolute love along the lines of the Judeo-Christian God.

If I'm right that the space of possible worlds is vast in this way, the question is not (a) how can we demonstrate that all possible worlds have X as their ultimate metaphysical nature? Rather, the question is (b) how confident should we be that—from among the vastness of modal space—our world is a world of the X sort, rather than of the Y sort? In order to answer this question, it is not enough to consider pieces of theories in isolation—as though comparing individual puzzle pieces from two puzzles. We need to have fully fleshed-out theories, with all the pieces standing together, to hold side by side. We need to look at the total worldviews on offer, to see which overall offers the more compelling/plausible picture of our world.

Now that we have such a fleshed-out theory—a theory of the nature of the physical world, and of how conscious subjects like us fit into it and grasp it—we are in a position to evaluate it in relation to its materialist (and other) competitors as a complete account of the world and our place in it. Sections 6.1–6.3 compare the total idealist world view with the rival materialist picture. In §6.1, I consider three prima facie advantages that idealism has over its materialist alternatives: (i) It offers us a picture of reality on which the nature of reality is intelligible (*Fundamental Intelligibility*). Not only is reality intelligible, (ii) it is as it appears (*Edenic Reality*), and (iii) its nature and character is something that we can grasp directly (*Open Window*). If our world is an idealist world, we live in David Chalmers's (2006) perceptual Eden. §6.2 argues that these putative benefits are uniquely available to idealists—contrary to what naïve realists would have us believe. §6.3 makes the case that these putative benefits truly are theoretical virtues—features that should increase our credence that we live in a world of the sort I've described. Finally, §6.4 compares my nontheistic idealism with other "mind-first" alternatives, including panpsychism, phenomenalism, and theistic idealism.

6.1 Living in Eden

If the physical world is a phenomenal tapestry of the sort described, then it is *Fundamentally Intelligible*, in a way that it isn't on standard materialist pictures. This point is a familiar one, which has been made by panpsychists (Russell 1927, 1948; Eddington 1928; Strawson 2006; Goff 2017) as well as idealists (Sprigge 1983; Foster 1982, 2008; Robinson 2022) to motivate the

150 THE VIEW FROM EVERYWHERE

idea that there is something intrinsically experiential about reality. As Foster (1993, 294–295) puts it, materialism

> imposes a severe limit on the scope of our knowledge of [the physical world]. For, within the realist framework, we can at best acquire knowledge of the structure and organization of the physical world, not, at least at the fundamental level, of its content. Thus while … we may be able to establish the existence of an external space with a certain geometrical structure (one that is three-dimensional, continuous, and approximately Euclidean), we can never find out what, apart from this structure, the space is like in it-self: we cannot discover the nature of the thing which has these geometrical properties and forms the medium for physical objects.

Physics is likewise unable to provide an account of the natures of the objects that fill space, giving us only a relational characterization of these objects. Fundamental physical properties—mass, charge, spin—are all characterized by physics in terms of how they dispose entities to relate to one another. Fundamental physical objects are characterized in terms of how these entities relate to other physical entities, that are themselves so-characterized.

But the challenge for the materialist is not simply that science fails to specify what the intrinsic nature of reality is. When we look about logical space for candidates, the only possibilities we seem to find are experiential. In experience, I seem to be presented with a substantial reality, not merely an empty structure. I can grasp the possibility that reality is as it appears, or that reality is very different from how it appears, but every contentful possibility that I can wrap my mind around is equally phenomenalistic: They all make reference to phenomenology to provide the content.

The point is not that phenomenology is the only thing that could be the intrinsic nature of reality, but that it is the only possibility that is *intelligible to us*. Insofar as it's a virtue of a metaphysical picture that it renders reality comprehensible, idealist (and other mind-first) accounts of reality have an advantage. (I'll argue that this intelligibility does in fact constitute a theoretical virtue in §6.3.)[2]

---

[2] Cf. T. S. L. Sprigge's (1983) fourth argument for panpsychism. Sprigge develops an argument (which he attributes to Bradley): "there are two main claims involved here: first, that no human subject, however much he tries, will be able to conceive of some 'piece of existence' which is not psychical; second, that we should take this as evidence that the notion of any other sort of existence is radically nonsensical, and that, therefore, there could be no such thing." I agree with the spirit of this claim, but my claim is weaker: first, we cannot form any positive conception of the nature of reality,

THE VIRTUES OF IDEALISM   151

But not only is reality intelligible on the idealist's picture: *reality is as it appears*. We live in an *Edenic Reality*.[3] Philosophers of mind are at constant pains to distinguish green (the property of the tree's leaves) from phenomenal greenness (the quality of my experience). This distinction flummoxes any number of undergraduate students, who continually run the two together. While materialists tell us that colors are either unreal or radically different from how they seem, the idealist can hold that the greenness of the leaves precisely *is* the look that I'm acquainted with when I gaze at them.[4] The greenness of the leaves *is* green—the vibrant greenish *look* that I'm acquainted with. As Berkeley writes, "I cannot for my life help thinking that snow is white, and fire hot" (D3, 172). And for the idealists, we needn't doubt this. Fire is hot in a way that goes beyond its having high molecular kinetic energy. It is *hot*. Snow is *white*. Leaves are *green*. And—as argued in §5.4.4— time *flows*. As Berkeley sums up his view at the end of the Third Dialogue,

> My endeavours tend only to unite, and place in a clearer light, that truth which was before shared between the vulgar and the philosophers:—the former being of opinion, that THOSE THINGS THEY IMMEDIATELY PERCEIVE ARE THE REAL THINGS; and the latter, that THE THINGS IMMEDIATELY PERCEIVED ARE IDEAS, WHICH EXIST ONLY IN THE MIND. Which two notions put together, do, in effect, constitute the substance of what I advance.

This point goes beyond the idea that reality is fundamentally intelligible on the idealist picture. Not only is reality intelligible; we live in a "world with

---

which is not phenomenal. (This is not surprising: to consciously grasp something, the something must be thought of consciously.) And second, *insofar as intelligibility to us is a theoretical virtue*, this is a point in favor of theories that take reality to be fundamentally phenomenal. I don't think that this shows that a material physical world is "unmeaning" (as Bradley [1893] puts it). I don't think this observation by itself demonstrates that the world is fundamentally phenomenal. It is but one point to weigh as we consider which is the overall more plausible worldview. But it is a point that tells in favor of idealism.

[3] Robert Smithson (2023) defends a view that he calls "edenic idealism" that is quite different from the "naïve idealist" account developed here. Smithson's edenic idealist "acknowledges the existence of a mind-independent external world. But in contrast to the realist, she maintains that our *ordinary object judgments* are about the manifest world: the world of primitive objects and properties presented to us in experience" (1–2, emphasis added).
[4] Materialist proponents of color naïve realism will insist that materialism is compatible with this intuitive view of color. We'll return to the simple theory of color in §6.2.2, where I'll argue that it faces serious challenges.

152 THE VIEW FROM EVERYWHERE

respect to which our visual experience is perfectly veridical" (Chalmers 2006, 75). This is a distinctive benefit that's arguably unique to idealism.

One might object that idealism does not give us a reality that is as it seems, as the world does not seem to be experiential. The cup before me seems to instantiate the *quality* blueness, but it does not seem to instantiate the *phenomenal property* blueness. It is undeniable that common sense does not tell us that the world is fundamentally experiential. But this is a high-level interpretation of our experience, and not something directly given to us in perception.

Edenic Reality is *not* the claim that the world is such that all of our common-sense views are true. Rather, it is the claim that the world is such that, generally speaking, our perceptual experiences are perfectly veridical— that the apple before me truly is *red* in just the way that my visual experience presents it as being, that snow truly is *cold*, that the table truly is *solid*.

The world as it is given to us in perception does not distinguish between qualities and phenomenal properties. You can see this by deliberately trying to imagine what it would seem like to veridically perceive a world constituted by phenomenal properties. I hazard that it would seem precisely as our world seems. Philosophers may *judge* that the world is not fundamentally experiential, but our visual experiences do not make such a claim. So it is not in tension with the idealist's ability to secure an Edenic world—a "world with respect to which our visual experience is perfectly veridical."

Our perceptions do not merely *correspond* to reality. Given the theory of perception defended in Chapter 4, our perceptions of the world are unmediated: in perception, our minds are literally *constituted by* aspects of the physical world. The appearance is the reality. Perception is an *Open Window* through which we can reach out and grasp the world.

This also makes clear how naïve idealism accounts for makes good on Mark Johnston's (2011) neglected epistemic virtue. Johnston argues that veridical perception confers a distinctive epistemic virtue that (e.g.) a perfect blind-sighter would lack—a virtue that arises from the fact that I am consciously acquainted with the truthmakers of my perceptual judgments. Imagine a philosopher's fantasy of a blind-sight patient, who has no conscious experience of seeing the tree (or anything else), but who both has a reliable causal relation to their visual surroundings and can report reliably on all visible details. The blind-sight patient truly believes that the tree's leaves are a dark silver-green, is justified in believing this, and even (arguably) knows this. Nevertheless, Johnston argues, there is a sort of epistemic

THE VIRTUES OF IDEALISM   153

virtue that she lacks in making this judgment, and which my corresponding judgment has. When I form the perceptual judgment that the tree's leaves are a dark, silvery green, it is the dark silver-green of the leaves that is the truthmaker for this judgment, and which I recognize as the truthmaker for the judgment. By contrast, the blind-sighter has no such conscious awareness. Her beliefs may be just as reliable as mine, but I am in a more intimate contact with the truth of my belief. I don't merely know that the leaves are silver-green, I am *aware of* the silver-greenness that renders my belief true. As Johnston (2011, 205) puts it: "Thanks to this neglected virtue, we are in, and can see ourselves as being in, an epistemically reassuring situation, one not available to ... the blind-sighter."

Suppose perception is merely a matter of a causal chain connecting us with the truthmakers for our judgments—such that a conscious experience representing the truthmaker is had at the end of the chain. It's difficult to see how this representation of the truthmaker at the end puts us in a superior epistemic position to the blind-sighter. For perception to have Johnston's neglected virtue, we must be conscious of the truthmakers for our judgments in a stronger, more direct way. Naïve idealism gives us this: the dark silver-green of the tree's leaves is a *constituent* of my conscious experience. Awareness of the truthmaker grounds my perceptual judgment.

Thus, if naïve idealism is correct we are living in Chalmers's Eden (2006):

In the Garden of Eden, we had unmediated contact with the world. We were directly acquainted with objects in the world and with their properties. Objects were simply presented to us without causal mediation, and properties were revealed to us in their true intrinsic glory.

When an apple in Eden looked red to us, the apple was gloriously, perfectly, and primitively red. There was no need for a long causal chain from the microphysics of the surface through air and brain to a contingently connected visual experience. Rather, the perfect redness of the apple was simply revealed to us. The qualitative redness in our experience derived entirely from the presentation of perfect redness in the world.

Eden was a world of perfect color. (49)

As Chalmers continues:

[I]n the purest Edenic worlds, subjects do not perceive instances of perfect color by virtue of having color experiences that are distinct from but related

154　THE VIEW FROM EVERYWHERE

to those instances. That would seem to require a contingent mediating connection. Instead, Edenic subjects perceive instances of perfect colors by standing in a direct perceptual relation to them: perhaps the relation of acquaintance. Edenic subjects still have color experiences: there is something it is like to be them. But their color experiences have their phenomenal character precisely in virtue of the perfect colors that the subject is acquainted with.... We might say: in Eden, if not in our world, perceptual experience extends outside the head. (78)

While Chalmers presents Eden as a myth capturing our naïve intuitions—a place (or a mindset) we departed from when we ate from the trees of science and illusion—it could just as well be a statement summarizing the joint metaphysical/perceptual theory developed in this book. The idealist lives in Eden. And life in Eden is sweet.

6.2　Why Not Naïve Realism?

I've argued that the idealist can offer an attractive picture of reality and our connection to it, on which perception affords us an *Open Window* into an *Edenic Reality* whose nature is *Fundamentally Intelligible* to us. But is idealism *uniquely* able to offer such a picture? Or could we embrace materialism and still reap these benefits? Naïve realists embrace the virtues I've claimed on behalf of idealism but take such virtues to be perfectly compatible with materialism.

Naïve realists about perception take the physical world to be material yet take themselves to account for our direct grasp of the character of the world. If they are right, *Open Window* perceptual experience is not unique to idealism, undercutting it as an advantage of idealism. And naïve realists about color take colors to be simple, sui generis properties of objects, rather than the complex physical or dispositional properties we learn about from science. But these properties are held to be mind-independent. If this naïve view is coherent, it would show that materialists can embrace an intuitively plausible account of the nature of the world we live in: one on which leaves are primitively green (and, extending the argument from color to other sensible properties, fire is primitively hot, desks are primitively solid, and so on). Thus, an *Edenic Reality* could also be captured by the materialist. This would

THE VIRTUES OF IDEALISM   155

significantly weaken the appeal of idealism and the motivation for revising our metaphysical assumptions.

We'll begin by considering naïve realism about perception. I'll argue that the naïve view can only be rendered intelligible if the external world has the correct nature: if it's fundamentally phenomenal. This is because the acquaintance relation on which the naïve view depends can only intelligibly relate us to phenomenal items. In §6.2.2 I'll return to consider the naïve view of color (and other sensible properties), arguing that it faces serious challenges that undercut its ability to account for the world being as it appears.

6.2.1 Perceptual Naïve Realism

According to naïve realists, our perceptions—or at least the phenomenal characters of our perceptions—are constituted by objects in the world.[5] As Michael Martin (1997, 83) puts it:

> the actual objects of perception, the external things such as trees, tables and rainbows, which one can perceive, and the properties which they can manifest to one when perceived, *partly constitute one's conscious experience*, and hence determine the phenomenal character of one's experience. (emphasis added)

Fish (2009, 14–15) concisely summarizes the naïve relevant feature of the naïve realist's position:

> The distinctive feature of naive realism lies in the claim that, when we see the world, the subject is *acquainted* with the elements of the presentational character-the mind-independent objects and their features-where "acquaintance" names an irreducible mental relation that the subject can only stand in to objects that exist and features that are instantiated in the part of the environment at which the subject is looking. Moreover, the naive realist also claims that it is the particular elements of the environment that the subject is acquainted with that shape the contours of that subject's conscious experience. . . . Why is it like *that* to have that experience? Because

---

[5] Different naïve realists describe this idea slightly differently. Martin (1997) writes that these objects partially constitute *the experience*. Campbell (2002) writes that they constitute the *phenomenal character* of the experience. Nudd (2009) writes that they constitute experiential *episodes*.

156 THE VIEW FROM EVERYWHERE

in having the experience, the subject is acquainted with thus-and-such objects and their properties....

[A]ccording to the naive realist, the *phenomenal* character of the experience—the property of the experience that types the experience by what it is like to have it—is the property of acquainting the subject with such-and-such a presentational character. In this way, we can see how this thesis accommodates the idea that the very elements of one's environment can be said to shape the contours of one's conscious visual experiences.

The naïve realist's account of perception and the theory of perception defended in Chapter 4 agree about much: (a) Both hold that perception involves a direct relation of acquaintance with the distal objects of perception. (b) Both hold that when we stand in this relation to an object, the object thereby (partially) constitutes our perceptual experience. And (c) both hold that—because of this direct relation to the object—we have special epistemic access to the object. Where the views disagree is in the nature of the objects that we have direct acquaintance with. This might seem like a separate issue, that can be evaluated independently from (a)–(c). But I will argue that— contrary to naïve realism—direct acquaintance with reality is only open to us if reality is fundamentally phenomenal, since it's only if reality is phenomenal that we can account for the acquaintance relation that makes such contact possible.

Naïve theories of perception are predicated on the possibility of our standing in a relation of direct acquaintance with the real objects in the world that we perceive. The acquaintance relation is not just any old relation. It's a relation that affords us a special epistemic contact with objects, by putting us in direct contact with the truth-makers of our perceptual judgments. But how does it yield the epistemic benefits that naïve theorists take it to afford? *What is it that this acquaintance relation consists in?* I will argue that the naïve idealist, but not the naïve realist, can offer an account of this central relation.

Asking for an account of acquaintance might seem unreasonable—like too much to demand. Naïve realists generally take acquaintance to be a primitive relation. Perhaps there simply isn't any more that can be reasonably said of it beyond an account of the epistemic benefits it yields. After all, while some relations can be further explained, others are bedrock. One might be a sibling in virtue of having the same biological parents or having been raised together with another child by the same parents. But nothing illuminating can be said

THE VIRTUES OF IDEALISM 157

to explain the identity relation to one who doesn't understand it. Can't naïve realists maintain that we've hit bedrock? If so, surely it's unreasonable to expect further elucidation that renders the relation intelligible?

While it would be ridiculous to demand an explanation of how the identity relation works, it would also be a mistake to think that the existence of such bedrock relations absolves the naïve realist from any obligation to offer an account of acquaintance.

Holding that a relation is sui generis does not always absolve those who appeal to the relation from the need for further explanation. Suppose you're told that there's a relation such that when three things stand in it, it makes them both three and one, simultaneously. Call this the trinity relation. It's a sui generis relation, you're told, so you can't reasonably expect any further illumination of it. Should we believe that there is such a trinity relation? Perhaps. But belief in such a relation relies on faith: faith in God and faith in the veracity of divinely inspired texts. And I don't think our theory of perception should be predicated on faith in this sort of way.

The identity relation does not seem mysterious. Once we're told what the identity relation is, there's no further vexing sense of mystery or need to explain how it could obtain. By contrast, the trinity relation leaves us with just such a sense. In this, the acquaintance relation is more akin to the trinity relation: it beckons for an explanation. This is reminiscent of the explanatory gap that we find between phenomenal and physical truths. There seems to be no explanation forthcoming for why CFF feels hurty. While anti-physicalists maintain that physicalism requires there to be such an explanation, physicalists have noted that there are plenty of other cases of identity claims that do not have explanations: instances where we have simply hit explanatory bedrock and it would be ridiculous to ask for more. (Why is now = 2025) But the fact that there are *some* identity claims that are bedrock does not itself dispel the need to say more for every proposed identity claim. When we're told that now = 2025 we feel no sense of mystery. This does not beckon for further explanation. By contrast, the question of why some neural state should *feel like this* is the stuff that keeps us awake at night. Likewise, the trinity relation beckons for an explanation;[6] so, too, the acquaintance relation calls out for explanation. How can minds grasp physical objects? How can we gain this special epistemic access to the world outside of our minds?

---

[6] An explanation that we lack, but which the Christian will take to exist and to be understood by God.

158   THE VIEW FROM EVERYWHERE

Martin (1997) tells us that trees and tables partially constitute conscious experiences. But *how* could that be? We open our eyes and direct our gaze to the scene before us, and then ... magic happens? Given the central role that the relation plays for naïve realists and idealists—the work that is done by the relation—the need for an explanation is all the more pressing.

So let's see if either idealism or naïve realism can offer an account of how the acquaintance relation works: an account that will render our contact with reality *intelligible*. If neither can, we'll need to assess whether an essentially mysterious naïve view (on which perception involves a direct relation of acquaintance with the world, but it's unintelligible how) is preferable to an unmysterious representationalism (which makes no claim of putting us in direct contact with reality). But if, as I'll argue, the idealist is uniquely able to offer an account of acquaintance that renders our contact with the world intelligible, then idealism will constitute a clear win for idealism over its competitors.

According to idealism, the apple before me is a unified collection of phenomenology. Some of the phenomenal "threads" making up the apple are qualitatively identical to the experiences I have as I look at the apple. In perception, psycho-physical bridging laws function as laws of phenomenal fusion: ensuring that some of the phenomenology that is unified with my mind is numerically one and the same as the phenomenology making up the tapestry. Much as it's intelligible for the unity of consciousness relation to bind together (a) the pain in my arm with (b) my proprioceptive sense of my arm and (c) my wondering what's causing the pain, so too it's intelligible that the unity of consciousness could bind together (d) the greenness of the apple with (e) my imagining its sweet-tartness. For although the greenness is a property of the apple, it is also genuinely phenomenal. Assuming phenomenal unities can overlap (as I argued in §4.1.1), there is nothing remarkable about this phenomenal greenness being a component of my mind. Thus, it's unmysterious what it is for my mind to overlap with the world. The world is the stuff of minds. The apple's[7] being an element of my mind is no more baffling than my hallucination's being a part of my mind, for both are fundamentally phenomenal. And there is no mystery as to what it is that renders the apple part of my mind: it is the same relation that we all agree unifies our phenomenology—the unity of consciousness relation.

---

[7] The perceived aspects of the apple.

THE VIRTUES OF IDEALISM 159

Given that the perceived facets of the world are elements of my mind in precisely the same sense as my pains and musings, it should be no surprise that accounts of our acquaintance with our own minds are equally available for the idealist to account for our acquaintance with the physical world. To find an intelligible account of perceptual acquaintance, idealists need look no further than the well-developed literature on introspective acquaintance.

We've seen that naïve idealists (alongside naïve realists) hold that (a) perception involves a direct relation of acquaintance with objects of perception; (b) when we stand in this relation to an object, the object thereby constitutes our perceptual experience; and (c) because of this direct relation to the object, we have special epistemic access to the object. Acquaintance theorists about introspection embrace analogous claims about phenomenal judgments and our introspective access to our minds: (a′) Introspective phenomenal judgments involve our standing in a direct relation of acquaintance with our phenomenology. (b′) In forming such phenomenal judgments, our phenomenology partially constitutes our phenomenal judgments. And (c′) because of this direct acquaintance with our phenomenology, we have an especially intimate epistemic access to it. As Balog (2012, 30) writes:

We know our conscious states not by inference but by immediate acquaintance which gives us direct, unmediated, substantial insight into their nature. If phenomenal concepts are partly constituted by phenomenal states, our knowledge of the presence of these states (in the first person, subjective way of thinking of them) is not mediated by something distinct from these states. Rather the state itself serves as its own mode of presentation.... [A]cquaintance, on this account, is the special, intimate epistemic relation we have to our phenomenal experience through the shared phenomenality of experience and thought. Shared phenomenality produces the sense that one has a direct insight into the nature of the experience. Hence the unique epistemic standing of acquaintance.

In what follows I'll show how this can help the naïve idealist to give an intelligible account of acquaintance. Let's start with the question of how we are related to the objects of our introspective (and perceptual) judgments. I am partial to the constitutional account of phenomenal judgments, developed by Gertler (2001, 2012), Papineau (2002), Chalmers (2003), Levine (2006), and Balog (2012). But given the idealist's account of reality and subjects, we

160 THE VIEW FROM EVERYWHERE

should expect that any suitable account of introspective acquaintance will be equally suitable to the naïve idealist's task.

Here is the basic idea of the constitutional account of phenomenal judgments: our thoughts—and ultimately our knowledge—of our experiences are *partially constituted* by the relevant experiences. Much as I can refer to the word d-o-g by embedding it in quotation marks, the idea is that there is a kind of "mental quotation mark" that can be used to turn a mental object into an expression referring to that object. When you find yourself thinking of a piece of music by humming it—"what's that song that goes *dum dum dum, duuu du-dum*?"—you embed the music as a part of your thought.[8] Likewise, we can think about our experiences by mentally "quoting" them. You might think: *pain* feels horrible! Here, it's not a word or a description of pain that's an element of your thought, but an instance of the very experience itself. As Balog (2012, 30) puts it:

> If phenomenal concepts are partly constituted by phenomenal states, our knowledge of the presence of these states (in the first person, subjective way of thinking of them) is not mediated by something distinct from these states. Rather the state itself serves as its own mode of presentation. . . . When I focus on the phenomenal quality of that visual perception—not on what it represents but on the qualitative character of the visual experience—my representation contains that very experience. Thinking about it and simply having the experience will then share something very substantial, very spectacular: namely the phenomenal character of the experience.

This account renders it intelligible how there could be a relation between subjects and objects, that puts subjects in direct contact with the object in a way that gives them privileged epistemic contact with the object. When I judge *pain* feels horrible, my thought is itself composed from the objects of my belief. I do not stand "at a distance" from its truth-makers, as with a causal relationship. Rather, the nature of the object of my belief—the essence of pain—is directly presented to me (it is a constituent of me) as the means by which I think about pain. Because the very phenomenal experience that

---

[8] While many who embrace the quotational/constitutional account of phenomenal concepts take our experiences to be essentially representational, this is not essential to the account, as the case of mentally "quoting" music makes clear.

THE VIRTUES OF IDEALISM   161

is the object of my thought is being used to do the thinking, the truth of my judgment is especially secure.

This is precisely the sort of account we need. It renders the acquaintance relation intelligible by explaining it in terms of another, well-grasped, prosaic relation. This makes it clear how this relation can do the important epistemic work that philosophers are putting it to.

Just as my pain is a part of my mind, for the idealist, the tree I see outside my window is also a part of my mind. Just as I can "mentally quote" pain to form a phenomenal judgment that gives me direct insight into the nature of pain, I can also "mentally quote" tree to form a perceptual judgment that gives me direct insight into (the perceived features of) the tree. So the idealist can offer precisely the same account of introspective and perceptual judgments.

What conditions must be satisfied for this kind of mental quotation to be possible? What is it that enables us to stand in this relation to the objects of judgment?

Two conditions seem obvious to me: the quoted item must be (i) a phenomenal item (ii) of the subject who quotes it. Starting with the first condition: a material apple cannot be a constituent of my mind, and so cannot be a literal constituent of my *thought*, any more than a material apple can be a constituent of a video game. And second, I cannot mentally "quote" *your* thoughts, as they stand at a distance from me. It is only those thoughts that are *present within my mind* that I can use to form referring expressions (cf. Calkins [1927]).[9]

---

[9] This argument bears strong similarities to an argument that Kris McDaniel (2017) identifies in the work of Mary Whiton Calkins (1927). As McDaniel summarizes:

> The first argument for idealism is based on the premise that, in general, no relation can obtain between two things unless there is a qualitative commonality between the two things; relations are not instantiated independently of the "inner properties" of things, and hence in this sense all relations are "internal." The second premise is that a necessary condition of qualitative commonality is being of the same basic ontological kind. The third premise is that we are not material entities, but rather are mental entities, and that mental entities and material entities do not belong to the same basic ontological kind.... The fourth premise is that there is a relation of knowing between a person and an object of knowledge, the latter of which is a thing rather than, e.g., a proposition. (Perhaps the kind of knowledge invoked here is better described as one that involves acquaintance with things, since it does not seem to be straightforwardly a propositional attitude.) It follows from these four premises that everything that we have knowledge of is a mental entity rather than a material entity. (152–153)

The premises of this argument are more general than those I have endorsed. In particular, I have not argued that relations *in general* can only obtain between things that share a qualitative commonality. But it seems to me that the relation of constitution is such that it requires qualitative commonality and sameness of basic ontological kind.

162 THE VIEW FROM EVERYWHERE

If mental quotation is what acquaintance consists in, clauses (i) and (ii) are the enabling conditions for the relation. But arguably this explanation carves things up wrong. One might think that mental quotation here is not *explaining* acquaintance, but rather is a further thing that is *enabled by* acquaintance. Acquaintance, rather, is the more primitive relation that I stand in to objects that satisfy (i) and (ii). If this is right, acquaintance itself affords epistemic access only in that it is the enabling condition for gaining a certain sort of direct knowledge—knowledge that is gained when one forms a direct phenomenal judgment. Acquaintance is a precondition for knowledge-by-acquaintance but does not itself afford such knowledge.

On this way of understanding the acquaintance relation, standing in the relation is a matter of satisfying (i) and (ii)—the conditions for mental quotation. Hence, the acquaintance relation would be better understood as the unity of consciousness relation, which takes phenomenal items and binds them together as part of the unity of me. On this model, I'm acquainted with the peripheral experiences that I'm not currently attending to, by virtue of being phenomenally unified with these experiences. But it's only when I come to attend to them in the right way—forming a direct phenomenal judgment—that I gain privileged knowledge of them. Whereas on the mental-quotation-as-acquaintance model, I'm only acquainted with these peripheral experiences once I form the correct sort of judgments.

I don't think it much matters which of these we think of as the "acquaintance relation" and which we think of as mere enabling conditions. The upshot is the same. I can have privileged access to only those entities that I'm phenomenally unified with, and I actually get such privileged access only when I engage in an act of mental quotation. And neither mental quotation itself nor phenomenal unity (*with phenomenal items*) is mysterious. The constitutional analysis described above explains the former, and the accounts of the unity of consciousness relation discussed in Chapter 2 dispel the mystery of the latter.

Where does this leave us? Acquaintance, as we have seen, has been appealed to in order to play two roles in the philosophy of mind: accounting for the epistemic access we have to our own minds, and accounting for our relation to distal objects of perception.

If the apple is a collection of experiences, then (provided that the experiences are ones with which my mind is phenomenally unified) the same theory of acquaintance can play both roles. I can stand in precisely the same relation to the apple as I do to my pain. Idealist apples (at least the aspects of

THE VIRTUES OF IDEALISM   163

them that I perceive) can be constituents of my mind in precisely the same way as my pains. When I judge that there is an apple before me, I no more stand at a distance from my thought's truth-maker than I do to the truth-makers for sensation judgments (Yetter-Chappell 2018a, 2024a, 2024b).

So idealists are able to give a *unified* account of the acquaintance relation—one that renders it *intelligible* what acquaintance with distal objects consists in, and how it yields the epistemic benefits that relational accounts of perceptual experience are supposed to afford.

By contrast, for the analogy to introspective acquaintance to help the naïve realist, it would have to be intelligible that a non-mental item could be phenomenally unified with my mind. Unfortunately, this is not only mysterious, but *manifestly incoherent*. Minds can contain sensations, thoughts, feelings, and desires. But a mind cannot have a (non-mental) material apple as a constituent. Only the right sorts of things—phenomenal things—can be bound together by phenomenal unity relations. Only the right kinds of things—mental things—can be components of minds. And a material apple cannot form a constituent of my mind any more than a material apple can be a constituent of a computer simulation.

Insofar as mental quotation is essential to acquaintance, it might be noted that there is a sense in which it is possible to quote material objects: I can hold up an apple and think "is red"—thereby thinking of the apple that it's red. But this physical holding up of an apple does not render the apple itself a part of my mind or my thought. It does not entail any sort of epistemic access to the apple. The naïve realist might well agree with this: it's *perceiving* the apple that renders it a part of your experience, not holding the apple up. But this just brings us back to the original problem. The challenge we're considering is that of explaining how perception could render us acquainted with objects in this way. And it doesn't seem that the analogy to quotation helps to advance our understanding of this in the slightest.

Of course, just because the account of acquaintance that naïve idealists give is not open to naïve realists, this doesn't show there aren't any intelligible accounts that are open to them. I take it that naïve realists have a very different conception of experience from that of idealists. Experiences are not qualia. (Apples are not constituents of qualia.) Experiences are not brain states. (Apples are not constituents of brain states.) As Keith Allen puts it, perceptual experiences "*consist in* the obtaining of a conscious relation of awareness or acquaintance between perceiving subjects and mind-independent objects and properties in their environment" (Allen 2021, 43, emphasis

164 THE VIEW FROM EVERYWHERE

added). If this is our analysis of experience, apples can be constituents of experiences, insofar as they are constituents of a subject-acquaintance-apple completion.[10]

Unfortunately, characterizing experience in this way does not dispel the mystery. The acquaintance relation is not just any old relation. It's one that has a special epistemic significance. It's one that renders us directly *aware* of the object, *disclosing* the object of our awareness to us. How can it do this? Why is it that I can be related to objects in this way, whereas my car (with its pedestrian-detecting back-up camera) can't? What is it that distinguishes me from my perfect blind-sight twin, such that I am acquainted with the apple while she is not? As Mark Johnston (2011) might put it, the blind-sighter lacks the attentive *sensory* episodes that I have. But how is it that a material apple comes to be a constituent of an attentive sensory episode? Allen's conception of perceptual experience does not address this. The fundamental challenge remains.

If we are to have direct acquaintance with a material world, one way to do so would be to embrace a version of the Extended Conscious Mind Hypothesis according to which (i) experiences are material, and (ii) they extend into the world such that they include the distal objects of experience. Unlike local materialism, which holds that the experience of an apple is grounded in a brain state (perhaps of apple-fires-firing [AFF]), this naïve ECM view would hold that the apple experience is grounded in *AFF + material apple*. The relation between my experience and the apple would, thus, be one of constitution.

This proposal allows us to say that the apple and its properties are constituents of my experience. The trouble is that it doesn't account for the distinctive epistemic benefits that naïve realism is supposed to yield. Compare this view to an indirect view on which the experience of the apple is grounded in AFF (where these are merely caused by the apple). Why does the former, but not the latter, *disclose* the apple to the subject? It seems we've done no more than engage in some word-play, carving off "experience" in a different way. On one view, AFF is the experience, and is caused by apples. On the other, AFF + causally-related-apple is the experience. But it's hard to see why individuating experiences in one way or the other should come with the epistemic differences naïve realists take there to be between naïve views

---

[10] Where, following Kit Fine's (2000, 4) terminology, "[t]he completion of a relation R by the objects a1, a2, . . . is the state of the objects a . . . standing in the relation R."

THE VIRTUES OF IDEALISM   165

and indirect ones. We still are left with no explanation of the central mystery: if subjects are not material, how can a material world be directly related to them? And if subjects are material, how can we relate a material world to them in a way that goes beyond the material relations that fail to be world-disclosing for the representationalist?

The naïve realist asserts that perception involves a direct relation of acquaintance with the world, where this relation confers special epistemic benefits. But it is mysterious at best (and incoherent at worst) how a relation could provide such contact with a material world. Such a relation sounds like magic: a magic that is supporting the theory of perception and conferring all alleged benefits over rival theories. By contrast, if the world is fundamentally phenomenal—if the world is the sort of thing that minds are, and the sort of thing that mind-unifying relations unify—then we have a clear, intelligible account of what this acquaintance consists in.

Reality is only intelligible as something we can directly relate to and grasp if it is fundamentally experiential. If we want to account for the epistemic status we naïvely take ourselves to have on the world, we must embrace a phenomenal conception of reality.

6.2.2 Color Naïve Realism

According to the naïve realist view of color, colors are mind-independent primitive properties possessed by physical objects.[11] These primitive color properties supervene on microphysical properties but are not themselves revealed by scientific investigation. Naïve realism about color is often paired with perceptual naïve realism (e.g., Allen 2016)—the resulting view being one on which perception directly acquaints us with these primitive color properties.

Color naïve realism faces two major challenges. First, there is the question of *which* color properties objects have (Cohen 2009; Hardin 2004, 2008). The very same leaf may appear green to me, yellow-green to you, and red to my inverted twin. Which primitive color property(s) does the leaf have? The naïve realist about color has two options. They can privilege one of these appearances as the true one, or they can try to embrace the idea that

---

[11] See, e.g., Cavendish (1668); Hacker (1987); Campbell (1993); McGinn (1996); Gert (2006, 2008); Allen (2016).

166 THE VIEW FROM EVERYWHERE

objects can have many color properties at once. The first option seems arbitrary. For the same reason that we should not privilege human experiences or HYC experiences in constructing an idealist reality, there's no basis for a color naïve realist to include any one perceiver's color experiences in our ontology, to the exclusion of all others. The second option—color pluralism—is intriguing but faces serious difficulties. Color pluralism entails that the leaf is simultaneously red all over and green all over. This is not a problem per se. (Nontheistic idealism holds the same, accounted for by the indexing of phenomenal threads.) The challenge lies in whether a *materialist* can successfully account for this.

Mark Kalderon (2007) offers an elaborate defense of color pluralism, which is in many ways closely aligned with the view developed in this book. He writes:

> If there is more to the sensible qualities of an object than is manifest in a given perception, then not only might different sensible qualities of an object be perceptually available only in different circumstances of perception, but different sensible qualities of an object might be perceptually available only to different perceivers. (573)

I wholeheartedly agree. The question is whether this is compatible with the mind-independence of color. For an idealist, there was no problem holding that multiple conflicting color properties can be simultaneously instantiated, as we could intelligibly index these to different *perspectives*. But perspectives essentially require minds, at least of the thin sort discussed in §1.3.[12]

Kalderon continues:

> this raises the question whether, in veridically perceiving the object to be one color, it might also be another color. . . . From the fact that nothing can appear red all over and green all over at the same time to a given perceiver, it does not follow nothing can be red all over and green all over at the same time. (573)

Particular colors can only be able to be detected by particular apparatus. This, of course, is no different from any other (apparently) mind-independent property. Only certain systems can detect acids (or heat or

---

[12] But see Mark Johnston (2007) for dissent. I'll discuss Johnston's view in §6.2.3.

THE VIRTUES OF IDEALISM 167

pitches of 30,000 Hz). And only certain observers can perceive red. One might have thought that an object can be both red and green all over, but that we can only perceive one of these because we are simply not a system equipped to detect both.

But this cannot be the color pluralistic materialist's picture. Normally, when an object has two properties, it is at least *possible* for them to be perceived simultaneously (even if not every creature is capable of doing so). An appropriately designed agent could perceive that an object is both red and hot all over. But the same is manifestly *not* true for colors—at least if what we mean by color is the appearances that are manifest to us in perception. It is simply incoherent for there to be redness-all-over and greenness-all-over perceived of an object at a single time. (At least, this is not coherent without each color apprehended being indexed to a separate perspective. But if perspectives are essential to color, this is tantamount to colors being experiential!)

In recognition of this, Kalderon distinguishes between *colors* and the *appearance of colors*. The appearance of colors may be mind-dependent—depending on the observer together with the object. But, he argues, it doesn't follow that the color itself is. Particular colors may only be able to be detected by particular visual apparatus—but, of course, that is no different from any other mind-independent property. So the leaf is simultaneously red and green (mind-independently), but it only *appears* red or green *to minds*.

The difficulty is that this response requires that we deny that *colors* are manifest to us in perception. It requires denying that the nature and character of colors something that we can grasp directly. As Kalderon (2007, 589) writes:

> if the appearance of unique green depends on the visual system of the perceiver, then it is hard to understand how it could be the manifestation of a mind-independent quality. It is hard to understand how, as Campbell (1997, 189) puts it, "the qualitative character of a colour-experience is inherited from the qualitative character of the colour."

So even if color pluralism is able to salvage color primitivism, it does so at the expense of *Open Window*: we must deny that the nature and character of the world can be grasped directly. Worse than this, we seem to lose *Edenic Reality* as well. If *green* is distinct from *the appearance of green*, and the latter is dependent on the visual system of the perceiver, there is no reason to think

168   THE VIEW FROM EVERYWHERE

that reality is as it appears regarding color. This should not surprise us, as Berkeley is surely right that nothing can be like an idea but an idea. It's difficult to see how the materialist could hope to embrace an Edenic world.

Moreover, in addition to losing two central pretheoretic virtues, the color pluralist is forced to accept all the costs of idealism. The leaf not only has a certain microphysical structure, it also has the primitive property of greenness, and of yellow-greenness, and of redness, ... and so on. Any ontological profligacy that idealism faced confronts this view as well.

And the problem generalizes. While we've considered a primitivist view of color, color properties are only a tiny fraction of the sensible qualities we're acquainted with in perception. The same reasoning that leads some to embrace color primitivism might similarly lead one to embrace temperature primitivism, texture primitivism, and so on. And for each of these, we'll find the same push to embrace pluralism, and the same challenges that come with it. The materialist following this path will find none of the virtues of idealism, but all of the proliferation of sui generis properties. A lose, lose situation.

A second problem faced by color primitivism concerns whether (and how) such primitive properties could have causal powers (given a robust conception of causation). For color primitivism to be well motivated—and for it to have any hope at accounting for perception as an *Open Window*—we must be *aware* of these primitive colors. This, arguably, requires causation. Vision scientists have an explanation of how the surface properties of objects affect our brains (and thereby, our us). But this explanation seems complete without any reference to primitive color properties. As such, it seems there's no role left for primitive properties in affecting our sensory system.

This is structurally analogous to the problem of mental causation. We don't need to appeal to anything nonphysical to explain our behavior. As such, it doesn't seem like there's room for nonphysical properties to do causal work. So unless mental states are physical, there's no room for them to play a causal role. But our mental states intuitively do affect our behavior. (We are aware of them, after all.) Consideration of the problem of mental causation will prove illuminating to the problem of color causation.

Mental causation looks very different depending on the precise relationship between mental and physical properties. Functionalists take mental properties to be higher-level properties that are possessed in virtue of the lower-level physical properties that realize them. It's natural for functionalists to hold that mental (functional) properties are nothing over and above the physical properties but are mere abstractions from them. As such, the mental

THE VIRTUES OF IDEALISM 169

properties inherit the causal powers of the physical properties. The physical and the functional are not ontologically distinct. There are not two wholly separate properties——two separate potential causes—any more than the leaf's greenness is a wholly separate property from its lime-greenness or its $green_{255}$-ness. They are simply different levels of abstraction.

By contrast, no such account is available to property dualists. For the dualist, mental properties are wholly distinct from physical properties. There may be a nomological relationship between the two, but this is not sufficient for the inheritance of causal powers. Were there fairy-godmother-laws that caused my fairy-godmother to pop into existence every time I acted wickedly, my fairy-godmother would not thereby be the cause of my wickedness.[13] The problem is not that my fairy-godmother is *merely nomically* related to my wicked actions. Even if (somehow!) it were metaphysically necessary that she so come into existence, she would still in no way be responsible for my actions. The problem is that dualistic mental properties are ontologically distinct from the physical properties they are related to. (Compare with the metaethical case: metaethical nonnaturalists hold that normative properties supervene on natural properties. But it is not standardly held that normative properties inherit he causal powers of the physical properties that they supervene on.)

If dualistic mental states do not inherit the causal powers of the physical states that they supervene on, the dualist must offer a different response. In embracing epiphenomenalism (Yetter-Chappell 2022), I argue that dualists do not need phenomenal properties to affect physical reality in order to explain our awareness of our experiences. They can offer a different—more immediate—account of how we are aware of our phenomenal experiences: the constitutional account described in §6.2.1. If mental properties are primitive sui generis properties of the world, distinct from the physical properties, they cannot inherit the causal powers of their physical correlates. They lack causal efficacy. But we *can* be aware of them, because they are mental parts of *us*.

Let's return to the problem of color. On the naïve realist's view, (a) colors are primitive sui generis properties possessed by physical objects, which (b) supervene on physical properties of objects' surfaces. They are not abstractions from the physical properties, as functionalist mental states are.

---

[13] One might object that a simple regularity theory of causation (trivially) entails that the fairy-godmother is causally responsible for my wickedness. But this seems like a point against regularity theory, rather than a solution to the problem of mental causation.

170 THE VIEW FROM EVERYWHERE

As such, the functionalist's response to the causal problem is not available to the color primitivist. Colors, for the primitivist, are ontologically distinct from the physical properties on which they supervene; they are not mere abstractions from them.

Thus naïve realists about color are in a position more akin to that of the dualist. But naïve realists about color also hold that (c) colors are mind-independent. As a result, they also cannot embrace the dualist's response to the causal problem. For, as we saw in §6.2.1, mind-independent properties cannot be constituents of minds.

So the color primitivist cannot explain our awareness of color by causal means. Primitive colors do not inherit the causal efficacy of physical properties just by supervening on them (any more than moral properties do). Nor can they account for our awareness of color via the constitution relationship that dualists can appeal to.

It's worth considering how the idealist fares by contrast. The idealist agrees with the color primitivist that colors are primitive sui generis features of objects that nomologically supervene on the microphysical structure of objects' surface. As such, they cannot embrace the functionalist account of the inheritance of causal powers. But the idealist takes colors to be inherently phenomenal: precisely the sort of feature that constitutes minds. So an epiphenomenalist dualist account of our introspective access to qualia (Yetter-Chappell 2022) is equally well available to idealists to explain of our awareness of external color. The familiar causal picture of light reflecting off objects, together with the externalist bridging laws described in Chapter 3, causes the greenness of the leaf to become phenomenally unified with my mind. Once so-unified, my awareness of the greenness is direct and perfect.

We began with the question of whether materialists could accept that reality is as it appears. Reality appears to have primitive colors, temperatures, and sounds . . . while science reveals no more than surface reflectance properties, molecular kinetic energy, and vibrations, and the equally obscure effects that these physical phenomena have on our bodies and brains. We've looked at a materialist attempt to take color to be primitive and have found it lacking. We must either arbitrarily privilege certain appearances over others or abandon the idea that colors are manifest in their appearances. But it's no more palatable for a materialist to arbitrarily privilege certain appearance over others than it would be for the idealist to construct their world solely out of a single "privileged" perspective. (Screw your experience; *my* experiences are where it's at!) And denying that colors (and other such properties) are

THE VIRTUES OF IDEALISM 171

manifest in their appearances amounts to giving up on reality being as it appears.

Beyond this, color primitivists face a serious challenge in explaining how we can be *aware of* color. Sui generis color cannot inherit the causal powers of the physical properties they supervene on, and we cannot be aware of them directly as constituents of our minds, as the idealist can.

6.2.3 Johnston's Manifest World

The fundamental insight of naïve idealism is that naïve views of perception and color entail *metaphysical* commitments. If we are to have direct access to the world, *the world* has to be a certain way. We cannot simply embrace the standard materialist picture of reality and hope to account for special epistemic access to it. For the leaf to truly be *green* entails specific commitments regarding the nature of reality.

Mark Johnston (1998, 2007, 2011) is one philosopher who—while often characterized as a naïve realist—seems to embrace this fundamental insight. It's worth quoting from him extensively. As Johnston (2007), 247–248) puts it:

> [Our] experiences . . . are occasions of accessing objective modes of presentation of items. So our mental lives are filled with objective features of external items, namely their modes of presentation. But we get nowhere near exhausting the modes of presentation that there are. For example, there is a way things look to a being like you from three feet North East from here now, even if no one is ever occupying that perceptual standpoint. You could have accessed that way of looking if you had occupied that position; but your accessing this objective, if relational, mode of presentation would make no difference to its character or to what it presents.
>
> The transformed picture of reality associated with this idea can be brought out very simply. When you close your eyes, the objects before you are still looking the way they just did; more generally, without you on the scene they would still present in the whole variety of ways in which they now present to you. Furthermore, if that is not eerie enough, given that there are animals or conscious minds with sensibilities unlike ours, the objects before you now present in a host of ways which you could never access. . . . The specificity of your sensibility, the detailed structure of your

172 THE VIEW FROM EVERYWHERE

sensory and cognitive apparatus, in effect blinkers you to all but a very narrow range of modes of presentation of the items before you. You do not produce presence; you only selectively access it in your mental acts. What you call the contents of your mind are out there already.

Presence is therefore not a subjective phenomenon.... There is a host of events that fill our so-called "subjective" mental lives. These events are occurrent mental acts, which are objective psychological occurrences. Their contents are objective modes of presentation. These modes of presentation are standing properties of the objects themselves. It is because they have these standing properties anyway that the objects themselves are intelligible to the intellect, and available to be sensed in a variety of ways....

[T]he basic reality is not the fact of consciousness, understood as the inner achievement of a mind. It is the fact of the on-going and multifaceted disclosure of objects, which certain evolved animals are able to access.

Johnston doesn't merely offer a picture of perception as disclosure, but a picture of *how reality is* such that it can facilitate perception-as-disclosure. Reality contains *perspectival qualities*—qualities that disclose how objects appear from a particular point in space, and that are accessible only to suitably evolved creatures.

Johnston's reality is not one of empty structure. As such, it is not one that could be captured by science alone. But, Johnston assures us, it does not require subjectivity or—*shudder*—qualia. Does this show that naïve realism is a viable alternative to naïve idealism?

The answer depends on where one carves the boundary between naïve realism and naïve idealism. One obvious objection to Johnston's view is that presence requires presence-*to*; perspectivality requires a *subject* whose perspective it is. Johnston is well aware of the challenge, and responds thus:

Is presence fundamentally presence to something, a self or subject of experience, an essential third term of any mental act, besides the object of the act and the manner of presentation of the object? ...

Try as I might, I just do not find the third term of my mental acts. I do find objects presenting in this or that way, and in the perceptual case these manners or modes of presentation have an interesting property: they are perspectival. That is, they disclose how objects appear from a particular point in space.... but I do not find a self or a subject of experience, here. (2007, 257)

THE VIRTUES OF IDEALISM   173

Johnston's response to the challenge is to reject the existence of a Robust self, as a "third term" of mental acts. I have also rejected a Robust self. (Though, again, readers who disagree are free to modify my view to incorporate one.) Like Johnston (and Hume), I fail to find a self lurking about my mental acts, as something over and above what I experience. I find the computer before me, my hands typing, the thoughts running through my head, the sound of a bird, the ache in my left calf. I do not find the computer in its entirety, but a particular perspective on the computer. All these experiences are unified into the total experience of me at a moment.

But I take presence to be essentially presence-to. Much as Frege (1956) and Strawson (2003) take an experience to essentially require an experienc*er*, it seems to me that perspectives are essentially perspectives-*to*. But, as we saw in §1.3, accepting this doesn't require commitment to a Robust self. In addressing the question of who (if anyone) has the experiences of the phenomenal tapestry, I distinguished three possible answers:

(i)   Robust Mind view: there is a cosmic mind, which experiences the totality of external reality, and which is an addition to our ontology;

(ii) Thin Mind view: experiences are understood as essentially experienc*ed*, and hence as requiring an experienc*er*, but this is not taken to require any addition to our ontology beyond the experiences themselves (properly understood);

(iii) No Mind view: there can be free-floating phenomenology, independent of any experiencer, and reality is constituted by an experiencer-less phenomenal unity.

Like Johnston, I rejected (i) the Robust Minds view on Humean grounds. I opted instead to embrace (ii) the Thin Mind view. At this point, I must confess that I become murky on the difference between Johnston's view and my own. Insofar as (ii) is an option, one cannot dismiss the apparent connection between perspective and a subject-whose-perspective-it-is simply by dismissing Robust Minds. Given that Johnston does not consider the Thin Mind view—moving from the rejection of Robust Minds to the conclusion that presence is not fundamentally presence-to something—one might naturally interpret him as embracing something like the No Mind view.[14] But it

---

[14] Though insofar as his motivation is simply to reject Robust Minds, the Thin Mind view also seems compatible with what he writes.

174   THE VIEW FROM EVERYWHERE

may also be that Johnston has something radically different in mind, which is at odds with the basic picture presented in this book.[15]

However the views relate, the fundamental insight remains: Eden comes with metaphysical commitments. Put as neutrally as possible, I take these commitments to include a commitment to intrinsically *perspectival, qualitative* features of reality, which can be bound up so as to constitute (thin) minds. And these are points on which Johnston's view is (I take it) in agreement.

Does this commonality mean that Johnston is an idealist? That I am not an idealist? That naïve realists in general are off the hook? I don't think terminological discussions are interesting or fruitful. There is a core similarity between (a) the Robust Mind view of Berkeley; (b) the Thin Mind view developed in this book; and (c) the No Mind view (which perhaps corresponds to Johnston's view), in that they all embrace the Fundamental Insight. In this, (a)–(c) differ from standard materialism. Where we carve off the bounds of idealism is neither here nor there. What is important is the commonality that (a)–(c) share, and which—I take it—standard naïve realists (as materialists) reject. It is the rejection of this commonality that cuts us off from Eden.

6.3 Theoretical Virtues or Wishful Thinking?

I've argued that idealism together with the theory of perception developed in Chapter 4 has a number of noteworthy features. It entails:

(i)   *Fundamental Intelligibility*: that the nature of reality is intelligible to us,

(ii) *Edenic Reality*: that reality is (roughly) as it appears, and

(iii) *Open Window*: that the nature and character of reality can be grasped directly—such that we are directly acquainted with the truthmakers for our judgments about the world.

I've argued that these features are available to us only insofar as we embrace a picture of the world as fundamentally phenomenal. (i) Phenomenology is

---

[15] Johnston rejects qualia, while I'm inclined to embrace something of that name. But I'm not clear on whether this is a substantive disagreement or one of terminology. I don't take qualia to require Robust minds or subjectivity (in any sense that appeals to such minds). I take qualia to be essentially suitable for constituting (Thin) minds, and to be the conscious features of awareness me and my envatted twin share. I take it Johnston believes there are conscious features of awareness me and my envatted twin share—though he would describe them differently (Johnston 2011, 2004)—so perhaps the disagreement isn't a substantial one at all.

THE VIRTUES OF IDEALISM   175

the only intrinsic nature that we are capable of grasping, hence it is only if reality is fundamentally phenomenal that we are capable of grasping its nature. (ii) All of our awareness of the world is awareness of the way that it appears: the cold of the rain, the boom of the thunder, the strange greenness of the sky. If these appearances are not a part of the world, the world we live in is a very alien place. And (iii) it is only if reality is fundamentally phenomenal that direct acquaintance with the world is intelligible. In light of this, we might dub (i)–(iii) *the idealistic virtues.*

But are (i)–(iii) really virtues? Is it really a theoretical virtue that the world be intelligible to us or that it be as it appears? Are we rationally justified in putting more credence in our world being these ways? Or is the idealist's worldview simply better at capturing wishful thinking? While these putative virtues sound nice, so does cosmic justice, and we don't think that cosmic justice is a *theoretical* virtue. So why think that (e.g.) the world being as it appears *is* such a virtue?

First, consider the intelligibility of the nature of reality. There are many things that cats, dogs, elephants, and dolphins are not capable of understanding. It would be hubris to think that humans are capable of grasping all truths. Why should we think that the nature of reality is something that we *should* be able to grasp? Sure, consciousness is the only intrinsic nature we're directly acquainted with. But arguably this doesn't constitute evidence that it *is* the intrinsic nature of reality—rather, it constitutes a basis for thinking that the nature of reality is something that is *beyond* our ability to grasp.

And why think that reality is as it appears? It might seem to many readers that this is a positively *counterintuitive* claim. The sophisticated reader might insist that intuitively, we're only acquainted with how things appear to us. We don't know anything about the thing in itself.

Likewise, readers who embrace representationalism might find the idea that we *directly* grasp the world around us completely baffling. (This is certainly the position that I found myself in prior to writing this book.) What is intuitive about the idea that we directly—unmediatedly—grasp the redness of tomatoes? We all know that vision comes about by light bouncing off of objects in our surroundings, and carrying information about those objects to our retinas and brains. Sophisticated readers might find it thoroughly intuitive that experience is something that our brain produces at the end of this chain, reflecting the world (but not *grasping* it in any further sense). Likewise, they might find the suggestion that we can literally grasp or overlap with reality positively bizarre.

176   THE VIEW FROM EVERYWHERE

There is a sense in which I find each of these points quite compelling. When assuming materialism, I don't take myself to have any insight into the nature of reality (and don't find this problematic or counterintuitive); I don't presume that the world-in-itself is anything like my experience of it (and don't take this to be problematic or counterintuitive); I don't take perception to involve direct acquaintance with reality (and don't take this to be problematic or counterintuitive). So why is it that when confronted with idealism, we should take these features to tell in idealism's favor?

My son has a puzzle with pieces made out of hexagons conjoined in different configurations. There are countless ways the puzzle can be put together. But, of course, each piece you put down constrains the remaining pieces. Trying to make sense of the world around us, and our place in it, is a vast task, with many separate pieces and considerations. Like the hexagon puzzle, there are many different ways the physical world and conscious minds could be and fit together. And like the hexagon puzzle, each explicit position you take—and each implicit background assumption you leave in place—functions to constrain where the other pieces of the Cosmic Puzzle can go.

Once we put down the puzzle piece of materialism, that constrains where the other pieces go. Once we lay down materialism, it follows that the world is not as it appears. *Given* that we have laid down the materialism piece, this doesn't seem bizarre: it strikes us as how the world *must be*. But it would be a mistake to conclude from this that the world's being as it appears is something that we should reject as implausible *independently of materialism*. It would be a mistake to conclude that there is nothing intuitively more plausible about the world being how it appears *if there is another way of putting together the Cosmic Puzzle that renders this intelligible.*

I propose that, rather than considering the upshots of idealism in isolation, we should look at the complete worldview on offer—the completed Cosmic Puzzle—and that we should compare this to the completed Cosmic Puzzle on offer by materialists. These are package views, with pieces that cannot necessarily be mixed and matched, and we should compare them as such. Further, we should begin by suspending judgment about where individual pieces go, as these judgments may be implicitly based on presumptions that make sense within our original worldview but which should not necessarily be universally presumed. My claim is that when we do this—when we hold up the completed puzzles on offer from the idealist and the materialist, and assess them from a truly neutral starting point—we will find significant

THE VIRTUES OF IDEALISM   177

advantages to the idealist's worldview: things which, from a neutral starting point, we would take to be theoretical advantages.[16]

Suppose (setting aside preconceptions about what the world is like) that there are two coherent accounts of reality: according to one, reality is just as it seems; according to the other, reality is nothing like it seems. Which seems more plausible? Obviously, that the world is as it seems. Why would one take the world to be other than it seems, unless required to do so by the placement of some other piece of the Cosmic Puzzle?[17] *A win for idealism.*

Suppose (again setting aside preconceptions about what is possible) that there are two coherent pictures of reality. One picture offers an account of the nature of reality. The other says nothing positive about the nature of reality— but only "the nature of reality isn't like that other account says." The first theory clearly is at an advantage by offering a more complete picture of reality. It offers a positive account of a feature of the world on which the second theory is silent. *A win for idealism.*

The question of whether direct perceptual contact with the world is a theoretical virtue—as opposed to wishful thinking—seems less clear to me, but there is still a powerful case for thinking that idealism offers the more plausible theory. Certainly if you find the so-called naïve view of perception intuitive, the idealist's theory uniquely renders it intelligible that the world is as it appears in this respect. But what about those with entrenched representationalist intuitions? Imagine first coming to philosophy from a naïve starting point—prior to embracing the preposterousness of directly grasping reality—and finding that there are two coherent theories of perception that you could embrace. On the first view, perception is like an open window on the world. The world is there and we can simply reach out and grasp it. On

[16] And being guided by intuitions is, as Braddon-Mitchell and Jackson (1996, 81) put it, "nothing more than to follow the principle that it is better to say what seems plausible than to say what seems implausible."

[17] One might object that idealism does not give us a reality that is as it seems, as the world does not seem to be experiential. The cup before me, they might argue, seems to instantiate the *quality* blueness, but it does not seem to instantiate the *phenomenal property* blueness. It is certainly right that common sense does not tell us that the world is fundamentally experiential. But this is a high-level interpretation of our experience, and not something directly given to us in perception. The world as it is given to us in perception does not distinguish between qualities and phenomenal properties. You can see this by deliberately trying to imagine what it would seem like to veridically perceive a world constituted by phenomenal properties. I hazard that it would seem precisely as our world seems. Philosophers may *judge* that the world is not fundamentally experiential, but our visual experiences do not make such a claim. So it is not in tension with the idealist's ability to secure an Edenic world— a "world with respect to which our visual experience is perfectly veridical."

178 THE VIEW FROM EVERYWHERE

the second view, perception is more like a mirror, reflecting a world beyond our reach. Which theory would seem more plausible; more likely to be true?

It's generally accepted that that pretheoretical intuition favors the former. It's not surprising that naïve realists take this to be the intuitive pretheoretical view (Merleau-Ponty 1983; Martin 2006; Hellie 2007; Allen 2019). But even detractors from naïve realism rarely object to this claim and often allow that naïve realism best captures our intuitions about perception. C. D. Broad (1952) writes:

> In its purely phenomenological aspect *seeing* is ostensibly *saltatory*. It seems to leap the spatial gap between the percipient's body and a remote region of space. (5)
>
> It is a natural, if paradoxical, way of speaking to say that seeing seems to "bring one into direct *contact* with *remote* objects" and to reveal their shapes and colours, as feeling reveals the shapes and textures of objects which are literally in contact with one's skin. (6)

And from Joseph Levine (2018, 110), we're told

> another feature of the experience is the way that the ripe tomato seems immediately present to me in the experience. I am not in any way aware of any cognitive distance between me and the scene in front of me; the fact [as Levine sees it] that what I'm doing is *representing* the world is clearly not itself part of the experience. The world is just there.

If this consensus view is right, idealism puts us in the unique position to intelligibly capture another feature of how the world pretheoretically appears: the way we intuitively relate to our surroundings. *Another win for idealism.*

Naïve realists often take there to be further grounds for embracing a relational account of perception, over and above its capturing the pretheoretic view of what perception consists in. If I'm correct that the intelligibility of relational theories of perception presupposes idealism, then any additional theoretical benefits will also tell in favor of idealism.[18]

---

[18] Naïve realists have argued that there are other benefits of embracing a relational account of perception. McDowell (1986, 2006) and Johnston (2006, 2011) have argued that there is a response to skepticism that is only available if we can directly grasp reality. Campbell (2002) argues that a relational theory of perception is required to account for reference. While I am not convinced by either argument, inasmuch as you find the argument compelling, they would provide further support for the idealist's solution to the Cosmic Puzzle.

THE VIRTUES OF IDEALISM   179

But not all virtues of idealism are theoretical virtues. A relational account is required to capture Johnston's neglected epistemic virtue. But while it is an attractive aspect of idealism that it can so robustly account for this epistemic virtue, I'm not sure that this should raise our confidence that we live in an idealist world. Should we *expect* to find all epistemic virtues (or all moral virtues for that matter) instantiated? Surely not. A more minimal claim in this ballpark would be: for any (epistemic) virtue that we are capable of grasping, we should have a default presumption that we're capable of instantiating said virtue. If true, this would entail that theories that capture Johnston's neglected epistemic virtue have a theoretical virtue that other theories lack. But I'm not sure that I endorse this claim.

Unless forced by other commitments to hold otherwise, we should expect the world to be as it appears, we should expect reality to be directly grasped in perception, and we should expect to find the nature of this reality intelligible. Giving up on each of these is a cost—a cost we might have felt that there was no possibility of avoiding. You might have thought you simply had to resign yourself to death, taxes, and the veil of perception. But idealism, it turns out, can free us from the last. Idealism shows us that the world *can be* just as it appears, and that the world *can be* comprehended more thoroughly than merely understanding its structure. Once we see that it is possible to retain each of these intuitive claims, the failure to do so becomes apparent as a cost. Looking out at the space of possible worlds from a theoretically neutral starting point, it looks less plausible that our world is among the materialist worlds—ungraspable, unintelligible, nothing like anything that we're aware of—and far more plausible that ours is among the idealist worlds: worlds of color, heat, and flow, worlds that we can grasp and comprehend.

Of course, all this is predicated on idealism's offering a viable alternative to materialism. That's what the bulk of this book has been devoted to arguing. There may also be drawbacks to idealism when compared neutrally to materialism. Materialism certainly offers a simpler, sparser picture of reality. (We'll return, momentarily, to the question of whether this is a virtue from a neutral standpoint.) The point I'm making is just that the alleged virtues put forward in §6.1 are *genuine virtues*—that when we consider the idealist's Cosmic Puzzle against the materialist's, these are points (and not insignificant points) on which the idealist comes out ahead.

Most of us approach idealism from a materialistic starting point. Materialism (about the physical world) is implicit in our intellectual environment, such that materialism seems to be the default before we even set

180   THE VIEW FROM EVERYWHERE

foot in a philosophy classroom. We weigh the merits of idealism holding fixed the background assumptions of materialism. I've argued that we need to do away with these background assumptions.

But sometimes it's difficult to take a truly neutral starting point. Another way we could approach the merits of idealism, compared to materialism, is to turn the tables. Imagine that we all grow up indoctrinated with an idealist worldview. Young philosophers grow up reading *The View from Everywhere*, finding it as natural as you might the materialism of Lewis and Armstrong.

Ida is a young implicit idealist. She goes off to grad school, where she encounters materialism for the first time. Her initial encounter with Matt, the materialist, might go something like this:

Ida: So if the world isn't made of experiences, then what is it made of?
Matt: It's made of atoms.[19]
Ida: Of course it is; I agree. But what are atoms, on your view?
Matt: Oh, I don't know. But they're not experiences!
. . .
Ida: So . . . you don't think that snow is cold? Or that tomatoes are red?
Matt: Well, I mean, we can truthfully say that tomatoes are red. But that's just because they have a molecular structure that causes certain wavelengths of light to be reflected from them, and this affects our brains in a certain way.
Ida: Yeah, but according to you tomatoes aren't really red. Redness is all in our imaginations . . .
. . .
Ida: You're telling me that your theory is that tomatoes are not red things made out of not-experiences?! How is that a compelling alternative to idealism?!
Matt: Well, it's much simpler. We don't need to have all those experience that you say make everything up.
Ida: Yeah, but it's simpler because you got rid of the world! Tomatoes aren't red, fire isn't hot, violins don't make sounds. And the alternative picture is that it's all made up out of what? Not-experiences?! What the heck are those?
Matt: Well. . . .

[19] "Atoms" here used as filler for whatever the fundamental particles are.

THE VIRTUES OF IDEALISM   181

Ida can be forgiven for finding Matt's alternative worldview uncompelling. There are *costs* to embracing materialism. And while the materialistic picture is simpler, this is only a virtue if the materialist is right that they explain everything that needs explaining. Simpler theories are only better, all else being equal. As the idealist sees it, all else is not equal: the materialist has left color, temperature, sound, and all other sensible qualities out of our world. They have traded blue skies for photon dispersal, green fields for molecular structure.

Given a materialist starting point, idealism looks strange. Given an idealist starting point, materialism looks even more baffling. And given a neutral starting point, perhaps there are virtues to both.

So how should you weigh the views? I leave this to the reader to decide. I do not argue that you are rationally required to be an idealist. You aren't. The space of possible worlds is vast. I have no doubt that there are both materialist worlds and idealist worlds that roughly correspond to our own: worlds that their inhabitants perceive to be just as we perceive our world to be. What I am arguing is this: first, idealism is possible. That is, there are possible worlds that look from the inside just like our own, where idealism is the correct account of the metaphysics. Second, there are genuine virtues that idealist theories have over their materialist competitors. When we set aside our background commitments regarding the positions of individual pieces and compare the idealist's way of fitting together the Cosmic Puzzle with the materialist's, there are important respects in which the idealist has the upper hand. And hence, your credence that our world is an idealist world should not be insignificant—and should probably be much higher than it was prior to reading this book.

If the world is an idealist world, we live in a perceptual Eden. We did not fall from Eden. Rather, we deluded ourselves into believing that we couldn't possibly live in Eden when we committed to the materialism piece in the Cosmic Puzzle. With this in mind, it's time to reset our commitments. It's time to re-evaluate our solution to the Cosmic Puzzle.

6.4 Assessing the Competition

Thus far, I have made the case for idealism in relation to materialism.[20] Over the past fifteen years, there has been a resurgence of interest in metaphysical

[20] I use "materialism" here as a view about the nature of the physical world. Both physicalists/ materialists and dualists about the mind-body problem count as "materialists" in this sense, as they

182 THE VIEW FROM EVERYWHERE

theories that give phenomenology a central place in the world. This includes versions of panpsychism/cosmopsychism (Goff 2017; Strawson 2006), phenomenalism (Pelczar 2015, 2019, 2022), and theistic idealism (Foster 1982, 1993, 2008; Robinson 1985, 2009, 1994, 2022). In this section, I consider how my nontheistic realist idealism fares in relation to these other "mind-first" theories.[21]

6.4.1 Panpsychism

Panpsychism has attracted vastly more attention in recent years than idealism has. Given that both views hold phenomenology to be a primitive building block of reality, it's natural to wonder about the relation between the views. It's also a difficult question to give a straightforward answer to, as there are so many variants of the views and so little terminological consistency. I won't try to assess the many forms of panpsychism and whether or not they count as varieties of idealism. Instead, I'll use "experientialist worldviews" as an umbrella term for theories (such as idealism and panpsychism) on which the physical world is fundamentally experiential, and lay out the dimensions along which experientialist worldviews can differ. Then we'll be able to assess what subset of experientialist theories can capture the epistemic benefits described in §6.1.

(a) Consciousness: Exhaustive or Not
The first dimension along which such theories can differ is whether they take phenomenology to exhaust the fundamental nature of reality, or to merely be one such fundamental feature. The worldview developed in this book is one on which phenomenology exhausts the fundamental nature of reality. Berkeley also held such a view, as do many who identify as panpsychists.[22] By

---

both take the physical world of brains, stars, and quarks to be material—that is, not fundamentally phenomenal or mental.

[21] "Mind-first" is a term which I believe was coined by Michael Pelczar to capture what's in common between theories according to which reality is mind-dependent (e.g., idealism and panpsychism) along with phenomenalism (according to which reality is not dependent on actual experiences, but is constructed out of *potentials* for such experiences).

[22] As Strawson (2006) writes, "I think that the idea that some but not all physical ultimates are experiential would look like the idea that some but not all physical ultimates are spatio-temporal (on the assumption that spacetime is indeed a fundamental feature of reality). I would bet a lot against there being such radical heterogeneity at the very bottom of things. In fact (to disagree with my earlier self) it is hard to see why this view would not count as a form of dualism."

THE VIRTUES OF IDEALISM 183

contrast, Philip Goff's (Goff 2017) cosmopsychism takes "consciousness+" to be the fundamental nature of the universe, where consciousness+ "enfolds experiential and non-experiential aspects in a single unified property" (Goff 2017, 230).

(b) What's Fundamental: Small, Medium, Large

I've tried to remain neutral as to the question of what level of reality is fundamental—and, indeed, as to whether there *is* a single fundamental level. But panpsychism is often presented as the view that the *fundamental physical entities* are conscious. As such, panpsychists think it's important to know what the fundamental physical entities are. Canonically, panpsychism takes the fundamental physical entities to be microphysical entities. (This standard form of panpsychism has been dubbed *micropsychism* [Strawson 2006; Chalmers 2019].)

But we could also take the very biggest thing—the universe—to be fundamental, and take it to be the fundamental locus of consciousness, as on Goff's cosmopsychism: the universe is not built up out of little conscious bits. It is a single, unified conscious experience of which all else is but a part. While I have not taken a stand on whether the universe is fundamental, nontheistic idealism agrees with Goff in taking the universe to be a phenomenal unity.

One could also take mid-sized minds to be fundamental, and construct a world out of mid-sized consciousness (Chalmers 2019).

(c) Macro-Minds

There are also a variety of different positions that experientialist theories can take on the mind-body problem. Harking back to the discussion of the mind-body problem in Chapter 3, we can distinguish between reductive and nonreductive views of macro-experiences.[23] Reductive views hold that macro-experiences are fully grounded in other features of the physical world. Constitutive panpsychism is such a view. Nonreductive views deny that macro-experiences can be so reduced. Rather, they are primitive, with law-like connections between our brain (or other physical) states and the resulting macro-phenomenology. Emergent panpsychists embrace the nonreductive view, and I endorsed such a view in Chapter 3.

---

[23] I use "macro-experience" here to denote an intermediary between micro-consciousne (e.g., of quarks) and cosmic-consciousness (of the universe). I use it roughly as Goff uses "o-consciousness" as a catch-all to include mid-sized consciousnesses, such as human consciousness, animal consciousness, and AI consciousness.

184 THE VIEW FROM EVERYWHERE

So to return to the question of the relation between idealism and panpsychism, the answer is a definitive *meh*. They're both messy family resemblance terms, with a great deal of overlap. Is the view developed here panpsychism? Meh. I've embraced an experientialist theory on which (a) consciousness is exhaustive; (b) the universe is a locus of consciousness; and (c) macro-consciousness is sui generis. This is quite a different metaphysical picture from the canonical form of panpsychism: constitutive micropsychism. For traditional constitutive micropsychists: (a) consciousness is exhaustive; (b) microphysical particles are the fundamental loci of consciousness; and (c) human consciousness reduces to micro-consciousness. The view developed here is more akin to—but still bears striking differences from—Goff's (2017) cosmopsychism, according to which (a) consciousness is not exhaustive; (b) universe is the fundamental locus of consciousness;[24] and (c) macro-consciousness is an irreducible aspect of the cosmos.[25]

The question I think is more interesting is: what is essential to capturing the idealistic virtues laid out in §6.1? Here we can give a substantive account.

(i) To capture *Fundamental Intelligibility*, consciousness must exhaust the fundamental nature of reality. If phenomenology does not exhaust the fundamental nature of reality, then the nature of reality is not something that is wholly within our grasp. We may grasp part of the nature of reality—leaving us in a better position than materialism—but we have a less thorough grasp than I've argued for.

(ii) To capture *Edenic Reality*, macro-objects must have sensible (phenomenal) qualities. It is not enough that microphysical particles have an intrinsic phenomenal nature, if this doesn't combine to yield the sensible properties of physical objects that we know and love. If the world is to be as it appears, tomatoes must be *red*, tea must be *hot*, tables must be *solid*.

(iii) To capture *Open Window*, our minds must literally overlap with the perceived features of macro-objects. If they do not, then even if the

[24] Though there's no reason to believe that Goff envisions the phenomenal content of the universe to be anything like what I've argued for, or to include the sensible qualities necessary for the world being as it appears. Given the difference in motivation, Goff's primary concern is the mind-body problem, rather than capturing an Edenic world or solving the problem of perception.

[25] Goff distinguishes different kinds of aspect: (a) "vertical aspects," which are proper parts of the universe; (b) "horizontal aspects" of vertical aspects, which abstract away from some of the richness of the vertical aspects. While a brain is a vertical aspect of the cosmos; the computational properties of the brain or horizontal aspects. Human subjects are identified with horizontal aspects of the cosmos (2017, 240).

THE VIRTUES OF IDEALISM   185

world is as it appears, our grasp of this will be only indirect. This literal mind overlap can be achieved with a non-reductive account of our minds, together with externalist bridging laws (as described in Chapters 3 and 4).[26]

Canonical forms of panpsychism capture *Fundamental Intelligibility*, but not *Edenic Reality* or *Open Window*. Goff's cosmopsychism only partially captures *Fundamental Intelligibility*, but not *Edenic Reality* or *Open Window*.

This is not to say that no form of panpsychism could possibly capture virtues *Edenic Reality* or *Open Window*. The clearest dividing line between writers who identify as "panpsychists" or "idealists" is in philosophical motivation. Both are views about the nature of reality. But panpsychists tend to come to their view as a result of trying to make sense of the mind-body problem. Solving the mind-body problem is the aim, and the world being conscious falls out of it.[27] By contrast, idealists tend to be directly interested the nature of reality and our ability to grasp the world around us. In short: idealists tend to come to their position as a result of trying to capture the virtues described in this chapter. As Philonous says in Berkeley's Third Dialogue:

> I am of a vulgar cast, simple enough to believe my senses, and leave things as I find them. To be plain, it is my opinion that the real things are those very things I see, and feel, and perceive by my senses.... I cannot for my life help thinking that snow is white, and fire hot. (1996, 172)

This is a motivational difference, rather than a metaphysical one. But we should not be surprised to find that it leads to differences in the issues addressed by writers from both traditions and to how well suited the resulting theories are to capturing these virtues.

---

[26] For a reductive view to capture this overlap, the physical basis of the mind would need to be constantly shifting to include different objects in my environment. There would need to be some explanation of how/why this is. Whereas non-reductive views can appeal to bridging laws, reductive accounts don't have such a resource. So I find it difficult to see how such a view could work.

[27] This is not to say that this is the *sole* motivation for panpsychism. (*Fundamental Intelligibility* has motivated panpsychists just as they have motivated idealists.) But providing a novel solution to the mind-body problem—one that walks the fine line between dualism and physicalism (Chalmers 2013)—is clearly a (perhaps *the*) driving impetus. And panpsychists have not traditionally focused on *Edenic Reality* or *Open Window*. Conversely, Bernardo Kastrup (2018) is an idealist who is less interested in a naïve view of reality and perception, and more motivated by the prospect of a novel solution to the mind-body problem.

186   THE VIEW FROM EVERYWHERE

So is idealism theoretically superior to panpsychism? Meh. What we can say is that worldviews that capture the idealistic virtues thereby have an advantage over those that don't. And standard forms of panpsychism fail at this.

6.4.2 Phenomenalism

The relationship between idealism and phenomenalism is considerably more straightforward. As Michael Pelczar (2022, 8) succinctly puts it, "phenomenalism is the view that the physical world is a potential for things to be as traditional idealists . . . think things actually are." According to the phenomenalist, the tree is not a collection of actual experiences, as for the idealist, but a *potential for* such a collection of experiences. While materialists and idealists agree that there are such potentials, they take these potentials to be grounded in something else: *a tree*, where the tree is either a hunk of mind-independent matter or a structured collection of *actual* tree-ish experiences. The phenomenalist disagrees: the tree itself just is *the potentials* for tree-ish experiences. What it is for there to be a tree outside my office window is for there to be the potential for tree-ish experiences, given the appropriate circumstances (e.g., were I to look out my window). Why, according to the phenomenalist, are there such potentials? Apart from giving a causal story as to how the tree came to be planted there, there is nothing further to be said. Nothing grounds these potentials.[28] They do not exist in virtue of anything else existing. The world is all potentials all the way down.[29]

It seems to me that the phenomenalist can plausibly claim to capture *Edenic Reality* and *Open Window*—but that they do so in a less robust manner than idealists, and without other advantages that make up for this loss. Whether they can successfully capture *Fundamental Intelligibility* is less clear. Let's start by making the case for phenomenalism's ability to capture the idealistic virtues. Then we'll assess the case for phenomenalism in relation to the case for idealism.

Like idealism, phenomenalism has a story to tell about the intimate connection between the nature of the world and its appearance: the world is the

---

[28] Nothing save, in some instances, further potentials.

[29] This is the most radical and distinctive form of phenomenalism. Michael Pelczar embraces this account in (Pelczar 2019). Phenomenalism can also take a more modest form: identifying the world with potentials for world-like experience, while remaining neutral on whether there is anything that grounds these potentials. Pelczar adopts this more modest phenomenalism in (Pelczar 2022). For concreteness, I'll focus on the ungrounded version as the purest version of the view.

THE VIRTUES OF IDEALISM 187

potential for the sorts of experiences that could be had of it (Mill 1865). For the phenomenalist, it is not strictly true that the world *is* as it appears; rather, the world is a *potential for being* as it appears. While this does not capture the intuition (that the world is as appears) as literally as idealism, the distinction is a subtle one. And it's plausible that our intuitions aren't fine-grained enough to distinguish between these alternatives.[30] Much as the idealist can make the case that what we know of the world is the *experiences* we have of it, the phenomenalist can plausibly argue that what we know of the world is the *potentials* for such experiences. I know of my desk that there is a potential for desk-ish experiences. And the world literally is this way.[31]

And the phenomenalist has a claim on capturing the intuition that we directly grasp reality in perception. According to the phenomenalist, when I perceive the tree, the tree is not itself a part of my experience. (Potentials for tree-ish experience are not a part of my tree-ish experience.) Rather, perceiving the tree involves having an experience that *partially realizes* the tree. As Pelczar (2022, 173–174) puts it, perceiving is having "an experience that's among those for which the thing is a possibility."

I do not directly grasp reality in the sense of overlapping with it. But I do *realize* one of the very same sorts of potential that it is constituted by. While this is a less literal connection to reality than idealism affords us, it does make intelligible how we can have a considerably more robust connection to reality than that available to materialists. I find it a bit murky whether this instantiating-the-constituting-potential view captures our naïve intuitions, perhaps because the idea of the physical world being constituted by brute potentials for experience (as opposed to causing them) seems such a subtle philosophical distinction that my naïve intuitions start to lose their grip. Nevertheless, I'll argue in what follows that the idealist has the upper hand—though the phenomenalist certainly fares better on this front than the materialist does.

---

[30] One might further object that the world does not seem to be made out of brute potentials for experience. This is analogous to the objection to idealism considered earlier that the world does not seem to be experiential. As before, these are *philosophical judgment* about the nature of reality, and not something that our *experiences* of reality directly reveal.

[31] While it seems more natural to say that the desk causes the potential for desk-ish experiences, this is not strictly true for the phenomenalist. Much as behaviorists hold that pain is identical to a set of behavioral dispositions, not caused by them, phenomenalists take the desk to be identical to the desk-ish potentials for experience, not caused by them. This might constitute an objection to phenomenalism, insofar as the desk pretheoretically seems to us to be the *cause* of such potentials. But we're notoriously bad at identifying causes, and the distinction is sufficiently subtle that it's again plausible that our intuitions here aren't especially reliable.

188　THE VIEW FROM EVERYWHERE

It's less clear how the phenomenalist fares on the intelligibility of reality. I can certainly grasp experiences. And hence, I can grasp what the phenomenalist's potentials are potentials *for*. What's less clear is whether *brute potentials* themselves are fully intelligible—or intelligible at all. Whether they are or not, it's clear that for brute potentials to be coherent, they must be far more ontologically "heavy-weight" than one might have initially supposed. And I think this commitment to ontologically heavy-weight brute-potentials undercuts any apparent benefit phenomenalism might have seemed to have over idealism.

I take potentials to be ontologically "thin." They're not things that would exist in God's Big Book of basic elements needed to construct the world. Rather, potentials fall out of categorical things that are elements of God's Big Book, and so are ontologically insubstantial. But this is not the way that phenomenalists thinks about potentials. There is—on the purest form of phenomenalism—nothing grounding the potentials for experience, nothing that they "fall out of." Hence, the potentials themselves must appear in the Big Book. (Howard Robinson [2022] makes a similar point.[32])

So God's Big Book contains brute potentials for experiences of certain sorts. What these potentials are potentials *for* is intelligible. But it's not obvious that this is sufficient to render the potentials *themselves* intelligible. Many writers have certainly found such brute potentials mysterious (Prior, Pargetter, and Jackson 1982; Smith and Stoljar 1998). Still, let's grant that they are—at least, they're as intelligible as anything brute and nonexperiential is—although we clearly cannot grasp them in the direct and character-disclosing way that we grasp experience.

Given this, phenomenalism has a plausible case for capturing the idealistic virtues. (i) *Edenic Reality*: the world is a potential to appear just as it appears. (ii) *Open Window*: in perception we instantiate the potentials that constitute perceived objects. (iii) *Fundamental Intelligibility*: insofar as we can make sense of brute potentials, we can grasp what the world's nature is. Phenomenalism may not give us quite so neat and intuitive a view as idealism, but it still does a heck of a lot better than materialism.

---

[32] As Robinson (2022, 211–212) puts it, for Pelczar "these potentialities are objective probabilities. The question then arises of what the reality of these probabilities or potentialities consists in. . . . They seem to have to be self-standing truths, without any truthmaker. One way of giving this content might be to think of these potentialities as a complicated web of laws like those that a Berkeleian theistic phenomenalist would attribute to the mind of God, but treated in an abstract, Platonic way, and so dispensing with the theism."

THE VIRTUES OF IDEALISM   189

Pelczar (2022) takes phenomenalism to have distinctive advantages over idealism and materialism. Among the most interesting arguments he offers is a defense of the claim that

> If something explains why there exist the possibilities of sensation that do actually exist, then that "something" *explains why* there is a physical world, but isn't *identical with* the physical world. The physical world is identical with the possibilities. (28)

He defends this claim by considering a world with a changing ground for the experience potentials. We might imagine the ground of the world shifting from something material to 0s and 1s in the matrix to Leibnizian monads . . . perhaps disappearing all together. Pelczar thinks that as the ground of the experience potentials changed, we intuitively wouldn't think that the physical world disappeared and was replaced by a new one. Newspaper headlines would not read "Universe no longer exists." We'd take the world—the same world we've always known—to continue to exist just as before. If right, this means that the possibilities for sensations (what's remained constant over the shifting ground) are what we identified with the physical world all along.

I wholly share Pelczar's intuitions when the ground is a material world, or something completely unlike the world we're acquainted with. If the ground of our experience potentials begins as a material world (who knows what that is like), and then becomes 0s and 1s in a computer (who knows what that is like), and then becomes something else with no intelligible connection to the world as it appears . . . well, *these* grounds aren't the world we're acquainted with, the world we care about. What matters is that the grounds (whatever they are) somehow produce the relevant experiences. But I think the Pelczarian intuition loses its plausibility when the original ground was *actual* experiences.

Suppose the physical world is an idealist world: one that is as it appears, in which we overlap with reality, and thereby directly grasp it. Now imagine that the ground shifts or disappears. Yesterday when I looked out my window, I overlapped with the bit of reality that constitutes the tree, thereby directly grasping the tree. Today I simply have experiences as of a tree, caused by a mind-independent Something, or with no ground whatsoever. Yesterday, the *tree* was green. Today, I simply generate a green experience when I look out the window. I think that if we fully grasped the situation we were in here, we *would* take our world to have disappeared. Yesterday, there was a world

190　THE VIEW FROM EVERYWHERE

that I could reach out and grasp. Yesterday, there were *colors* out there, in the world. Today, this world that I understood so intimately, this world that I could comprehend as fully as my own pains, is gone. Today, I have fallen from Eden.

So while I think that Pelczar's argument is an ingenious way of making the case against materialism, I do not think it has the same force against idealism. Furthermore, while I granted that phenomenalism has a plausible claim to capturing the idealistic virtues (when compared with materialism), this thought experiment illustrates that it does not capture them as robustly as idealism. If moving from idealism to phenomenalism entails a fall from Eden, the phenomenalist's world could not have been Eden.

Phenomenalism has other apparent benefits over idealism, chief being that it appears to be less ontologically burdensome. According to idealism, reality doesn't just include all the actual experiences had by existing humans and other animals; there are potentially endless *actual experiences* making up all the facets of the tapestry. By contrast, phenomenalism takes there to be just the experiences had by ordinary actually existing creatures, along with a multitude of *potentials* for experience.[33] And intuitively, potentials for experience are ontologically lighter-weight than actual experiences.

I certainly think that potentials for experience are lightweight in this way. The potential for the experience of dark silver-green leaves simply falls out of the phenomenal tapestry and the bridging laws that connect me to it. This potential does not appear in God's Big Book. It's simply entailed by the things that are written there. The problem is that the phenomenalist cannot agree. If there is nothing grounding the potentials for experience, nothing that they "fall out of," the potentials themselves must appear in the Big Book.[34] So the idealist has a vast collection of actual experiences (or a single vastly complex actual experience) in the book, and the phenomenalist has a vast collection of potentials for experience (or a single vastly complex such potential).[35] Is one of these more ontologically "lightweight"? Less burdensome? It's difficult to see what such a claim could amount to. Are some sorts of entries

---

[33] Or perhaps, an extremely complex multifaceted single potential. This would be analogous to the priority monist reading of idealism.

[34] The more modest form of phenomenalism adopted by Pelczar (2022) entails agnosticism as to whether potentials are thick (and ungrounded) or thin (and grounded in some categorical nature). But it's difficult to assess the simplicity of a view that's agnostic about grounds.

[35] Idealists of the nonreductive sort that I defend will also posit bridging laws. But there seems just as much need for phenomenalists to posit something akin to bridging laws. There will need to be laws that explain why brains cause (or have) experiences: why does this collection of brain-y potentials for experience cause the realization of certain actual experiences?

in God's Big Book written in italics, and others in plain text, and only the italicized entries are really burdensome?

It's easy to see why one would have the intuition that potentials for experience were less ontologically burdensome. I myself have this intuition. But I think that it stems from holding a background view on which potentials are grounded in categorical features of the world. If this is not the case—if potentials are brute elements of our ontology—it's difficult to see why these would be any ontologically thinner than other candidate element of our ontology, or what such a claim would even mean.

Where does this leave idealism in relation to phenomenalism? Phenomenalism does not offer a more ontologically lightweight theory. The possibility of a shifting ground does not give reason to favor phenomenalism over idealism. And though phenomenalism has a plausible claim to capturing the idealistic virtues (in comparison with materialism), idealism seems to capture them in a more robust and straightforward way. This can be seen from the fact that losing the ground of an idealist world—going from a world of actual experiences, which we overlap with, to a world of mere potentials for experience—entails a loss. Moving from idealism to phenomenalism entails a fall from Eden.

6.4.3 Theistic Idealism

This book began with a move away from Berkeley's theistic idealism, on which an omnipotent, omniscient, omnibenevolent agent grounds the physical world, and toward a nontheistic idealism on which a more minimal phenomenal tapestry plays this role: a move from God to God-minus. My motivation in moving away from theism was two-fold: first, to make do with as narrow a range of assumptions as possible. Logically weaker claims are more likely to be true. And given that fewer than a fifth of philosophy professors identify as theists (Bourget and Chalmers 2023), it's worth being clear that idealism *does not entail theism*. Second, it's difficult to speculate freely about the structure and contents of the mind of God. (What business do I have—absent divine revelation, mystical insight, or theological training—speculating on the mind of God?) Once we embrace the idea that there is a traditional God who accounts for the persistence and stability of the physical world, it's tempting to leave things at that: to leave all the tricky details within the black box. Moving away from God to the phenomenal

192   THE VIEW FROM EVERYWHERE

tapestry gives us license to speculate about how such a fundamentally phenomenal world could hang together and what it could be like.

The theory I have developed is not essentially atheistic. It is perfectly compatible with there being a traditional Judeo-Christian God. In the same way that such a God could create a materialist world, so too he could create the world of the phenomenal tapestry. But it's compatible with God in another sense. The theist could circle back and insist that the view developed in this book is broadly correct . . . but that the phenomenal tapestry is an agent and has the traditional distinctive attributes of God. In effect, they could "plus" God-minus, where God-minus-plus = God.

I take it that all the benefits of the nontheistic idealism developed in this book can be captured equally well by theistic idealists. There is nothing essential to capturing these virtues that came from the absence of a Divine creator, and nothing essential to capturing these virtues that comes from the phenomenal tapestry being a *mere* unity of sensory experiences. So it seems to me that whether nontheistic idealism or its theistic counterpart is the better theory depends on whether you take there to be independent reason to believe in a traditional God.[36]

But if, at the end of all this, we reintroduced the traditional divine attributes into the tapestry, one might think that this book has been pointless. We have abandoned ship. We may as well just have stopped with Berkeley. I disagree.

The second benefit I claimed for moving away from theistic idealism is a methodological one: that it is far easier to speculate freely about the structure and contents of an impersonal phenomenal tapestry, than the mind of God. The benefits that come from doing so are retained even if, at the end of the day, one were to hold that the phenomenal tapestry actually has the divine attributes that I originally stripped from it—even if one were to change course and insist that the phenomenal tapestry is an agent and is omniscient and omnipotent and omnibenevolent.

Even if one returns to a more traditional theistic conception of the tapestry, we have fleshed out the details of a possible idealist world with far greater depth and precision. We have an account of the structure of reality (§2.2), an account of the sorts of contents that make up reality (§2.3), a new

---

[36] I myself am agnostic, but think that the problem of suffering is an insurmountable problem for a traditional conception of God. Whether there's a creator of some other sort or no creator is something I remain neutral on.

THE VIRTUES OF IDEALISM   193

account (divergent from Berkeley's) of subjects like us (Chapter 3), a fleshed-out account of perception (Chapter 4), and an account of how idealism is compatible with science (Chapter 5). This is far from nothing.

On the other hand ... why plus when you could minus?

Bibliography

Allais, Lucy. 2009. "Kant, Non-Conceptual Content and the Representation of Space." *Journal of the History of Philosophy* 47 (3): 383–413. https://doi.org/10.1353/hph.0.0134.

Allen, Keith. 2016. *A Naïve Realist Theory of Colour*. New York: Oxford University Press.

Allen, Keith. 2019. "Merleau-Ponty and Naïve Realism." *Philosopher's Imprint* 19 (2): 1–25. http://hdl.handle.net/2027/spo.3521354.0019.002.

Allen, Keith. 2021. "Bridging the Gap? Naïve Realism and the Problem of Consciousness." In *Purpose and Procedure in Philosophy of Perception*, edited by Heather Logue and Louise Richardson, 43–62. Oxford: Oxford University Press. https://doi.org/10.1093/oso/978019 8853534.003.0003.

Antony, Louise. 2011. "The Openness of Illusions." *Philosophical Issues* 21: 25–44.

Armstrong, D. M. 1982. "Laws of Nature as Relations between Universals and as Universals." *Philosophical Topics* 13 (1): 7–24. https://doi.org/10.5840/philtopics19821311.

Armstrong, D. M. 1983. *What Is a Law of Nature?* Cambridge: Cambridge University Press.

Balog, Katalin. 2012. "Acquaintance and the Mind-Body Problem." In *New Perspectives on Type Identity: The Mental and the Physical*, edited by Simone Gozzano and Christopher S. Hill, 16–43. Cambridge: Cambridge University Press.

Bayne, Tim. 2010. *The Unity of Consciousness*. New York: Oxford University Press.

Bayne, Tim, and David Chalmers. 2003. "What Is the Unity of Consciousness?" In *The Unity of Consciousness: Binding, Integration, Dissociation*, edited by Axel Cleeremans, 23–58. New York: Oxford University Press.

Beebee, Helen. 2009. "Review of *The Divine Lawmaker*." *British Journal for the Philosophy of Science* 60 (2): 453–457. http://www.jstor.org/stable/25592010.

Berkeley, George. 1996. *Principles of Human Knowledge and Three Dialogues*. Edited by Howard Robinson. Oxford: Oxford University Press.

Blake, Randolph, and Frank Tong. 2008. "Binocular Rivalry." *Scholarpedia* 3 (12): 1578. https://doi.org/10.4249/scholarpedia.1578.

Bourget, David, and David J. Chalmers. 2023. "Philosophers on Philosophy: The 2020 Philpapers Survey." *Philosophers' Imprint* 23 (11): 1–53. https://doi.org/10.3998/ phimp.2109.

Braddon-Mitchell, David, and Frank Jackson. 1996. *The Philosophy of Mind and Cognition: An Introduction*. Oxford: Blackwell.

Bradley, Francis Herbert. 1893. *Appearance and Reality: A Metaphysical Essay*. London: Oxford University Press.

Broad, C. D. 1952. "Some Elementary Reflexions on Sense-Perception." *Philosophy* 27 (100): 3–17. https://doi.org/10.1017/S0031819100019732.

Builes, David. 2024. "Modal Idealism." In *Oxford Studies in Philosophy of Mind*, edited by Uriah Kriegel, Vol. 4, 46–107. Oxford University Press.

Calkins, Mary Whiton. 1927. *The Persistent Problems of Philosophy: An Introduction to Metaphysics through the Study of Modern Systems*. 5th ed. New York: Macmillan.

Campbell, John. 1993. "A Simple View of Colour." In *Reality: Representation and Projection*, edited by John J. Haldane and C. Wright, 257–268. New York: Oxford University Press.

Campbell, John. 1997. "A Simple View of Colour." In *Readings on Color. Vol. 1, The Philosophy of Color*, edited by Alex Byrne and David Hilbert, 177–90. Cambridge, MA: MIT Press.

Campbell, John. 2002. *Reference and Consciousness*. Oxford: Oxford University Press.

196 BIBLIOGRAPHY

Cavendish, Margaret. 1668. *Margaret Cavendish: Observations upon Experimental Philosophy.* Edited by Eileen O'Neill. Cambridge: Cambridge University Press.

Chakravartty, Anjan. 2017. "Scientific Realism." In *The Stanford Encyclopedia of Philosophy*, edited by Edward N. Zalta, Summer 2017. Metaphysics Research Lab, Stanford University. https://plato.stanford.edu/archives/sum2017/entries/scientific-realism/.

Chalmers, David. 2003. "The Content and Epistemology of Phenomenal Belief." In *Consciousness: New Philosophical Perspectives*, edited by Quentin Smith and Aleksandar Jokic, 220–272. Oxford University Press.

Chalmers, David. 2006. "Perception and the Fall from Eden." In *Perceptual Experience*, edited by Tamar Szabó Gendler and John Hawthorne. Oxford: Oxford University Press.

Chalmers, David. 2010. "The Matrix as Metaphysics." In *The Character of Consciousness.* Oxford: Oxford University Press. https://doi.org/10.1093/acprof:oso/9780195311 105.003.0013.

Chalmers, David. 2013. "Panpsychism and Panprotopsychism." *Amherst Lecture in Philosophy* 8: 1–35.

Chalmers, David. 2016. "The Combination Problem for Panpsychism." In *Panpsychism: Contemporary Perspectives*, edited by Godehard Bruntrup and Ludwig Jaskolla, 179–214. New York: Oxford University Press. https://doi.org/10.1093/acprof:oso/9780199359943.003.0008.

Chalmers, David. 2019. "Idealism and the Mind-Body Problem." In *The Routledge Handbook of Panpsychism*, edited by William Seager, 353–373. New York: Routledge.

Chudnoff, Elijah. 2013. "Intellectual Gestalts." In *Phenomenal Intentionality*, edited by Uriah Kriegel, 174. Oxford: Oxford University Press.

Clark, Andy. 2009. "Spreading the Joy? Why the Machinery of Consciousness Is (Probably) Still in the Head." *Mind* 118 (472): 963–993. https://doi.org/10.1093/mind/fzp110.

Clark, Andy, and David J. Chalmers. 1998. "The Extended Mind." *Analysis* 58 (1): 7–19. https://doi.org/10.1093/analys/58.1.7.

Cohen, Jonathan. 2009. *The Red and the Real: An Essay on Color Ontology.* Oxford: Oxford University Press.

Coleman, Sam. 2006. "Being Realistic—Why Physicalism May Entail Panexperientialism." *Journal of Consciousness Studies* 13 (10–11): 40–52.

Cusimano, Maddie, James Traer, and Josh McDermott. 2017. "Auditory Perception of Object Properties as Inverse Acoustics." *Journal of the Acoustical Society of America* 141 (5): 3898. https://doi.org/10.1121/1.4988762.

Cutter, Brian. 2016. "Review of *Phenomenal Qualities: Sense, Perception, and Consciousness*," July. https://ndpr.nd.edu/reviews/phenomenal-qualities-sense-perception-and-consci ousness/.

Dainton, Barry. 2000. *Stream of Consciousness: Unity and Continuity in Conscious Experience.* London: Routledge.

Downing, Lisa. 2011. "George Berkeley." *Stanford Encyclopedia of Philosophy*, January. https://plato.stanford.edu/entries/berkeley/.

Eddington, Arthur Stanley. 1928. *The Nature of the Physical World.* Cambridge: University Press.

Farkas, Katalin. 2013. "Constructing a World for the Senses." In *Phenomenal Intentionality*, edited by Uriah Kriegel, 99–115. Oxford: Oxford University Press.

Fine, Kit. 2000. "Neutral Relations." *Philosophical Review* 109 (1): 1–33. https://doi.org/10.1215/00318108-109-1-1.

Fish, William. 2009. *Perception, Hallucination, and Illusion.* Oxford: Oxford University Press.

Foster, John. 1982. *The Case for Idealism.* London: Routledge.

Foster, John. 1991. *The Immaterial Self: A Defence of the Cartesian Dualist Conception of the Mind.* London: Routledge.

Foster, John. 1993. "The Succinct Case for Idealism." In *Objections to Physicalism*, edited by Howard Robinson, 293–313. Oxford: Clarendon Press.

BIBLIOGRAPHY 197

Foster, John. 2004. *The Divine Lawmaker: Lectures on Induction, Laws of Nature, and the Existence of God.* Oxford: Oxford University Press.

Foster, John. 2008. *A World for Us: The Case for Phenomenalistic Idealism.* Oxford: Oxford University Press.

Fraassen, Bas C. Van. 1980. *The Scientific Image.* Oxford: Oxford University Press.

Fraassen, Bas C. Van. 1989. *Laws and Symmetry.* Oxford: Oxford University Press.

Frankish, Keith. 2016. "Illusionism as a Theory of Consciousness." *Journal of Consciousness Studies* 23 (11–12): 11–39.

Frege, Gottlob. 1956. "The Thought: A Logical Inquiry." *Mind* 65 (259): 289–311. https://doi.org/10.1093/mind/65.1.289.

Gatto, Elia, Olli J. Loukola, Maria Elena Miletto Petrazzini, Christian Agrillo, and Simone Cutini. 2022. "Illusional Perspective across Humans and Bees." *Vision* 6 (2): 28. https://doi.org/10.3390/vision6020028.

Gert, Joshua. 2006. "A Realistic Colour Realism." *Australasian Journal of Philosophy* 84 (4): 565–589. https://doi.org/10.1080/00048400601079128.

Gert, Joshua. 2008. "What Colors Could Not Be." *Journal of Philosophy* 105 (3): 128–155.

Gertler, Brie. 2001. "Introspecting Phenomenal States." *Philosophy and Phenomenological Research* 63 (2): 305–328. https://doi.org/10.2307/3071065.

Gertler, Brie. 2012. "Renewed Acquaintance." In *Introspection and Consciousness*, edited by Declan Smithies and Daniel Stoljar, 93–128. New York: Oxford University Press. https://doi.org/10.1093/acprof:oso/9780199744794.003.0004.

Goff, Philip. 2011. "A Posteriori Physicalists Get Our Phenomenal Concepts Wrong." *Australasian Journal of Philosophy* 89 (2): 191–209. https://doi.org/10.1080/00048401003649617.

Goff, Philip. 2015. "Real Acquaintance and Physicalism." In *Phenomenal Qualities: Sense, Perception, and Consciousness*, edited by Paul Coates and Sam Coleman, 121–143. New York: Oxford University Press. https://doi.org/10.1093/acprof:oso/9780198712718.003.0005.

Goff, Philip. 2017. *Consciousness and Fundamental Reality.* New York: Oxford University Press.

Hacker, Peter Michael Stephan. 1987. *Appearance and Reality: A Philosophical Investigation into Perception and Perceptual Qualities.* Cambridge: Blackwell.

Hanna, Robert. 2005. "Kant and Nonconceptual Content." *European Journal of Philosophy* 13 (2): 247–290. https://doi.org/10.1111/j.0966-8373.2005.00229.x.

Hardin, C. L. 2004. "A Green Thought in a Green Shade." *Harvard Review of Philosophy* 12 (1): 29–38. https://doi.org/10.5840/harvardreview20041212.

Hardin, C. L. 2008. "7 Color Qualities and the Physical World." In *The Case for Qualia*, edited by Edmond Wright, 143. Cambridge, MA: MIT Press.

Hellie, Benj. 2007. "Factive Phenomenal Characters." *Philosophical Perspectives* 21: 259–306. https://www.jstor.org/stable/25177205.

Hoffman, Donald. 2019. *The Case against Reality: Why Evolution Hid the Truth from Our Eyes.* New York: W. W. Norton.

Hofweber, Thomas. 2022. *Idealism and the Harmony of Thought and Reality.* Oxford: Oxford University Press.

Holcombe, Alex O., Donald I. A. MacLeod, and Scott T. Mitten. 2004. "Positive Afterimages Caused by a Filled-in Representation." *Journal of Vision* 4 (8): 485. https://doi.org/10.1167/4.8.485.

Horridge, Adrian. 2009. "What Does an Insect See?" *Journal of Experimental Biology* 212 (17): 2721–2729. https://doi.org/10.1242/jeb.030916.

Hume, David. 2000. *A Treatise of Human Nature.* Edited by David Fate Norton and Mary J. Norton. Oxford Philosophical Texts. Oxford: Oxford University Press.

Hurley, Susan L. 1994. "Unity and Objectivity." In *Objectivity, Simulation and the Unity of Consciousness: Current Issues in the Philosophy of Mind*, edited by Christopher Peacocke, 49–77. Oxford: Oxford University Press.

198 BIBLIOGRAPHY

Hurley, Susan L. 1998. *Consciousness in Action*. Cambridge, MA: Harvard University Press.

Hurley, Susan L. 2003. "Action, the Unity of Consciousness, and Vehicle Externalism." In *The Unity of Consciousness: Binding, Integration, Dissociation*, edited by Axel Cleeremans. New York: Oxford University Press. https://doi.org/10.1093/acprof:oso/9780198508 571.003.0004.

Johnston, Mark. 1998. "Are Manifest Qualities Response-Dependent?" *The Monist* 81 (1): 3–43. https://doi.org/10.5840/monist199881110.

Johnston, Mark. 2004. "The Obscure Object of Hallucination." *Philosophical Studies* 120 (1–3): 113–183. https://doi.org/10.1023/b:phil.0000033753.64202.21.

Johnston, Mark. 2006. "Better than Mere Knowledge? The Function of Sensory Awareness." In *Perceptual Experience*, edited by Tamar Szabó Gendler and John Hawthorne, 260–290. Oxford: Oxford University Press. https://doi.org/10.1093/acprof:oso/9780199289 769.003.0008.

Johnston, Mark. 2007. "Objective Mind and the Objectivity of Our Minds." *Philosophy and Phenomenological Research* 75 (2): 233–268. https://doi.org/10.1111/ j.1933-1592.2007.00075.x.

Johnston, Mark. 2011. "On a Neglected Epistemic Virtue." *Philosophical Issues* 21 (1): 165–218. https://doi.org/10.1111/j.1533-6077.2011.00201.x.

Kalderon, Mark Eli. 2007. "Color Pluralism." *Philosophical Review* 116 (4): 563–601. https:// doi.org/10.1215/00318108-2007-014.

Kammerer, François. 2019. "The Illusion of Conscious Experience." *Synthese* 198 (1): 845–866. https://doi.org/10.1007/s11229-018-02071-y.

Kant, Immanuel. 2003. *Critique of Pure Reason*. Translated by N. Kemp Smith. Basingstoke: Palgrave Macmillan.

Kastrup, Bernardo. 2017a. "An Ontological Solution to the Mind-Body Problem." *Philosophies* 2 (2): 10. https://doi.org/10.3390/philosophies2020010.

Kastrup, Bernardo. 2017b. "On the Plausibility of Idealism: Refuting Criticisms." *Disputatio* 9 (44): 13–34. https://doi.org/10.2478/disp-2017-0025.

Kastrup, Bernardo. 2018. "The Universe in Consciousness." *Journal of Consciousness Studies* 25 (5–6): 125–155.

Landau, Elizabeth. 2019. "Black Hole Image Makes History; NASA Telescopes Coordinated Observations—NASA Science." https://science.nasa.gov/universe/black-holes/black-hole-image-makes-history-nasa-telescopes-coordinated-observations/.

Leonard, Anne S., and Pavel Masek. 2014. "Multisensory Integration of Colors and Scents: Insights from Bees and Flowers." *Journal of Comparative Physiology A* 200 (6): 463–474. https://doi.org/10.1007/s00359-014-0904-4.

Levine, Joseph. 2006. "Phenomenal Concepts and the Materialist Constraint." In *Phenomenal Concepts and Phenomenal Knowledge: New Essays on Consciousness and Physicalism*, edited by Torin Andrew Alter and Sven Walter, 145–166. Oxford: Oxford University Press.

Levine, Joseph. 2018. "Conscious Awareness and (Self-)Representation." In *Quality and Content*, 105–126. Oxford: Oxford University Press. https://doi.org/10.1093/oso/978019 8800088.003.0007.

Lewis, David. 1973. *Counterfactuals*. Malden, MA: Blackwell.

Lewis, David. 1983. "New Work for a Theory of Universals." *Australasian Journal of Philosophy* 61 (4): 343–377.

Lewis, David. 1986a. *On the Plurality of Worlds*. Oxford: Blackwell Publishers.

Lewis, David. 1986b. *Philosophical Papers Vol. II*. New York: Oxford University Press.

Maier, A., M. A. Cox, J. A. Westerberg, and K. Dougherty. 2022. "Binocular Integration in the Primate Primary Visual Cortex." *Annual Review of Vision Science* 8 (1): 345–360. https:// doi.org/10.1146/annurev-vision-100720-112922.

Majid, Asifa, Niclas Burenhult, Marcus Stensmyr, Josje de Valk, and Bill S. Hansson. 2018. "Olfactory Language and Abstraction across Cultures." *Philosophical Transactions of the Royal Society B: Biological Sciences* 373 (1752). https://doi.org/10.1098/rstb.2017.0139.

BIBLIOGRAPHY 199

Martin, Michael. 1997. "The Reality of Appearances." In *Thought and Ontology*, edited by M. Sainsbury, 81–106. Milano, Italy: Franco Angeli.

Martin, Michael. 2006. "On Being Alienated." In *Perceptual Experience*, edited by Tamar Szabó Gendler and John Hawthorne, 354–410. Oxford: Oxford University Press.

Maudlin, Tim. 2007. *The Metaphysics within Physics*. Oxford: Oxford University Press. https://doi.org/10.1093/acprof:oso/9780199218219.001.0001.

McDaniel, Kris. 2017. "The Idealism of Mary Whiton Calkins." In *Idealism: New Essays in Metaphysics*, edited by Tyron Goldschmidt and Kenneth L. Pearce, 142–157. Oxford University Press. https://doi.org/10.1093/oso/9780198746973.003.0009.

McDowell, John. 1986. "Singular Thought and the Extent of 'Inner Space'." In *Subject, Thought, and Context*, edited by Philip Pettit, 137–168. Oxford: Clarendon Press.

McDowell, John. 2006. "The Disjunctive Conception of Experience as Material for a Transcendental Argument." In *Disjunctivism: Perception, Action, Knowledge*, edited by Fiona Macpherson and Adrian Haddock, 376–389. Oxford: Oxford University Press.

McGinn, Colin. 1996. "Another Look at Color." *Journal of Philosophy* 93 (11): 537–553.

McLear, Colin. 2015. "Two Kinds of Unity in the Critique of Pure Reason." *Journal of the History of Philosophy* 53 (1): 79–110. https://doi.org/10.1353/hph.2015.0011.

Merleau-Ponty, Maurice. 1983. *The Structure of Behavior*. Pittsburgh: Duquesne University Press.

Mill, John Stuart. 1865. *An Examination of Sir William Hamilton's Philosophy, and of the Principal Philosophical Questions Discussed in His Writings*. London: Longman, Green, Longman, Roberts & Green.

Montague, Michelle. 2017. "Perception and Cognitive Phenomenology." *Philosophical Studies* 174 (8): 2045–2062. https://doi.org/10.1007/s11098-016-0787-z.

Mørch, Hedda Hassel. 2020. "The Phenomenal Powers View and the Meta-Problem of Consciousness." *Journal of Consciousness Studies* 27 (5–6): 131–142.

Nadis, Steve. 2011. "The Strange Physics—and Singular Sights—Inside Black Holes." https://www.discovermagazine.com/the-sciences/the-strange-physics-and-singular-sights-inside-black-holes.

Nagel, Thomas. 1986. *The View from Nowhere*. New York: Oxford University Press.

Nolan, Daniel. 1997. "Quantitative Parsimony." *British Journal for the Philosophy of Science* 48 (3): 329–343. https://doi.org/10.1093/bjps/48.3.329.

Nudds, Matthew. 2009. "Recent Work in Perception: Naïve Realism and Its Opponents." *Analysis* 69 (2): 334–346. https://doi.org/10.1093/analys/anp039.

Palmer, Stephen E. 1999. *Vision Science: Photons to Phenomenology*. Illus. ed. Cambridge, MA: MIT Press.

Papineau, David. 2002. *Thinking about Consciousness*. Oxford: Oxford University Press. https://doi.org/10.1093/0199243824.001.0001.

Parfit, Derek. 1984. *Reasons and Persons*. Oxford: Oxford University Press.

Pelczar, Michael. 2015. *Sensorama: A Phenomenalist Analysis of Spacetime and Its Contents*. New York: Oxford University Press.

Pelczar, Michael. 2019. "Defending Phenomenalism." *Philosophical Quarterly* 69 (276): 574–597. https://doi.org/10.1093/pq/pqy064.

Pelczar, Michael. 2022. *Phenomenalism: A Metaphysics of Chance and Experience*. Oxford: Oxford University Press.

Pitcher, George. 1977. *Berkeley*. London: Routledge.

Prior, Elizabeth W., Robert Pargetter, and Frank Jackson. 1982. "Three Theses about Dispositions." *American Philosophical Quarterly* 19 (3): 251–257.

Robinson, Howard. 1985. "The General Form of the Argument for Berkeleyan Idealism." In *Essays on Berkeley: A Tercentennial Celebration*, 163–186. Oxford: Oxford University Press.

Robinson, Howard. 1994. *Perception*. New York: Routledge.

200 BIBLIOGRAPHY

Robinson, Howard. 2009. "Idealism." In *The Oxford Handbook of Philosophy of Mind*, edited by Ansgar Beckermann, Brian P. McLaughlin, and Sven Walter, 189–205. Oxford: Oxford University Press.

Robinson, Howard. 2022. *Perception and Idealism: An Essay on How the World Manifests Itself to Us, and How It (Probably) Is in Itself.* Oxford: Oxford University Press. https://doi.org/10.1093/oso/9780192845566.001.0001.

Roelofs, Luke. 2016. "The Unity of Consciousness, within Subjects and between Subjects." *Philosophical Studies* 173 (12): 3199–3221. https://doi.org/10.1007/s11098-016-0658-7.

Roelofs, Luke. 2019. *Combining Minds: How to Think about Composite Subjectivity.* New York: Oxford University Press.

Rowlands, Mark J. 2010. *The New Science of the Mind: From Extended Mind to Embodied Phenomenology.* Cambridge, MA: A Bradford Book.

Russell, Bertrand. 1915. "On the Experience of Time." *The Monist* 25 (2): 212–233. https://doi.org/10.5840/monist191525217.

Russell, Bertrand. 1927. *An Outline of Philosophy.* London: George Allen & Unwin, Ltd.

Russell, Bertrand. 1948. *Human Knowledge: Its Scope and Limits.* London: Routledge.

Schaffer, Jonathan. 2010. "Monism: The Priority of the Whole." *Philosophical Review* 119 (1): 31–76. https://doi.org/10.1215/00318108-2009-025.

Sendłak, Maciej. 2018. "On Quantitative and Qualitative Parsimony." *Metaphilosophy* 49 (1–2): 153–166. https://doi.org/10.1111/meta.12286.

Siegel, Susanna. 2006. "Which Properties Are Represented in Perception?" In *Perceptual Experience*, edited by Tamar Szabó Gendler and John Hawthorne, 481–503. Oxford: Oxford University Press. https://doi.org/10.1093/acprof:oso/9780199289769.003.0015.

Smith, Michael, and Daniel Stoljar. 1998. "Global Response-Dependence and Noumenal Realism." *The Monist* 81 (1): 85–111. https://doi.org/10.5840/monist19988115.

Smithson, Robert. 2023. "Edenic Idealism." *Australasian Journal of Philosophy* 101 (1): 16–33. https://doi.org/10.1080/00048402.2021.1981804.

Sprigge, Timothy L. S. 1983. *The Vindication of Absolute Idealism.* Edinburgh: Edinburgh University Press.

Stoneham, Tom. 2002. *Berkeley's World.* Oxford: Oxford University Press.

Strawson, Galen. 2003. "What Is the Relation between an Experience, the Subject of the Experience, and the Content of the Experience?" *Philosophical Issues* 13: 279–315. http://www.jstor.org/stable/3050535.

Strawson, Galen. 2006. "Realistic Monism: Why Physicalism Entails Panpsychism." *Journal of Consciousness Studies* 13 (10–11): 3–31.

Treisman, Anne. 2003. "Consciousness and Perceptual Binding." In *The Unity of Consciousness*, edited by Axel Cleeremans, 95–113. New York: Oxford University Press.

Tye, Michael. 2003. *Consciousness and Persons.* Cambridge, MA: MIT Press.

Van Cleve, James. 1999. *Problems from Kant.* New York: Oxford University Press.

Wilson, Jessica M. 2014. "No Work for a Theory of Grounding." *Inquiry: An Interdisciplinary Journal of Philosophy* 57 (5–6): 535–579. https://doi.org/10.1080/0020174x.2014.907542.

Winkler, Kenneth P. 1989. *Berkeley: An Interpretation.* Oxford: Oxford University Press.

Yetter-Chappell, Helen. 2018a. "Idealism without God." In *Idealism: New Essays in Metaphysics*, edited by Tyron Goldschmidt and Kenneth L. Pearce, 66–81. Oxford: Oxford University Press.

Yetter-Chappell, Helen. 2018b. "Seeing through Eyes, Mirrors, Shadows and Pictures." *Philosophical Studies* 175 (8): 2017–2042. https://doi.org/10.1007/s11098-017-0948-8.

Yetter-Chappell, Helen. 2019. "Idealization and Problem Intuitions: Why No Possible Agent Is Indisputably Ideal." *Journal of Consciousness Studies* 26 (9–10): 270–279.

Yetter-Chappell, Helen. 2022. "Dualism All the Way Down: Why There Is No Paradox of Phenomenal Judgment." *Synthese* 200 (2): 99. https://doi.org/10.1007/s11229-022-03654-6.

BIBLIOGRAPHY 201

Yetter-Chappell, Helen. 2024a. "Get Acquainted with Naïve Idealism." In *The Roles of Representations in Visual Perception*, edited by Robert French and Berit Brogaard, 263–274. Cham, Switzerland: Springer.

Yetter-Chappell, Helen. 2024b. "Idealism and the Best of All (Subjectively Indistinguishable) Possible Worlds." In *Oxford Studies in Philosophy of Mind*. Vol. 4, 144–172.

Index

For the benefit of digital users, indexed terms that span two pages (e.g., 52–53) may, on occasion, appear on only one of those pages.

afterimages, 113–16
Allen, Keith, 163–64
Antony, Louise, 101–4

Balog, Katalin, 159
Bayne, Tim, 37–39, 91–93
Berkeley, George, 3–4, 6–12, 16, 110–12, 119, 151, 167–68, 185
black holes, 57–60

Campbell, John, 155n.5, 167, 178n.18
Chalmers, David, 1, 68, 129–30n.10, 149, 153–54, 183, 185n.27
cognitive phenomenology, 13–14n.16, 28n.4, 62–63, 109, 111–12
coherence, 55–56, 103, 136–39
cosmopsychism. *See* panpsychism, cosmopsychism

Dainton, Barry, 37–39, 46, 89–91
dualism, 60–61, 68–73, 84, 97–98, 128–29, 168–70

eden, 129–30n.10, 149–54, 167–68, 174, 180–81, 184n.24, 184–85, 186–87, 188, 189–90, 191

Farkas, Katalin, 55–56, 103
Foster, John, 4, 5n.9, 9, 122–23, 148, 149–50
Fraassen, Bas van, 126

God, 6–7, 8–16, 26–27, 28–29, 119, 122–23, 133, 191–93
Goff, Phillip, 96, 127n.8, 182–83, 184, 185

hallucination, 71–72, 75–78, 84–88, 100, 104–6, 113, 115–16, 127–28, 158
hidden assumptions, 95–96n.10, 99–113
Hoffman, Donald, 5n.9
Hurley, Susan, 45–46

illusion, 95–96n.10, 103–4, 110–16

Johnston, Mark, 152–53, 171–74, 178–79

Kalderon, Mark, 166–67
Kant, Immanuel, 42–45, 47, 50, 51
Kastrup, Bernardo, 80–81, 185n.27

laws of nature, 9, 15, 20, 119–24, 136–39
    contingent necessitation relation, 120–22
    primitivism, 123–24
    regularity theory, 120, 121
    See also realism, about laws
Levine, Joseph, 178
Lewis, David, 119–20, 121, 132–33

Martin, Michael, 155, 157–58
materialism
    mind-body (*see* physicalism)
    nature of reality, 3, 6, 20–21, 82, 104, 119–21, 124, 125, 130–33, 135, 140, 144, 146–47, 150–51, 154–55, 166–68, 170–71, 176–77, 179–82, 188, 189–90
Maudlin, Tim, 121–22, 123–24
Mill, John Stuart, 13, 186–87

Nagel, Thomas: xi, 5n.8
naïve idealism, 19, 85–99, 106, 116–17, 152–53, 171, 172–74
naïve realism:
    color naïve realism, 22, 165–74
    property naïve realism, 21–22, 116–17, 154–65, 171–74, 177–78
nonreductive idealism:
    immanent nonreductive idealism, 67–68, 73–74, 79–83, 96
    transcendent nonreductive idealism, 68–69, 70–73, 80–83, 84, 96

panpsychism, 66–68, 69, 79–81, 182–86
    cosmopsychism, 95–96, 183, 184–85
Pelczar, Michael, 22n.19, 50–51, 186–90
Perception. *See* illusion; veridical perception

204 INDEX

phenomenalism, 12, 186–91
physicalism, 3n.2, 5, 19, 67, 78–81, 157–58
property binding, 28–30, 48–51, 64, 68, 131, 137–38, 140
psychophysical bridging laws, 60–61, 69–73, 75, 84–85, 87–88, 97–98, 129, 184

realism, 4–5
  about laws, 122 (*see also* laws of nature)
  scientific, 126–27, 131
reductive idealism, 66–67, 74–83
Robinson, Howard, 4, 55–56, 103, 122, 188

spacetime, 21, 59–60, 139–46
Strawson, Galen, 2, 16–17, 78–79, 173, 182n.22

subjects, 15–18, 48n.26, 65, 75–76, 91–93, 160–61, 162–63, 164–65, 172–74

theistic idealism, 6–10, 61, 122–23, 191–93
theoretical virtues, 11–12, 21, 149–54, 174–81
Tye, Michael, 26n.1, 39–41, 94

unity of consciousness, 27–28, 30–51, 88–96, 140, 158, 162–63
  co-consciousness, 37, 38, 89–91
  experiential parts, 39–42
  Kantian, 42–48
  subsumptive unity, 37, 38
  transitivity of, 38–39, 88–96

veridical perception, 55, 57, 59, 66–74, 85–88, 98–110, 113, 115–17, 129, 152–53